Jerer ....ans.
Andrew Roberts described him as the 'most underrated thinker in Britain'. He is Professor of History at Exeter University and a renowned expert on the history of war. He appears regularly on TV and radio, including BBC Radio 4's *In Our Time*. This title is his 100th single-author book.

Highlights from the series

A Brief History of British Kings & Queens
Mike Ashley
A Brief History of the Crusades
Geoffrey Hindley
A Brief History of the Druids
Peter Berresford Ellis
A Brief History of the Dynasties of China
Bamber Gascoigne
A Brief Guide to the Greek Myths
Stephen Kershaw
A Brief History of Henry VIII
Derek Wilson
A Brief History of the Hundred Years War
Desmond Seward
A Brief History of Life in the Middle Ages
Martyn Whittock
A Brief History of Mankind
Cyril Aydon
A Brief History of the Middle East
Christopher Catherwood
A Brief History of the Private Lives of the Roman Emperors
Anthony Blond
A Brief History of Secret Societies
David V. Barrett
A Brief History of the Universe
J.P. McEvoy
A Brief History of Venice
Elizabeth Horodowich
A Brief History of the Vikings
Jonathan Clements

A BRIEF HISTORY OF

BRITAIN 1851–2010

JEREMY BLACK

ROBINSON

Constable & Robinson Ltd
3 The Lanchesters
162 Fulham Palace Road
London W6 9ER
www.constablerobinson.com

First published in the UK by Robinson,
an imprint of Constable & Robinson Ltd, 2010

A copy of the British Library Cataloguing in Publication
data is available from the British Library

ISBN: 978-1-84529-700-8

Printed and bound in the EU

1 3 5 7 9 10 8 6 4 2

For Sarah

CONTENTS

Preface and Acknowledgements   ix

Prologue: An Imperial Presence   xi

PART ONE: 1851–1931

1. Changing Country   3

2. The Culture of Power   35

3. Changing People   85

4. Imperial Strength   117

PART TWO: 1931–2010

5. Changing Country   149

6. Changing People   173

7. Empire to Europe   207

8. To the Present   261

9. Contesting the Past   307

Selected Further Reading   327

Index   333

PREFACE AND ACKNOWLEDGEMENTS

Historians are of two types. One, pretending Olympian detachment and Delphic omniscience, tells you the answers and pretends that there is only one way to look at the past: their way. That is not my approach. I think it important to be frank about the difficulties of covering the past, about the choices made in what is covered, and how it is treated and organized, and about the degree to which others will take different approaches. That is particularly true of the treatment of the recent past.

The key choices here are coverage and organization. In coverage, there is a determination not to put politics first but, instead, to focus on changes in country and people that reflected broader pressures as well as those arising from government policy. The two 'changing country' chapters cover environmental issues in the broadest sense and use this approach to discuss such topics as economic and transport history and the spread of the cities. The two 'changing people' chapters cover demographic history, including migration and health, but also social structure and such trends as the rise of the independent voice of youth.

In each part, there is also a chapter on Britain's international position, a key element of its lasting importance, as well as a chapter that seeks to link political and cultural developments. Political and cultural developments are often treated as different, but that is mistaken as they can be closely related. This is particularly the case if culture is understood in the widest sense, namely to include public activities such as sport. In Britain, the key characteristics of the two relevant sections in this book, Chapters 2 and 8, is that the first saw the triumph of the market, while, in the second, the state became more significant. The book closes with a chapter-length conclusion that includes the way in which public history has presented the nation's past.

I am most grateful to Bill Gibson, David Gladstone, Keith Laybourn, Thomas Otte, Murray Pittock, Bill Purdue, Richard Toye and Michael Turner for their comments on all or part of an earlier draft. None is responsible for any errors that remain. Nor is Leo Hollis, who has been a most encouraging editor, or Jaqueline Mitchell, an exemplary copy-editor.

This work takes me to my 100th single-author book, and I close the preface by recording my heartfelt thanks to Sarah, who has been there throughout all the books. I would also like to note my gratitude to the many others who have provided help and encouragement, a goodly number. I hope they take pleasure in what has resulted.

PROLOGUE

An Imperial Presence

The Great Exhibition in 1851 was to speak for Britain past, present and future. Opened at the specially built Crystal Palace in Hyde Park, it was intended as a demonstration of British achievement, and was a proclamation of the nation's mission, duty and interest to put itself at the head of the diffusion of civilization, and thus to take forward history. The exhibition was seen as an opportunity to link manufacturing and the arts, in order to promote a humane practicality and inspired, progressive society in which Britain would be foremost, and from which the British people and economy could benefit. The exhibition proclaimed the supposed triumph of free trade which was linked to manufacturing supremacy. It also symbolized the coming of a less fractured and more prosperous society after the often divisive and difficult experiences of the 1830s and 1840s, notably the contentious repeal of the Corn Laws and the pressure from the Chartist movement for political reform.

The exhibition, thus, reflected an attempt to embrace and to channel the country's dynamic industry, the New Britain; an attempt in part arising from the visit to the manufacturing centre of Birmingham in 1843 of Queen Victoria's husband, Prince Albert (1819–61) a key promoter of the exhibition. With its 24-ton (24.4-tonne) block of coal by the entrance, the exhibition was a tribute to British manufacturing skill, prowess and confidence in the future, one abundantly displayed in its central space, the first wonder of the modern world, Joseph

Paxton's (1803–65) iron and glass conservatory, which was 1,850 feet (564 metres) long (over three times the length of St Paul's Cathedral), 460 feet (140 metres) wide and 108 feet (33 metres) high. It included 294,000 panes of glass and contained almost 1 million square feet of space. This was a public palace of Britain's prowess and future, one that was more impressive than the royal palaces nearby. As a tribute to the importance of this British initiative, other countries sent exhibits, while the British public celebrated their future with their presence: some of the 6.2 million visitors in the 140 days of the exhibition came to London by means of the recent and expanding rail system.

Public improvement was a key goal of the exhibition and its profits appropriately led to the building of a series of museums and learned institutions in South Kensington, to the south of Hyde Park. The South Kensington Museum, later renamed the Victoria and Albert, was followed by the Natural History Museum (1873–81) and, in 1907, by the Science Museum. The Royal College of Music and the Imperial College of Science were part of the same development, while the Royal Albert Hall (1870) was added by a private developer. The Albert Memorial (1876) in Kensington Gardens contributed to the townscape of knowledge, the statue of Prince Albert shown holding the Great Exhibition's catalogue and presiding over industry and the arts.

The Crystal Palace itself was moved to Sydenham in 1852, and its use was championed by the railway baron Samuel Laing, but it hit repeated financial problems as its varied fare – concerts to dog shows, imperial festivals to balloon flights – attracted few. Partially damaged by fire in 1866, the building was totally destroyed by another in 1936.

In 1851, the year of the exhibition, Britain's rule, protected by the world's greatest navy, stretched to include Australasia, Canada, India and much else besides, not least Sri Lanka, Hong Kong, Singapore, Aden, Cape Town, the Falklands, Mauritius, St Lucia and Jamaica, most of which had been conquered or otherwise acquired over the previous seventy years. In 1852, Britain commemorated the life of the general who had helped create that empire, Arthur, Duke of Wellington (1769–1852), victor over the Marathas in India in 1803, Napoleon's vanquisher at Waterloo in 1815, and later Prime Minister (1828–30). His state funeral, carefully arranged by Prince Albert and the Prime Minister, Edward, 14th Earl of Derby (1799–1869), celebrated national greatness, and provided an opportunity to link people, state and Church in an exuberant patriotism. The *Illustrated London News* of 20 November 1852 declared:

> The grave has now closed over the mortal remains of the greatest man of our age, and one of the purest-minded men recorded in history. Wellington and Nelson sleep side by side under the dome of St Paul's, and the national mausoleum of our isles has received the most illustrious of its dead. With a pomp and circumstance, a fervour of popular respect, a solemnity and a grandeur never to be surpassed in the obsequies of any other hero hereafter to be born to become the benefactor of this country, the sacred relics of Arthur Duke of Wellington have been deposited in the place long since set apart for them by the unanimous decision of his countrymen.

In the 1850s, meanwhile, technology and enterprise were helping remould the country, and were doing so with a confidence in the future and in Britain's role in it that was very different to the reluctance of today. On 29 August 1850, Queen Victoria (1819–1901) opened the Royal Border Bridge over the River Tweed at Berwick. Designed by Robert Stephenson (1803–59), one of the greatest engineers of the day, this viaduct of twenty-eight arches cost £253,000 and is still impressive today, the height of the bridge and the curve of the approach providing a fine vista. Moreover, this was a man-made vista, as those of Victoria's reign increasingly were. Proving that technology can unify the state, the bridge provided the last railway link between London and Edinburgh; there, in 1853, 2,000 people came to the first meeting of the National Association for the Vindication of Scottish Rights, its support for Scottish rights not extending to nationalist pressure for separatism – again a marked contrast to the situation today.

Stephenson also showed talent and social mobility in operation. His father, George, a colliery workman, had been a central figure in the development of railway locomotives, a development in which Britain led the world. Robert designed bridges across the empire, including the Victoria Bridge at Montreal (1859), was Conservative MP for Whitby, a sign of the openness of politics to wide-ranging talent, and was buried in Westminster Abbey, a recognition of the importance of engineering. As a reminder of the rush, freneticism and changes of these years, the Calais–Dover telegraph cable, another key sign of progress in communications, was laid in 1851, which was also the year when Charles Morton (1819–1904), seen as the 'father of the music hall', founded the Canterbury Theatre at Lambeth. Mass leisure for the popular urban audience was greatly taken forward by the music hall, which was more immediate, inclusive and populist than the pleasure gardens, such as Vauxhall, that had been so important a century earlier.

In addition, the emphasis on public provision and governmental reform as the solution to problems was shown in 1851 when the Wiltshire asylum was opened in Devizes. Such asylums were to replace private madhouses run for profit and typified the Victorian belief in exemplary regulation. Similar public institutions, for these and other purposes, were built across the country, testimonies to the Victorian confidence that the community should and could provide for the weak.

The progress of the world's leading economy, an economy visibly transforming both country and people, was seen as calling forth a regulation of society directed on moral lines. The *Western Luminary* newspaper in its issue of 5 June 1855 pressed the case for legislation that amounted to a caring set of

Victorian values, which is not the usual view of these values:

> The Factory Act set limits to the demands of the mill-owner upon the strength and endurance of young people; the statute abolishing the use of children in the abhorrent practice of climbing, in the process of cleansing, chimneys; and the salutary provision of interdicting the employment of females in coal mines; – all these prove that the instincts of humanity are not only alive in us, but have been aroused and actively exerted in vindication of our character as considerate and civilized beings. ... of a people who, above all others, feel it a duty to succour the oppressed, and pride themselves upon a ready and liberal redress of grievances and suffering.

Optimism in the expansion and application of knowledge was widespread. The narrator in Edward Bulwer Lytton's (1803–73) ghost story 'The House and the Brain' (1859) explained his theory that 'what is called supernatural is only a something in the laws of Nature of which we have been hitherto ignorant'. A sense of the congruence of Christianity, reform and science played a major role in this optimism, although the Religious Census of 1851 produced a major shock, suggesting that Britain was not a truly Christian country and revealing that Christian belief and observance varied greatly. In the Welsh county of Radnor, half of the population attended no place of worship. Indeed, the need to support the consolations of religion was an aspect of the Victorian cult of progress, which was not seen as anti-religious by its protagonists.

To contrast 1851 with the present is to be aware both of the extent of change over only a few generations and also of changes unanticipated at the high tide of Victorian glory. The empire is no more, a fundamental change not only for the world but also for Britain. The importance of this change explains why 1931 has been chosen as the chronological dividing point for this book. The divide at 1931 reflects more than the convenience of a midway year, for there are other years that are possible, for example 1918 with the universal male franchise and votes for women. The year 1931, however, has been selected because of the great importance of Britain's global position. Although 1901, the year of Queen Victoria's death, and 1914, when the First World War broke out, might seem tempting, much of the world of late-Victorian Britain continued into the early twentieth century despite the savage and deep disruption of the First World War (1914–18). Indeed, Britain's international position reached its imperial and colonial height after the war, and that position provided much of the context for the history of the British Isles, not least as it contributed to the impression and reality of the nation's extraordinary importance and range. Britain ruled the world's most populous and extensive empire.

1931, however, saw the successful Japanese invasion of Manchuria, the key industrial region in China. This invasion proved a major breach of the liberal post-war order over which Britain had presided, and one that saw the beginning of a period in which Britain was to be reactive and on the defensive. Two years later, this process was taken further with Hitler's rise to power in Germany, a rise that led directly to the Second World War (1939–45). Although Hitler talked of friendly relations with Britain, everything he sought and stood for was fundamentally opposed to the liberal and tolerant assumptions of British public culture and society.

Hitler (1889–1945) was defeated in a war that exhausted Britain and strained the cohesion of its empire, but this hostile international environment was to continue after the Second World War, with the threat from the Soviet Union in the Cold War; and this environment provided the backdrop for Britain's decline, first in imperial power, and then in relative consequence. We are still in that situation of decline today, and it reflects the way in which we look at the past. Stemming from this decline is the loss of any sense of Britain as having an historic mission or as being special: in a religious sense or as a governmental system or as a society. Whereas in the 1920s and 1930s there was still a feeling of particular value, and strong identity, in the British constitution, governmental system and national character, this feeling has largely ceased, and the once strong belief that Britain and the British had special God-given roles to fulfil has gone.

To compare modern celebratory occasions, the Millennium Dome at Greenwich in 2000 or the preparations for the Olympics at Stratford, London in 2012, with the Great Exhibition of 1851 or with the British Empire Exhibition at Wembley in 1924, an exhibition that encapsulates the world that was to be swept away from the 1930s on, is to be aware of a totally different situation, both within the country and as far as Britain's international position is concerned. That change is the theme of this book, our history, a nation transformed. The very weakness of the Dome as an image alongside Paxton's iron and glass creation, at once sparkling and dominant, reflects the sense of present-day weakness and uncertainty.

This transformation is also that of image and identity, and that change is an important part of the story. It is valuable, and ironic, to note the comments of George Orwell (1903–50), a leading novelist and key public intellectual of the 1940s. In his essay 'The Lion and the Unicorn', which he reworked as *The English People* (1947), Orwell wrote:

> ... there is something distinctive and recognisable in English civilisation. It is a culture as individual as that of Spain – it is somehow bound up with solid breakfasts and gloomy Sundays, smoky towns and winding roads, green fields and red pillar-boxes. It has a flavour of its own. Moreover, it is continuous, it stretches into the future and the past, there is something in it that persists, as in a living creature ... The suet puddings and the red pillar-boxes have entered into your soul.

Yet, in 2010, none of these definitions resonates in the same way, and even talking about 'the English people' would be seen as non-inclusive and inappropriate in many quarters. Diet has become lighter, with muesli replacing bacon and eggs. Sundays have become less gloomy because changes in law and custom have ensured that Sunday observance is far less common and, indeed, possible, while the television schedules make Sunday much like any other day. Towns have become less smoky as a result of the Clean Air Acts of 1956 and 1968 and the creation of smokeless zones.

Moreover, winding roads have been superseded by motorways. If they are now less commonly driven straight through the countryside with scant allowance for its topography than was the case a generation ago, and are more sensitive to the landscape, motorways and bypasses still are certainly not Orwell's winding roads. Instead, they represent the triumph of town over country which is a theme in this book. Furthermore, as another aspect of change, traditional crops and green fields have been replaced by oilseed rape or maize, or, more seriously, housing. The role of the post has been lessened by the internet and many post offices have been closed.

Thus, Orwell's piece serves as a pointed reminder of the porosity and changeability of manifestations of national civilization. Its points will be reflected upon in the final chapter of the book where we examine the changing and different ways we look at our past. These changing ways are central aspects of our history.

PART ONE:

1851–1931

I

CHANGING COUNTRY

... the Station has swallowed up the playing-field. It was gone. The two beautiful hawthorn-trees, the hedge, the turf, and all those buttercups and daisies had given place to the stoniest of jolting roads ... The coach that had carried me away, was melodiously called Timpson's Blue-Eyed Maid, and belonged to Timpson at the coach-office up-street; the locomotive engine that had brought me back, was called severely No. 97 and belonged to SER [South Eastern Railway], and was spitting ashes and hot-water over the blighted ground.

Charles Dickens (1812–70), a writer who frequently dwelled on the presence and pressure of change, captured, in his short story 'Dullborough Town' (1860), the train as a cause of lost innocence as well as a source of new experiences. He also recorded the extent to which the sights, smells and much else of life were transformed and created anew as Britain modernized.

This modernization reflected the extent to which Britain in 1851 was closer, literally and metaphorically, to the world of

William III and Sir Isaac Newton in the 1690s than to today. Indeed, it is necessary to underline the strangeness of the mid-nineteenth century because it is all too easy to treat the Victorians of 1851, with their railways and photographs, as like us. Indeed, as a result, one way to look at the period 1851–2010 is as if it was one period, our period, an age in which differences exist, but in which such differences can be traced against a background of essential similarity.

That approach is mistaken. In fact, Britain in 1851 was profoundly dissimilar in many respects to today. The powerful grip of Christian worship, with religious observance by most of the population, and attitudes in the nineteenth century regarding social values and legal codes are core differences.

Another major contrast arose from the country itself. Balloon flights across Britain were not a method of transport practised in 1851 as balloons did not yet have the benefit of the engines that were to make long-distance journeys possible in the 1920s. Such a flight in 1851 would, however, have revealed a country in which the urban imprint was far smaller than today, with less of the country covered by buildings. The census of that year was certainly the first in which the majority of the population lived in towns, but these towns were far more compact than their modern successors, both smaller and more densely populated. In particular, despite entrepreneurs taking advantage of rail services reaching settlements near London like Deptford (1836) and Surbiton (1838), there was as yet little suburban sprawl, in part because most people still walked to work.

Moreover, the human imprint on the landscape was different in emphasis to now because in the 1850s it mostly related to working the land, largely by agriculture, but with forestry and quarrying also playing important roles. As a result, there was little of Britain that did not bear evidence of the direct impact of human activity, but, equally, that activity was closely linked to the practicalities created by terrain, soils, climate and other physical factors. Thus, long-lasting patterns of land use remained important, as knowledge of which fields or slopes were best for wheat or other crops, or sheep or cattle, were rocky or easy to cultivate, or were well or poorly drained, was handed down.

By 1931, the situation was very different. The country could be readily, rapidly, reliably and predictably crossed by aircraft, and the view was of a landscape more directly affected by the human imprint, and of activities less conditioned by the practicalities of the landscape, than in 1851. The history of this transition is fundamental to that of Britain because it created not only a transformed environment but also a different mental picture of national life. The urban experience became more significant at all levels of society, and while ruralism was an important cultural theme, it was largely so as a conscious and hostile response to the sway of this experience, and, indeed, as an attempt to deny its sway.

Population Growth

A key driver of change was population growth and urbanization. Thanks to a high birth rate and a falling death rate, the population grew rapidly in this period, sustaining earlier increases in a way that appeared to defy the idea that the country could support only so many people. Despite large-scale emigration, especially outside the empire to the US, but also within the empire, notably to Canada and Australasia, England and Wales had a population of 17,928,000 in 1851 and 32,528,000 in 1901; the figures for Scotland were 2,889,000 and 4,472,000. Most of this growth occurred in the cities, while the rural population declined in absolute and relative terms: from just under 50 per cent of the total population in 1851 to just under 30 per cent in 1911, although the latter percentage was still far greater than that today.

This growth posed a grave challenge to assumptions about society, leading as it did to concern that the new urban masses would prove a source and means of crisis, whether crisis was understood in terms of revolutionary politics, social violence, large-scale irreligion, demographic degeneration or epidemic infection, or several or all of these. The city as danger as well as source of pride and progress was a central theme in Victorian thought, and this remained pertinent for much of the twentieth century, although the 1960s were to bring forward a set of social and cultural values that was more clearly focused on the urban experience, and this remains the case today.

Urbanization entailed unprecedented growth for London (the population of the Greater London area rose to 7.2 million in 1911) as well as for the growing cities of the north, especially Manchester, a key centre of industrialization; Liverpool, the empire's second port (behind London, which had the largest and busiest port in the world); and Glasgow, a major empire port, Scotland's principal population centre, and the leading centre of engineering and shipbuilding. Most of the urban population, however, lived in more modest-sized cities and towns, for example Newcastle, which had a population of 215,328 by 1901; Sunderland, the world's leading shipbuilding town in the 1850s; and the Lancashire and Yorkshire mill towns, such as Bolton, Bradford, Bury, Halifax and Preston. In Ireland, Belfast developed as a great port with manufacturing industry based on linen, shipyards and tobacco, although its expansion saw the development of patterns of urban segregation based on religion.

Population growth was also seen in key centres of industry and mining, as both activities required large amounts of labour. The population in County Durham, a major centre of coal mining and related industry, rose from 390,997 in 1851 to 1,016,562 in 1891, with growth of 34.7 per cent in 1861–71 alone. Glamorgan and Monmouthshire, the centres of Welsh coal and iron production, contained about 20 per cent of the Welsh population in 1801, but 57.5 per cent in 1901. Within this area, the population of the coal mining Rhondda Valley rose from under 1,000 in 1851 to 153,000 in 1911. Much of this expansion was fed from rural Wales, but there was also significant migration from Ireland and England: 11 per cent of Swansea's population in 1861 had been born in south-west

England, which lacked comparable industrial growth. As is often the case, immigrants were blamed for crime in Wales.

Industrialization

The growth of the rapidly expanding centres and areas was based on a key element in the changing country: industrialization. Industry had been an important element in Britain's economic development in the eighteenth and early nineteenth centuries, but the widespread application of steam power and factory methods of production across most of the range of industrial activity did not occur until the mid-nineteenth century. Employment opportunities drew labour to expanding industrial cities and, in turn, their populations provided multiple opportunities for industries, services and agriculture.

Economic transformation was seen across the economy – in industry, trade, finance, transportation and agriculture, with the impact of what was later called the Industrial Revolution proving particularly impressive. The British economy had not only changed greatly from the early eighteenth century, but had also developed powerful advantages over foreign states, notably France, in manufacturing and trade. A culture of improvement lay at the heart of much British economic, intellectual and other innovation, and this belief in the prospect and attraction of change moulded and reflected a sense of progress. These and other advantages greatly impressed informed overseas visitors, helping to lead them to a cult for 'Britishness' as a testimony to progress; though these visitors were prone to ignore the extent and impact of periodic economic depressions.

Alongside production, the consumption of goods and services also developed. In particular, a national market was created for producers. This market owed much to the way investment in improved communications increasingly affected local production, with trends in national and local consumption being encouraged by new media, such as newspapers. In turn, developments in consumption helped drive both trade and industrial activity. This serves as a reminder of

the need to avoid viewing industrialization as a process solely
dependent on industrial technology. Alongside manufacturing,
commerce became a defining characteristic of British society,
and one that was particularly important in townscapes, where
weekly markets were supplemented, and then largely replaced,
by permanent shops. Some of the shopping names of the
period are still found on British high streets. John Sainsbury
(1844–1928) opened his first dairy in London in 1869, Thomas
Lipton (1850–1931) his first grocery in Glasgow in 1871, and in
1894 Marks and Spencer was founded. By 1900, Sainsbury had
47 provisions stores and by 1914 Lipton had 500.

The nature of industrial activity also changed, with more
specialization, as well as a greater division of labour and the
growth of capital. A stronger emphasis on the need for
constant, regular and predictable labour led to different forms
of labour control, including factory clocks, which, like the
train system, increased the emphasis on time, and thus pressure
for reliable systems for measuring time, the latter on the
national scale. For rapid industrial growth, the essentials were
capital, transport, markets and coal; and their availability
enabled Britain to avoid the limitations of the organic
economy – that based on the growth of plants, notably wood
for fuel. Instead, it was possible to exploit the plentiful supplies
of fossil fuels in the shape of coal that gave Britain a powerful
edge in industrial activity.

The use of coal, a readily transportable and controllable fuel
(unlike water and windmills), and an efficient power source,
was exploited in a host of industries such as metallurgy, soap
production, glassworks and linen bleaching. Partly as a result
of the development of large-scale coal mining, cheap energy
made possible a rise in per capita living standards in the nineteenth century, despite the major increase in population. Coal-
based steam power ensured that coalfields were key centres of
economic growth, notably those of north-east England, south
Lancashire, the West Riding of Yorkshire, South Wales, and
central Scotland, but also smaller coalfields elsewhere, for

example in the Midlands, Somerset and Kent. Moreover, the significance of coal was seen in the importance of its movement, notably from north-east England to London, for long by sea but increasingly by rail.

The statistics still impress. The average annual production of coal and lignite for Britain in 1855–9 was 67 million tons (69 million tonnes), compared to 31.5 million tons (32 million tonnes) for France, Germany, Belgium and Russia combined. The scale of activity was also measured by the number of pits. The year 1910 was the peak one for the number of collieries in South Wales: 688 in all. That coalfield produced 10.25 million tons (10.4 million tonnes) in 1860, but 57 million tons (58 million tonnes) by 1913, by when improvements in drainage and ventilation had made possible the working of deeper seams. Coal also meant large-scale employment, indeed of a third of the Welsh male labour force.

Heavy industries such as iron and steel, engineering and shipbuilding, were also attracted to coal and iron-ore fields, leading to a local geography of activity with the location of mines, manufacture, and transport in the same areas. Thus, Workington on the Cumbrian coast developed as a major centre of iron and steel production from 1857. Reflecting the way in which increased production was a response to, and in turn encouraged, the flexibility of the factors of production, railways built in the 1840s and 1850s created ready access for Workington to nearby iron-ore fields and to the coke supplies of County Durham on the other side of the Pennines, a journey that was not feasible by sea; while many of the migrant workers for the town came from Ireland. Similarly, metallurgy and the chemical industry were found on and near the Welsh coalfields.

Once iron replaced wood in shipbuilding, the industry took off as Britain had major competitive advantages with ships built of iron and powered by coal. The annual average of tonnage launched at Sunderland rose from over 60,000 (c. 61,000 tonnes) in the 1860s to 190,000 (193,048 tonnes) by the 1890s. In 1881, 341,000 tons (346,471 tonnes) were launched on the Clyde (Glasgow) and 308,000 (312,942 tonnes) on the Tyne (Newcastle) and Wear (Sunderland) combined; and in 1914 the figures were 757,000 (769,148 tonnes) and 666,000 (676,687 tonnes). Belfast, Barrow-in-Furness, the Humber and the Mersey were also important centres of shipbuilding. Shipyards employed large numbers of people, as did ancillary concerns such as engine manufacturers. Whereas there were 4,000 employed in Scottish shipbuilding in 1841, the number had risen to 51,000 by 1911.

Conversely, previously important manufacturing areas, such as East Anglia and south-west England, suffered de-industrialization, in part because they lacked coal, and, as a result, lost people both to industrializing areas and abroad. Thus, Norfolk's large textile industry collapsed in the face of competition from factory-produced textiles from northern England. Many small Norfolk market towns, such as Diss and Swaffham, saw little growth and were not to change greatly until they expanded again from the 1960s, leading to the joke, 'When it's 12 o'clock in London, it's 19.53 in Norfolk.' The previously large textile industry in the south west also collapsed, and this greatly affected the prosperity of local cities and towns, such as Exeter and Trowbridge; although factory production developed at Tiverton.

Machines were increasingly the key to economic activity, mechanization bringing profit and larger factories. The concentration of machine power became important to production. In 1850, there were 17,642 automatic looms in Bradford, mass-producing women's dress fabrics in what was the world centre of worsted wool production and exchange. Manchester was also a city of power looms, although small workshops were more common in mid-century in Birmingham, London, or even Sheffield, which, by then, was producing half of Europe's steel.

Mechanization was crucial to uniformity, the production of low-cost standardized products. As a result, brands of mass-produced goods, such as chocolate and soap, could be consumed and advertised nationally, which encouraged a transformation in retailing. New distribution and retail methods, particularly the foundation of department and chain stores, helped to create national products. Local products, in contrast, fell away.

Mechanization had a major impact on many industries. For example, newspaper production was transformed by the use of steam-powered presses, which increased the rapidity of printing. As in other industries, competition spread the new technology, which had been introduced in London in 1814 for *The Times*. The first issue of the *Wiltshire County Mirror* (10 February 1852) announced that it was due to 'the first introduction into Salisbury of Printing by Steam'. In response, the *Salisbury Journal* immediately adopted steam-printing. In 1854, the printer-proprietor of the *Staffordshire Sentinel* declared, in his first issue, that he had purchased a similar 'printing machine' so as 'to execute his work both expeditiously and at the cheapest possible rate'. The manufacture of paper also became a large-scale industry, with paper based on wood pulp replacing that based on rags.

These and other changes were followed in a country newly aware, through mass literacy and frequent publication of statistics, of developments across the nation. The statistics of industrialization were part of the utilitarian, measurement-based, outcome-oriented mentality that economic change led to. This mentality was depicted by Charles Dickens in his novel *Hard Times* (1854), where he contrasted the variety of human experience with the obsession on mathematical facts of the new world: 'So many hundred hands in this Mill; so many hundred horse steam power. It is known, to the force of a single pound weight, what the engine will do.'

The Train
The railway, in which Britain led the world in inventing and disseminating the new technology, greatly increased the effectiveness of the country in both manufacturing and marketing,

and thus helped make industrialization national in its impact, even if it was regional in its character. By 1851, a national rail system had been created, although there were still gaps that were to be filled later. Both the local landscape and geography were transformed as tunnels were blasted through hills, while rivers were bridged: the Tamar in 1859 and the Forth in 1890, both bridges that remain dramatic to this day. Another key link, the Severn Tunnel on the route from Bristol to Cardiff, was opened in 1886.

Because railways caught the popular imagination, with railway novels proliferating and widespread coverage of railway crimes, pictures of trains, and accounts of speed records, the press also devoted much space to the opening of new links and facilities, and to other railway news. For example, on 11 July 1855, the first number of Chudleigh's *Weekly Express* provided the London–Plymouth timetables. The scale of travel was immense. The number of passenger journeys measured in million miles rose from 60 in 1850 to near 300 in 1870. Moreover, the spread of the network continued, and in 1911, there were 130 staffed stations in Devon and Cornwall alone.

The manufacture and maintenance of trains became an important aspect of Britain's industry, with major workshops at towns that were founded or greatly expanded because of the railways, such as Crewe, Doncaster, Swindon and Wolverton. Even towns that are no longer noted for their railway works, such as Eastleigh, in Hampshire, could be heavily dependent on them. In Brighton and Gateshead, for example, the railway was the largest employer. Conversely, towns that missed out on railway development or that at best were on spur lines became of lesser consequence. Thus, Stamford was obscured by Peterborough.

The volume of freight carried rose from about 38 million tons (38.6 million tonnes) in 1850 to 513 million (521 million tonnes) in 1912, and industries were transformed by the new communications. For example, use of the railway enabled the brewers of Burton-upon-Trent to develop a major beer empire across much of England, and also helped speed North Wales slate towards urban markets, which greatly changed town-scapes. Thanks to the train, London newspapers could be transported rapidly around the country, while perishable goods were sent to the cities. In the 1870s, the rail companies opened up urban markets for liquid milk, encouraging dairy farmers to produce 'railway milk', rather than farmhouse cheese. Over 15,000 tons (c. 16,000 tonnes) of Cornish broccoli were sent by train annually by 1900, and a special daily refrigerated van carried Devon rabbit carcasses to London before the Second World War. Fresh fish was moved from North Sea fishing ports such as Aberdeen, Peterhead, Hull and Lowestoft to inland markets.

Companies and towns that wished to stay at the leading edge of economic development had to become, and remain, transport foci. In Carlisle, Jonathan Dodgson Carr (1806–84) adapted a printing machine to cut biscuits, replacing cutting by hand; helped by the city's position as a major rail junction, he sold his products, notably Carr's table water biscuits, throughout the country. Similarly, Huntley and Palmer, suppliers of sponge fingers to the nation, were based in Reading: another major biscuit-maker in another key rail junction. As a result of such activity, economic patterns changed, not least the nature of marketing. Small market towns without railways collapsed and the position of towns in the urban hierarchy therefore altered.

The impact of rail was also psychological. 'Space' had been conquered. As in America today, people could analogize space and time, such that, for example, a place became two hours away, rather than a certain distance. Moreover, the very building of the railways, with large gangs of migrant workers moving across rural Britain, disrupted local social patterns and assumptions. Maintaining and running the system also became a major source of employment. By 1873, there were 274,000 rail-workers. New sounds and sights, notably of the train passing, contributed to a powerful sense of change, and this change was overwhelmingly presented as progress. Such a perception encouraged the venture capital that was so important to the expansion of the railway system, as well as ensuring that local opposition was lessened. A key element in the process of conciliation was the winning over of landowners by re-routing lines and by building stations, or establishing stops, to serve their estates.

The impact of rail was powerfully visual. Major railway stations, such as St Pancras – built by Sir George Gilbert Scott (1811–78) and W.H. Barlow (1812–1902) in 1873 – were designed as masterpieces of iron and glass, and large railway shed-like stations, as in Darlington, York and Newcastle, became key urban structures. Moreover, alongside accompanying buildings and spaces, notably marshalling yards, the train took over important parts of the townscape. Railway lines also altered local landscapes with their embankments and cuttings, and transformed street plans, each to an unprecedented extent. The stations reflected the importance of functionalism in the search for effective designs, an importance already seen with Paxton's Crystal Palace. Railways and other examples of new industrial technology brought a requirement for new buildings and in dramatically new forms.

The railway, moreover, brought uniformity, as time within Britain was standardized. The railways needed standard time for their timetables, in order to make connections possible, and, in place of the variation from east to west in Britain, they adopted the standard set by the Greenwich Observatory as 'railway time'. Clocks were kept accurate by the electric telegraph that was erected along lines. Thanks to the train, the meaning of place changed. Edinburgh and Glasgow were now closer to London as an aspect of a national network for which York and Manchester were merely important stages. Dublin was brought closer, with expresses from London to Holyhead (crossing the Menai Straits on a dramatic bridge) followed by steamships thence to Ireland. Rail also brought a new speed to news and changing fashions. Local trends and towns were eclipsed by metropolitan fashions.

Rail, in addition, spread familiarity with the country. In 1864, the original fort at Fort William was demolished to make room for the railway station through which English tourists reached the Scottish Highlands. This demolition was a symbolic change of function and an aspect of the way in which new-build was often at the expense of the most prominent sites of the past, including, in the case of the railway, Berwick and Newcastle castles and Launceston Priory.

In the second half of the nineteenth century, industrial growth increasingly focused on engineering, shipbuilding and chemicals, rather than the textiles and metal smelting of earlier industrial development. The pace of scientific advance and technological change was unremitting, and British scientists led in a number of fields. In electricity, James Clerk Maxwell (1831–79), the first professor of experimental physics at Cambridge, and Lord Kelvin (1824–1907) expanded on the earlier work of Michael Faraday (1791–1867), and the development of commercial generators led to the growing use of electricity. As industrialization gathered pace, the contrast between industrialized regions and the rest of the country increased, for example between South and central Wales, notably Glamorgan and Merioneth, although, in turn, South Wales was to suffer because it saw little of the new industry of the early twentieth century, such as car-making.

Housing

The populations of the industrial cities had to be housed, and one of the ways in which the changing country of the late nineteenth and early twentieth century is still with us is that much of the housing stock today derives from that period, whereas a relatively small percentage of the current stock survives from earlier periods, notably so in urban areas. By the 1860s, the terraced streets we know today were being built in England and, to an extent, Wales, and by the 1870s, a standard version of working-class housing was the two-up-two-down 'through terrace' – with its access at both front and rear, solid construction and adequate ventilation, and sometimes small gardens or back yard. Increasingly, this was becoming the standard dwelling, although, in Scotland, housing remained tenemented across the classes until the collapse of private building and its displacement by local authority building after 1919. Houses are rare in Scottish city architecture prior to 1920, with Aberdeen a partial exception.

The traditional terraced house reflected the rise in average real wages in the 1850s–60s as the economic boom of industrialization brought prosperity. These houses were a great improvement on the back-to-back, the lodging-house and the damp cellar in which all too many had lived. In part, this was because terraced houses were built at a time of prosperity and rising construction standards when covered sewerage systems and adequately piped clean water were being included in new residences. Indeed, from 1875 it was mandatory to provide lavatories on the same plot as a new house. These houses, with their separate rooms, enabled greater definition of the spheres of domestic activity, from chatting or reading to eating or sleeping, all of which had major implications for family behaviour and gender roles, as well as for a sense of privacy.

Terraced houses were usually built in straight streets. This pattern replaced an earlier style of layout frequently described in terms of a warren. This earlier style had been difficult to keep clean or to light because it contained so many self-enclosed alleyways, closes or courts. In contrast, the straight streets of terraced houses, equally apportioned and relatively spaciously laid out, were easier to light and to provide with supplies of gas, water and drainage. This situation was true not only of areas as a whole, but also of individual properties. Legislation was important. The removal of the Brick Tax in 1850 encouraged the large-scale utilization of bricks in construction, and their use helped keep damp at bay. Similarly, the end of the Wallpaper Tax in 1861 affected the interior of houses. Technology also played a role, as in the provision of inexpensive linoleum from the mid-1870s as an effective floor covering.

Nevertheless, many of the urban poor and casually employed still lived in one-roomed dwellings, tenements, back-to-backs, rookeries and courts, and would continue to do so until the Second World War. Their walls frequently ran with damp, sanitation was often primitive, lighting was limited, and poorly swept chimneys contributed to the fug in many homes. Health was greatly affected as a consequence. Prominent and wealthy individuals derived income from areas of poor housing, including Robert, 3rd Marquess of Salisbury (1830–1903), Prime Minister in 1885–6, 1886–92 and 1895–1902. This housing was deplored by social commentators and contributed to the growing concern with the environment in which the bulk of the people lived, a concern that led to social surveys and also to missions to the poor in slum areas, especially in the East End of London. George Bernard Shaw's (1856–1950) first play, *Widowers' Houses* (1892), concerned the relationship between the aristocratic Henry Trench and Blanche Sartorius whose father gains his wealth by slum landlordism. Trench is appalled, only for Sartorius to point out that Trench's money came from similar sources.

Townscapes and Architecture
The new townscapes were in part achieved by clearing existing areas, and, more generally, changes in the urban landscape reflected shifts in society. Paintings such as Myles Foster's (1825–99) *Newcastle upon Tyne from Windmill Hill, Gateshead* (c. 1871–2) showed formerly prominent buildings – the castle keep and cathedral – now joined by the new buildings representing change, in this case, factory chimneys and the railway bridge.

There was also extensive civic architecture, for example the big, high-ceilinged banking halls and post offices that took up prominent sites. During the post-1945 Modernist vogue,

Victorian architecture was much castigated and many buildings were destroyed, famously the Euston Arch outside the London railway station, or left stranded amid a new world of concrete and cars. Nevertheless, an enormous amount of this architecture survives in city centres, and this remains an aspect of the Victorian culture that can be readily approached. Greek Revival was the dominant style in the first half of the century, and can be found in many cities, but it was challenged in the mid-nineteenth century by Gothic Revival (or neo-Gothic), a style advocated by Augustus Pugin, who presented it as the quintessential Christian style. It was readily adapted for the extensive church-building by Protestants and Catholics in the second half of the century. Significant architects in the style included Sir George Gilbert Scott, William Butterfield (1814–1900), G.E. Street (1824–81), Norman Shaw (1831–1912) and Alfred Waterhouse (1830–1905).

The influential cultural commentator John Ruskin (1819–1900) also proved important as, in place of classical order, he advocated varied skylines and steeply pitched roofs. There was also much secular building in the neo-Gothic style from the 1850s, including Waterhouse's bulky and imposing Manchester Town Hall (1869–77), as well as St Pancras Station in London. The neo-Gothic style was seen as conveying solidity and permanence. As the century waned, however, the neo-Gothic became increasingly repetitive in England, although Scottish baronial style ensured that Victorian domestic, and to an extent civic, architecture reached its apogee in the Glasgow region.

Yet Gothic Revival did not enjoy an unchallenged ascendancy. Other styles included the neo-Renaissance of Sir Charles Barry (1795–1860). His range indicated the eclecticism that was a pronounced feature of the period. Barry's output ranged from the neo-Gothic Houses of Parliament to the Greek Revival Manchester Athenaeum.

The variety of the Arts and Crafts movement associated with William Morris (1834–96) helped to lighten the neo-Gothic.

The influential Morris popularized an interest in craftsmanship and design skills. As was typical of the Victorians, entrepreneurship and production played a major role, with Morris and Co., established in 1861, producing wallpapers, furnishings and stained glass windows that influenced fashionable style.

Other architectural styles and themes included, at the end of the century, Art Nouveau, which drew on Continental developments and was particularly associated with Glasgow architects, especially Charles Rennie Mackintosh (1868–1928), who stressed functionalism and modernity and criticized the revival of past styles. His 1896 design for the Glasgow School of Art was a triumph of functionalism, as were the houses he built in Glasgow in the early 1900s. Mackintosh also played an important role in furniture and design, offering interiors that were far from the opulent, often cloying, heaviness frequently associated with the period.

The Sense of Change

The spread of towns outwards was more significant than changes in the pre-existing urban area. This spread was accompanied by the improvement of transport links and led to the development of commuting as an aspect of daily life. The railway played the key role, but omnibuses, first horse-drawn, and later motor-powered, joined by trams, swiftly expanded the new urban transport systems. Life became a matter not only of the extent of the built environment, but also of the intense web of connections that gave it drive.

Prefiguring the modern communications revolution of the internet and the mobile phone, the Victorians had daily postal services covering the country, as well as the telegraph to send messages even faster at home and abroad. Life was particularly speeded up in and by the cities. In 1899, Sir J.W. Barry (1836–1918) estimated that eight horse-drawn buses a minute would pass an observer on Tottenham Court Road in central London.

This process of change did not stop or slow with Queen Victoria's death in 1901, yet another instance of the danger of placing too great a weight on supposed turning points and significant moments. Instead, the new power sources, electricity and the internal combustion engine, provided continuing opportunities for entrepreneurs and advocates of change. New industries developed and created new links between regions. By 1907, the Britannia Foundry at Derby included a motor-cylinder foundry making 400–500 cylinders weekly for car manufacturers, such as Jowett Motors of Bradford, an output that indicated the cascading benefits of industrial production and demand.

The sense of new possibilities was captured in the name of the cinema opened in Harwich in 1911, the Electric Palace. In addition, science fiction was increasingly potent in the imaginative landscape: *The Time Machine* (1895) was the first major novel by H.G. Wells (1866–1946), prophet of New Liberalism, whose scientific futurism seemed increasingly appropriate in the rapidly changing world. The Time Traveller goes to the year 802,701 where he finds a dystopia with two human species: the aesthetic Eloi and the crude Morlocks, the latter the descendants of subterranean labourers. This vision, a warning about the social and cultural divisiveness of modern Britain, reflected Wells' interest in evolution.

The Rise of Suburbia

As a result of the pace of economic activity, the process of urban expansion continued to be rapid over subsequent decades. Inexpensive land, a product of the downturn in the agricultural economy from the 1870s, and the availability of cheap credit, combined to satisfy the demand from the increasing population. The new housing was linked to a change in the nature of industry. The growth of factory employment and factory districts meant the decline of workshops, and thus of the industrial nature of the inner city. The new factory districts were linked to the establishment of housing estates, both these aspects of a form of development zoning that became a more apparent feature of the differentiation of cities by area. Thus, the west end of Newcastle had industry and working-class housing in marked contrast to the middle-class suburbs of Jesmond and Gosforth to its north.

Industry was generally kept at a distance from suburbia. Indeed, the growth of suburbia reflected the desire for a life away from factory chimneys and inner-city crowding, a desire catered to in the publicity advocating life in the new suburbs. Place and movement were particularly susceptible to change, as the cities altered and the motor car spread in the early twentieth century in a symbiotic development: cars encouraged housing of a lower density, while the new suburbs were shaped by the road systems constructed for these cars. The tightly packed terraces characteristic of Victorian England, for the middle as well as the working class, were supplemented by miles of 'semis': semi-detached houses with some mock-Tudor elevations, red-tiled roofs, and walls of red brick or pebbledash, with a small front and a larger back garden. Each house had a small drive and a separate garage, which was often structurally linked to the house. This was a suburbia, later eulogized by the poet John Betjeman (1906–84), representing the application of pre-First World War ideas of garden suburbs, notably with an emphasis on space, calm and the separateness expressed in individual gardens.

Earlier, suburbia had spread in the late nineteenth century with the railways, but development then had generally not moved far from the stations. In contrast, car transport permitted less intensive development, although, in practice, this often meant more extensive estates that were otherwise as densely packed by the developers as the basic housing model permitted. As with the car, the semi expressed the desire for freedom: a freedom to escape the constraints of living in close proximity to others, as most people did, and, instead, to enjoy space. Semis were not the more individual and larger suburban villas for the wealthier members of the middle class built round

Victorian cities in up-market suburbs such as London's St John's Wood, which continued to exist in what were now enclaves, but they reflected a similar aspiration for space and privacy. Moreover, semis captured the aspirations of millions, and offered them a decent living environment, including a garden. Stanley Baldwin's speeches in the 1920s helped to capture suburbia for the Conservatives by emphasizing that its inhabitants were country dwellers, and hence custodians of the core English values.

Semis were certainly far more a realization of the suburban ideal than terraced housing. In *English Journey* (1934), J.B. Priestley (1894–1984) wrote, alongside the old industrial and rural Englands, of the new England of suburbs and road houses: pubs built along trunk roads. In Scotland, in contrast, the cities remained more like Continental ones, as to an extent they still do, with the well-to-do living quite close to the centre and the poorest in peripheral housing schemes.

In part, suburbia was a response to the cult of the outdoors, one mediated through, and in, the suburban garden (which greatly attracted the middle class) and the parks of new suburbs. I grew up in a 'Parkside Drive', built in the 1930s alongside a new suburban park taken from farmland. Suburbia, moreover, was linked to a ruralist image of England that was found across the arts. In music, it was seen in the positive response to Edward Elgar (1857–1934) and Ralph Vaughan Williams (1872–1958), notably pieces that became iconic such as *Enigma*, *Pomp and Circumstance* and *The Lark Ascending*, and, in painting, in the popularity of 'authentic' rather than modernist works.

Suburbia, which came into use as a pejorative noun in the 1890s, certainly reflected sameness and national standardization. Indeed, a predictability of product helped to make the new housing sell: the houses were mass-produced and had standardized parts and they looked similar, as did their garages. A degree of individuality was provided by the gardens, but they generally had similar plantings. The Garden Cities also allowed only a very narrow diversity.

In part, the similarity of the new housing was because of the role of brick as the standard building material and the dominance of much brickmaking by the Fletton process using the Jurassic clays of the East Midlands, whose high carbon content cut the cost of firing. Feeding the new suburbia, brickmaking developed as a massive industry between Bedford and Bletchley and also near Whittlesey on the Cambridgeshire–Huntingdonshire border. Bricks, and other products for the housing market, such as prefabricated doors and windows, could be moved not only by rail, but also by the new expanding road system; and profit was made from mass-production and long-range distribution, rather than from local sources.

Much new building was by private enterprise (rather than local councils), and often by speculative builders, such as Richard Costain (1839–1902) and John Laing (1879–1978). They were largely responsible for the plentiful supply of inexpensive houses by the mid-1920s. The ability of purchasers to borrow at low rates of interest from building societies was also important. In the mid-1920s, houses cost between £400 and £1,000. This new housing was crucial to the process by which suburban culture became increasingly defined and important within Britain, and this importance was true for both politics and social assumptions. The suburbs had fairly standard mock-Tudor parades of shops on their high streets and also enormous and lavishly decorated picture palaces – cinemas – which represented the move to the suburbs of leisure. The cinema also proved a fashionable, standardized, mechanistic and cheaper alternative to the music hall, and one that by offering the same product justified national advertising.

Council house building was also important to the spread of suburbia, as well as providing a crucial link between housing and local politics. Treasury loans for local authority building had been available from 1866, but most local authorities had been reluctant to incur debts. From 1919, however, as a consequence of the Housing and Town Planning Act introduced by Christopher Addison (1869–1951), grants replaced loans, and council house building expanded. This expansion was designed to give bricks and mortar to the Prime Minister David Lloyd George's (1863–1945) promise of 'Homes fit for Heroes' for troops returning home at the end of the First World War.

Following many of the recommendations made in the Tudor Walters Report of 1918, the Housing and Town Planning Act of 1919 sought to provide lower-density housing for the working class. Minimum room sizes were decreed, as was the inclusion of internal bathrooms. Indeed, the public housing of the period was generally of good quality, and much of it is regarded as more desirable than a lot of 1960s public housing, not least because of its human scale.

Rural Transformation
While Britain urbanized, the countryside was also changing. Agriculture was hit hard by growing international competition and by the end of protectionism with the repeal of the Corn Laws in 1846, a move which was designed to help ensure cheap food for the increasingly urban people. Technological advances were to help provide this food in the shape of steamships, refrigerated ship holds, and the railways and barbed wire that enabled the exploitation of large areas for agriculture. As a result, grain from North America, mutton and lamb from Australasia, and beef from Argentina, all enjoyed competitive advantages over home production, and this ensured that Britain, which could not anyway feed its rapidly growing population, became even more of a food importer. Most of the imports were not from Europe. Grain from Germany, Poland and Russia was only bought in significant quantities in some years, although German sugar beet was important, while, by the end of the century, Danish bacon and eggs was the staple of the British breakfast. Nevertheless, it was products from the New World and Australasia that were crucial, all, ironically,

opened up by British technology, particularly railways and steamships, and helped by British finance.

Britain, the dominant player in the expanding and intensifying global economic order, was itself changed greatly by this new economy. The consequences moulded the shape of rural Britain and its relationship with the remainder of the country. Agriculture remained significant, especially for products such as milk and vegetables that were not convenient or economic to import, but its importance to British life and the economy diminished, while, thanks to international competition, there was a severe and sustained agricultural depression from the 1870s. Combined with new technology, such as combined reaping and mowing machines, and mechanization, as electric power and the internal combustion engine were applied in agriculture, this depression ensured falling labour demands for workers on the land. Partly as a result, only 10.4 per cent of the United Kingdom's workforce was employed in agriculture in the 1890s, compared to 40.3 per cent in France.

This fall contributed greatly to the migration to the cities that was such an important aspect of the population growth there. Rural counties lost population: Anglesey's population fell from 57,000 in 1851 to 49,000 in 1931. This depression and migration are not generally appreciated today, not least due to the presentation of rural life in terms of the National Trust stately homes visited and seen as television and film settings, but they were important to the changing character of both the countryside and the country. In novels such as *Far from the Madding Crowd* (1874) and *The Mayor of Casterbridge* (1886), Thomas Hardy (1840–1928) recorded the bleaker side of country life, the sway of folklore and customs, a countryside prey to North American grain imports, and the corrosive pressure of urban values on rural ways. Casterbridge was based on Dorchester.

There was, however, a clear regional dimension to these changes. The cheap, readily imported, food that fed the growing workforces of the industrial north helped to lead to a sustained depression through much of the more agrarian south, a regional disparity that was to be reversed in the twentieth century. Moreover, thanks to cheaper food, industrial workers were able to spend a lower proportion of their wages on food than hitherto, thus becoming important consumers, as well as producers, of manufactured goods.

Emigration from the countryside looked towards a feature that would have been increasingly apparent in the twentieth century to a visitor from earlier ages, its emptiness. The dense pattern of settlement across lowland Britain was transformed, with villages shrinking and farmsteads being abandoned. Moreover, the total area devoted to agriculture in Britain fell by half a million acres (202,343 hectares) between the 1870s and 1914. These changes proved the background to a series of changes in land use. Rural areas near cities and towns were increasingly suburban, with villages becoming the base for commuting by the affluent. In turn, the village poor, landless labourers without jobs, and unemployed rural craftsmen, moved abroad or to the towns. Thus, villages were now places of residence, not work. More marginal farmland was abandoned, and the leisure use of land grew greatly from the Victorian period.

The New Elite
This usage greatly reflected the character of British society and politics. Most of the land used for leisure, and notably so in Highland Scotland, was for shooting, stalking and fishing. It was at the disposal of very small numbers but required an appreciable workforce, for example as gamekeepers. This use of the land also reflected a shift in the self-image of much of the landed elite, as well as the change in this elite as the long-term process by which new money purchased old land and thus acquired status, speeded up with the large fortunes made from industry, commerce and finance.

Thus, William Armstrong (1810–1900), the grandson of a Northumberland yeoman farmer and the son of a Newcastle corn merchant, who created the Elswick Ordnance Company, one of the largest engineering and armaments concerns in the world, built a mock-baronial stately home at Cragside in Northumberland and in 1894 purchased Bamburgh Castle, a great medieval royal fortress. In turn, Armstrong was at the forefront of technological application. Cragside, now owned by the National Trust, was in 1880 the first house to be properly lit by light bulbs, while Armstrong was also responsible for the hydraulic lifts that were necessary if the London underground railway system was to expand with deep stations and thus serve the spreading city and also encourage its spread.

The purchase of old land by 'new money' was further encouraged by the increase of death duties in 1894 and by the dire impact of the casualties and taxation of the First World War on landed families and the resulting post-war surge in land sales; although some of this land was sold to tenant farmers. These developments provided opportunities for social change, but the key factor was socio-cultural: money saw status in terms of the old landed order and was eager to embrace fashionable rural hobbies, notably shooting. The contrast with the late twentieth century was readily apparent, because then new money tended to follow a metropolitan lifestyle and, if it bought into rural living, did not generally have much to do with the aristocracy or with aristocratic lifestyles.

If the wealthy of 1851–1931 sought the grouse moors, the comfortably off pursued the links. Unlike Scotland where it was more socially inclusive, golfing developed greatly in England as a middle-class hobby with membership in golf clubs serving to affirm and defend status: in most cases, only men could be members and in England the clubs were overwhelmingly middle-class. Jews, moreover, were generally excluded. Cities were circled by clubs, and they also became a key feature in wealthy suburban areas. The increased use of cars encouraged the use of suburban and rural golf courses.

Yet, the countryside was also the site of less exclusive leisure activity. Taking advantage of rail, bus and steamship excursions, and of holidays, notably bank holidays, working families saw parts of Britain as they had never done before. Much of this involved trips to the seaside resorts that rapidly developed, such as Blackpool, Ilfracombe, Rothesay, Skegness and Southend. As part of the pattern by which distinctive local characteristics were eroded, these holidays affected the places visited. Thus, the decline of the strong Methodist temperance (teetotalism) movement in Whitby in the 1930s owed much to the need to earn money from tourists who wanted alcohol.

There was also an interest in scenic Britain. This was explored further by ramblers, cyclists and a host of organizations that sought to take townspeople into the countryside, notably the Boy Scouts, the Girl Guides and the Youth Hostelling Association. Their Britain was not that of the shoot, but there were similarities, not least a belief that quality rested in the outdoor lifestyle as did a notion of national integrity, whether seen as British, English, Scottish or Welsh.

The outdoors was of course a contested space, to use a modern jargon that is not without value. Just as ramblers challenged the 'closure' of moorland for the sake of private shoots, and did so in an increasingly prominent fashion after the First World War, so cycling provided young women from the late nineteenth century with an opportunity to pursue a degree of unchaperoned independence, a prospect that filled some commentators with concern. There was also social tension, tension that affected those at the height of society. In 1888, the 3rd Earl of Sheffield (1832–1909), a Sussex landowner, received a letter including the passages:

> ... my duty to let you know, as I do not think you do, or you would not have the heart to turn out an old tenant like poor Mrs Grover out of her home after such a hard struggle to maintain and bring up her family ... you and your faithful steward want it all. ... My knife is nice and sharp.

The letter was signed Jack the Ripper, then at his brutal work among the prostitutes of poverty-stricken Whitechapel. In fact, nothing happened to the Earl: Mrs Grover was staying with her children after a fall, and Edward Grover, a failed butcher, admitted writing the letter. This was not, however, an isolated episode. Indeed, in 1889, the Earl wrote an open letter to the Secretary of Sussex County Cricket Club, explaining his resignation as president, in which he referred to two-and-a-half years of pestering by anonymous threats. Social deference was clearly limited, and in Oscar Wilde's (1854–1900) play *The Importance of Being Earnest* (1895), the fictional Lady Bracknell, the arbiter of social status, was fearful of acts of violence in Grosvenor Square, the centre of fashionable London.

Rural Identity and the National Problem

Not only landowners were at risk. Changing agricultural pressures and leisure priorities had varied consequences for the animals that shared the country with humans. As yet, the impact from intensive land use and chemical fertilizers was relatively limited, but railways had significant effects on local habitats and animal routes. The motor car, moreover, had a major impact in rural Britain thanks to the damage done by asphalting roads, as well as the marked growth in road-kill. Yet, the growing interest in preserving the landscape, especially supposedly exemplary parts, had beneficial consequences for animals who lived in those areas.

The myriad constituencies involved in pursuing rural interests indicated the extent to which agriculture and other traditional rural occupations no longer controlled the landscape, and this lack of control was rapidly followed by the development of urban interest in deciding what should happen to this landscape. The foundation of the National Trust in 1895 gave institutional form to a widespread concern about the disappearance of rural England and Wales but also to a belief that something could be done and that this did not necessarily involve action through the traditional rural order. Modern manifestations of this attitude include the hunting ban and the assertion of a 'right to roam'.

Although it was to come in part to be about tourism and consuming 'heritage', the National Trust was initially about preservation, and, as such, reflected the ruralism that was increasingly common in British attitudes. As the countryside came to encapsulate national values, so there was a desire to preserve it either free from obvious human impact or as a worked environment on what was seen as a human scale. The landscape as the repository and inspiration of national history and identity, and as the key medium between past and present, became a frequently advanced concept. Much of this drive owed little to any real knowledge of the countryside but, instead, was an expression of anxiety about the nature of British society.

Such anxiety could be seen across a range of sectors. Urban life, especially, but not only, that of the poor, was discussed in terms of irreligion, physical, mental and moral degeneracy, and the supposedly deleterious consequences of a political system in which the franchise (right to vote) was progressively expanded. Poor urban housing, sanitation and nutrition were widely blamed for what was seen as the physical weakness of much of the population, and this perception encouraged the Liberals, Labour and, also, Conservative paternalists to support measures for social welfare, notably the New Liberalism of the 1900s and 1910s. Thus, concern about the country as a physical space was related to anxieties about it as a moral sphere and political system: Britain and the British were seen as linked and under threat.

The Early Twentieth Century

By 1931, Britain, its landscape and its cities were spanned by new transport and power systems. Aircraft and electricity generation represented very different relationships between man and the environment to those of 1851. The former was not dependent on the terrain and thus looked towards a general disjuncture between man and environment that was to be a characteristic of modern life. Moreover, the National

Electricity Scheme launched in the 1920s permitted a location of industries that was not as close to the coalfields as the industries of the nineteenth century. Indeed, electricity transmission transformed the power system in Britain. Technology was like a freed genie, bringing ever more changes, and the growth of the genre of 'scientific romance' in literature testified to the seemingly inexorable advance of human potential through technology. The potential for a new urban landscape was grasped by architectural development, not least with new buildings built with steel frames which allowed for more flexibility in design. Thus, the style of building began to change from the constrained Victorian background where technical tolerance limits had restricted the design.

There was also a substantial development of new technology by the 1920s: radio and telegraphic communications and the car transformed everyday life. The emergence of cars, for example, led to problems with new forms of crime and new types of accidents, and the police had to develop flying squads of cars to deal with these problems, which led to the need for control rooms and therefore radio communication. Cars rivalled horse and carts on the road, up to 7,000 people were killed annually on the roads, and the Highway Code had to be developed to establish the rules of the road. The 1920s and 1930s were a period of economic, social and technological transition which fundamentally changed many aspects of social life.

The new technology that made these changes possible was not uniquely British, and Britain did not play the leading role in the industrialization of the early twentieth century as it had done a century earlier. Instead, first the US, and then Germany, passed Britain in manufacturing output and put British industry under great pressure. Pressing the case for imperial preference in tariffs (customs duties), Joseph Chamberlain (1836–1914) argued in 1903 that free trade threatened Britain's economic position: 'Sugar has gone; silk has gone; iron is threatened; wool is threatened; cotton will go.' Nevertheless,

Britain remained a leading manufacturing power, its relative position enhanced by the extent to which East and South Asia were not yet leading industrial powerhouses, as is the case today. In 1910–14, Britain still built 62 per cent of the world's ships, although in 1892–4 the percentage had been 82.

Moreover, although its share of world trade fell prior to the First World War, Britain's trade was larger than hitherto. Britain was also the largest overseas investor and the greatest merchant shipper in the world, as well as the centre of the world's financial system: commodity prices, shipping routes and insurance premiums were all set in London. In Dickens' novel *Little Dorrit* (1855–7), society worships Merdle, a great but fraudulent financier, 'a new power in the country', and, at dinner at Merdle's, 'Treasury hoped he might venture to congratulate one of England's world-famed capitalists and merchant-princes ... To extend the triumphs of such men, was to extend the triumphs and resources of the nation.' Indeed, the expansion of the service sector, focused on the City of London, was fundamental to Britain's continued economic strength and influence, and became more so as British manufacturing was put under pressure. In 1914, 43 per cent of the world's foreign investment was British, and Britain was also the sole European state selling more outside the Continent than in European markets.

These advantages, however, were challenged by international competition, while the cost and disruption of the First World War proved highly damaging, not least leading to the large-scale sale of foreign assets. Thanks largely to the war, London's financial position was in part overtaken by that of New York in the 1920s.

In the 1920s, Britain sought to re-create the pre-war liberal international order, but with only limited success. Britain's economy grew less than that of the US, and, although it compared well with other major Western economies, there was a serious recession in 1920–1. GDP (Gross Domestic Product) rose above 1913 levels only in 1927, and the trade balance with most of the world, which had deteriorated since 1913, was used as a major argument against free trade and in favour of tariffs, an abrupt departure from the liberal, free trade assumptions of the Victorian order, which had already been challenged in the 1900s. For many years after the war, exports remained well below 1913 figures. To many contemporaries, the economy, already in difficulties prior to the worldwide slump of 1929 and the subsequent Depression, appeared to be in the doldrums; and this view was confirmed by subsequent economic analysis. However, there were positive developments, not least the growth of demand-led consumer industries, such as the production of cars, radios and domestic appliances, for example cookers and washing-machines, rather than the more supply-led heavy industrial sector which had been so important to nineteenth-century industrialization, for example shipbuilding and cotton-textiles.

This contrast between sectors of growth and decline, which was to be taken much further in the 1930s, led to a very different geography of prosperity and economic opportunity to that of the nineteenth century, one that would have been readily apparent to anyone flying over the country. Outside the prosperous cities, suburbia followed the new roads, while new industrial plant could be seen in self-contained estates served largely by roads. In contrast, there was already derelict industrial plant in the heavy industrial zones, such as the north east of England, although not yet on the scale that was to be seen in the 1980s.

In the inter-war years, the availability of jobs in expanding industrial centres in the south-east and the Midlands, such as Birmingham, Coventry, Letchworth, Luton, Slough, Watford and Welwyn, led to substantial levels of migration within Britain. Oxford as a major centre of population, and the new towns and expansion in Letchworth, Luton, Slough, Watford and Welwyn, were all indicators of a country whose geography had changed substantially since 1851, in large part due to economic growth in the south. Thanks to the Morris car works at Cowley, Oxford had only 5 per cent unemployment in 1934, and the car factories there employed 10,000 workers in 1939, producing on the American model that Morris sought to copy from Henry Ford.

These changes in Britain's geography were linked to those of the people, their circumstances and opportunities, and were understood by contemporaries in that light. This gives readers a choice, a choice that reflects the extent to which any division of the national history for purposes of description and analysis is of limited value if it neglects the extent to which experience was not readily fractured between different categories. It is possible to turn to Chapter 3 to consider the changing condition of the people but it is best to follow the order in this book as the next chapter includes a narrative intended to guide the reader as well as to show the importance of political developments, not least for the condition of the people covered in Chapter 3. For both, however, there are two key contexts – the economic growth which has been discussed in this chapter and the imperial primacy considered in Chapter 4.

2

THE CULTURE OF POWER

'The latest is best ... not to believe in the nineteenth century, one might as well disbelieve that a child grows into a man ... without that Faith in Time what anchor have we in any secular speculation.'

This remark, in 1857, by the painter William Bell Scott (1811–90), was exemplified in his painting *The Nineteenth Century, Iron and Coal* (1861), which was set in the vibrant industrial city of Newcastle. His canvas sought to capture, as Scott stated, 'everything of the common labour, life and applied science of the day'. Scott depicted workers at Robert Stephenson's engineering works, one of the largest manufacturers of railway engines in the world, as well as an Armstrong artillery piece which was made on the Tyne, the steam of modern communications and telegraph wires. This was culture depicting power, the power of the world's leading economy. Yet, the politics that this society was to follow were unclear, as was the culture that it would celebrate.

Triumphant Market

In the event, the triumph of the market is the major theme in nineteenth-century British cultural history. This triumph parallels the rise of the (male) democratic electorate as the franchise, or right to vote, was extended, the course and consequences of which is a key theme in the second part of this chapter. By the 'market', we mean that the role of consumers, not government, determined the success of particular art forms and artists. This cultural marketplace had come to the fore in Britain in the eighteenth century, as patronage by individual wealthy patrons was largely replaced by the anonymous patronage of the market. The latter entailed producing works for sale to individuals the artist had not met and also led to the cultural meeting points so important to Victorian and early-twentieth-century society: choral festivals, concert halls and art galleries.

The crucial links were provided by the entrepreneurs who flourished in this period, notably concert organizers, art auctioneers and publishers, men who treated culture as a commodity, a commodity whose value was set by the market. Many politicians were not all that dissimilar in their methods, notably Benjamin Disraeli (1804–81), David Lloyd George and Winston Churchill (1874–1965), all of whom made their personality a key popular commodity. Even the more dour William Gladstone (1809–98) became a master of public meetings and of addressing a far larger audience through the penny press. For, in politics, as in culture, there was a fluid market, in which style and novelty were important in enhancing value and attracting recognition and support.

In both culture and politics, the market greatly changed during the nineteenth century, largely owing to the movement of the bulk of the population into markets hitherto defined essentially (though not exclusively) in terms of the elite and the middling orders. In the Victorian period, the bulk of the male working class, especially the skilled artisans, gained not only the vote, but also time and money for leisure. Much of this time and money was spent on sport, and football, in particular, emerged as a very popular spectator sport. This was a national game and one that benefited from the Victorian zeal for organization alongside entrepreneurship, indeed for enterprising organization. The Football Association, formed in 1863, sought to codify the rules of the game. The scale of an industrial economy also played a growing role. Increasingly popular, football was organized on a large scale from the 1880s, and attendances increased markedly. An astonishing 111,000 spectators, most standing, were at Crystal Palace in 1901 to see Tottenham beat Sheffield Wednesday.

Other sports, such as horse-racing, also attracted a large working-class following, as did pigeon-racing. Greyhound-racing, however, which was to have such a following, was not introduced until 1926, although there had been a previous experiment. It rose quickly to well over 30 million attendances per year. To the authorities, these numbers presented a threat since on-course betting was legal under British law, and so gave a chance for the working classes to bet legally much as the middle classes did on horse racecourses. The resultant betting provoked an attempt by Winston Churchill and others to control greyhound-racing, though they failed. Churchill referred to the greyhound tracks as being 'animated roulette wheels'.

In the late nineteenth century, sporting activities, like other branches of leisure, became increasingly highly organized, competitive and commercialized, and with a much more distinct division between participant and observer. There was also a boom in middle-class sports, such as golf and lawn tennis, whose rules were systematized in 1874. Sporting institutions and facilities were created across Britain. Northumberland Cricket Club had a ground in Newcastle by the 1850s, while Newcastle Golf Club expanded its activities in the 1890s.

Sport, leisure, culture and politics all followed society in becoming more urban, although with significant enclaves of upper-class activity. Certain types of leisure facilities needed urban populations to finance and sustain them, for example libraries, reading rooms and bath-houses – the public baths helpful for cleanliness and hygiene in towns where most people lacked bathing facilities at home.

The same need for urban populations was true for music halls where the entertainment epitomized the culture of urban workers. The music hall was escapist on one level, yet it was also central to working-class life. Large music halls, such as the Alhambra in Bradford, providing song, music, acrobatics and dance, offered both spectator entertainment and an opportunity to participate by singing along or engaging in repartee with the performers, with stars such as Marie Lloyd (1870–1922) becoming national figures.

Yet, the impact of technology and entrepreneurship was such that, with the advent of 'moving pictures', many music halls were converted into cinemas which, by 1914, numbered some 4,000. That year, Manchester alone had 111 premises licensed to show films, while even the more rural, and far less affluent, county of Lincolnshire had fourteen cinemas in 1913.

Organized middle-class cultural activity also greatly expanded in the Victorian age and early twentieth century, an expansion that owed much to the growth of the middle class in the cities and also to its pursuit of culture not only for pleasure, but in addition, as a way of defining its purpose and leadership. Cities such as Birmingham, Glasgow, Leeds, Liverpool, Manchester and Newcastle founded major art collections and musical institutions, for example the Hallé Orchestra in Manchester in 1857 and the Laing Art Gallery in Newcastle. Such patronage helped support popular art movements, for example that of the Pre-Raphaelite painters, who enjoyed considerable popularity from the early 1850s.

Although much of the expansion of cultural expression was the product of commercial, urban, middle-class wealth, its purpose was more broad-ranging. Labouring men and women queued for hours to file past Ford Madox Brown's (1821–93) classic painting *Work* when it was finally finished in 1863, and many hung up cheap reproductions of paintings and bought sheet music. For these people, viewing art was like viewing a film première today. Thus, art informed the public as well as the elite.

Fiction

Moreover, fiction became a major prism through which the country was viewed, and consciously so on the part of both writers and readers. Novels such as Charles Dickens' *Hard Times* (1854) and Elizabeth Gaskell's (1810–65) *North and South* (1855) depicted the problems of industrial life, particularly labour disputes and worker misery. Social issues attracted other prominent writers such as Wilkie Collins (1824–89) and George Eliot (1819–80), the latter the pseudonym of Mary Anne Evans, who depicted the decadent mores of society in *Daniel Deronda* (1878). They were not alone. George Gissing (1857–1903) presented urban poverty and the harsh binds of heredity in *Workers in the Dawn* (1880), while Thomas Hardy's *Jude the Obscure* (1895) dealt with exclusion from education as a result of class.

The writers of the age sought a wide readership, not only for personal profit but also because they thought it important to write for the unprecedented mass readership being created by increased education. Such a goal was not seen as incompatible with literary excellence, and these attitudes reflected the distance between the literary world of the nineteenth century and that of two centuries earlier which had displayed a self-conscious elitism. William Wordsworth's successor as Poet Laureate in 1850 was Alfred Tennyson (1809–92), who held the post until 1892 and helped reconcile poetry and the Establishment. A favourite of Queen Victoria, who raised him to the peerage in 1883, Tennyson was no bluff rhymester, but, like many prominent Victorians, a neurotic and withdrawn figure who understood sadness. As a protagonist of morality and empire, Tennyson was also safe as well as a master of poetry as understood in the period. The self-sacrifice endorsed in poems such as his 'Enoch Arden' (1864) was very popular. It was self-sacrifice, not of the Byronic outcast, but of the servant of a social morality. Despite the importance of the prolific and talented Robert Browning (1812–89), Tennyson dominated the poetic world even more than Dickens did that of fiction.

The current theatrical repertoire includes very few works from the first four decades of the period of this book, and it is not until Oscar Wilde in the 1890s that one finds such works still frequently acted. Among the now forgotten plays that lacked the dexterity and style of Wilde's well-written works but that were successes for contemporaries, Thomas Robertson's (1829–71) comedies, for example *Society* (1865), *Ours* (1866), *Caste* (1867), *Play* (1868), *School* (1869), and *M.P.* (1870), plays described as 'cup-and-saucer drama', have been seen as offering a detailed account of domestic life that laid the basis for the latter revival of serious drama by Shaw. Opulent Shakespeare revivals, melodrama, Gilbert and Sullivan operettas, and farces, such as Charles Hawtrey's (1858–1923) *The Private Secretary* (1884) and Arthur Wing Pinero's (1855–1934) *The Magistrate* (1885), dominated the stage.

Theatre managers preferred long runs of single plays which could best be secured by prominent stars, such as Ellen Terry (1847–1928), uncontentious plots and spectacular productions with an emphasis on scenery and music. Augustus Harris (1852–96), manager of the Theatre Royal at Drury Lane, London, from 1879 until 1896, set the tone with spectaculars featuring avalanches, earthquakes, horse-races and snow-storms. The success of the run could be increased either by sending the company on a rail-borne tour round Britain or by using second and third companies at the same time as the main company coined the London market and ensured continued favourable publicity. This system scarcely encouraged adventurous drama but it brought profits, encouraging investment in new theatres which congregated in London's West End, increasing its importance as a focus for commercial glamour.

Wilde's plays, *Lady Windermere's Fan* (1892), *A Woman of No Importance* (1893), *An Ideal Husband* (1895) and *The Importance of Being Earnest* (1895), were ironic and brilliant portrayals of high society. *Salome*, which was refused a licence in 1892 and first performed in Paris in 1896, was a very different work: a highly charged, erotic account of the relationship between Salome and St John the Baptist. *Salome* represented Wilde's willingness to press the boundaries of polite society and conventional culture, and also indicated the range of even one playwright's work, a point also seen for example in Sir Arthur Sullivan's music.

The 1890s also saw the appearance of the first of the plays of George Bernard Shaw, which were far more socially realistic than those of Wilde. Several, *Widowers' Houses* (1892), *Mrs Warren's Profession* (1892) and *The Philanderer* (1893), were performed only privately as they were thought unlikely to obtain a licence: the Lord Chamberlain, through the Examiner of Plays, had to give a licence before any public performances on the stage. This, in particular, restricted new and different works. The series of Shaw's realistic works produced publicly began only with his *Arms and the Man* (1894). Politically committed, he pushed the notion of the dramatist as a public figure able to turn a searching light on society.

Art

Painting reflected the eclecticism and energy of British culture, although, yet again, there is the tension between what was popular at the time and what appears most significant today. A key established figure was Queen Victoria's (and her subjects') favourite painter, Edwin Landseer (1802–73), who was knighted in 1850 and offered the presidency of the Royal Academy in 1865. He had the Scottish links that were helpful in British society at the time (far more so than for Irish and Welsh counterparts), and could also offer both a sentimentality and an exemplary image of bravery that appealed to contemporary tastes. In 1851, Landseer exhibited *The Monarch of the Glen*, a dramatic depiction of a stag, in 1853 *Night* and *Morning*, pictures of a duel between stags, and in 1864 *Man proposes, God disposes*: polar bears amid the relics of Sir John Franklin's disastrous Arctic expedition. The last, an episode in the attempt to find a North-West Passage from the Atlantic to the Pacific, was presented in terms of the selfless, yet disciplined, heroism that Victorian society found exemplary. Engravings of Landseer's paintings were printed in large number. He was not noted as an explorer of the urban scene, although he left his mark on London when he sculpted the lions at the foot of Nelson's Column (1867), part of the process by which Trafalgar Square was scripted as the symbolic centre of empire.

A counterpart of Landseer, Daniel Maclise (1806–70), was much applauded as a great artist, although today he is far less well known. A close friend of Dickens, and an accomplished draughtsman who painted statuesque forms, Maclise illustrated themes from British history, such as *The Death of Nelson* (1864) for Parliament. Another prominent figure of the period, Sir Charles Eastlake (1793–1865), was President of the Royal Academy from 1850 to 1865 and was noted for portraits, historical scenes and picturesque displays of Mediterranean scenes and people. More generally, animals, sporting pictures and exemplary historical, religious and military scenes were popular with purchasers, as were scenes of rural bliss.

There were also paintings reflecting the less benign aspects of life, but most of them were tempered in their realism. For example, Thomas Kennington's (1856–1916) *The Pinch of Poverty* (1889) did not provide a picture of smiling joy, but poverty was generally far harsher in its consequences than this genteel scene with its charming flower-seller and romantically pale mother.

The year 1851 saw both the death of J.M.W. Turner (1775–1851), the leading British painter of the early nineteenth century, and the appearance of one of the great Pre-Raphaelite paintings, *The Hireling Shepherd* by William Holman Hunt

(1827–1910). The term Pre-Raphaelite had been adopted in 1848 by a group, or, as they called themselves, Brotherhood, of young English painters, the most prominent of whom were Hunt, John Everett Millais (1829–96) and Dante Gabriel Rossetti (1828–82). They attempted to react against what they saw as the empty formalism of the then fashionable 'subject' painting and, instead, offered a stress on the moral purpose of art. Millais and Hunt in particular sought their own revolution in art.

The Brotherhood had dissolved by 1855, but its themes remained influential, including among many of those who were not actually members of either the Brotherhood or the second Brotherhood, founded by Rossetti, Edward Burne-Jones (1833–98) and William Morris. Thus, Ford Madox Brown, although never a member, was sufficiently impressed to paint in the Pre-Raphaelite manner, most famously *Work*.

Among the Brotherhood, Hunt remained faithful to its aims. He travelled on several occasions to Egypt and Palestine, in order to ground his paintings of Biblical scenes accurately. The popularity of these paintings underlines the strong Christian commitment of Victorian society. Yet, as a reminder of variety, Millais followed a different course, becoming a fashionable painter and pillar of the artistic establishment, thanks to undemanding sentimental portraits, for example *The Blind Girl* (1886) and *Bubbles* (1886).

By the time of Millais' death, the contours of the artistic world were very different. A sense of *fin de siècle* affected the mood of the 1890s. Paintings such as *Circe Invidiosa* (1892) by J.W. Waterhouse (1849–1917) illustrate the appeal of the exotic and the erotic; although no painter made as great a success of mixing the exotic with the historical as did Sir Lawrence Alma-Tadema (1836–1912) with his vast output of highly detailed studies of Roman, Greek and Egyptian life in classical times. Alma-Tadema's paintings also emphasized the female form in as much detail as was permissible in Victorian society, a trait he shared with Waterhouse.

Middle-class Culture

The drive for interest and self-improvement did not only focus on sport, reading, listening to music and visiting art galleries. In addition, many enthusiasts were committed to natural history, astronomy and geology. Such activities were also institutionalized with numerous natural history societies and observatories around the country. Interest in geology and natural history helps explain the public engagement with the controversy over Darwin's theory of evolution, which was expounded in his *The Origin of Species* (1859).

Politics was part of this world of individual enthusiasm, group activity, civic concern and entrepreneurialism. Indeed, in his novel *The Moonstone* (1868), Wilkie Collins wrote 'The guests present being all English, it is needless to say that, as soon as the wholesome check exercised by the presence of the ladies was removed, the conversation turned on politics as a necessary result ... this all-absorbing national topic.' The growth of middle-class culture and consciousness, notably in the great northern cities, such as Leeds and Newcastle, followed by the rise of a self-consciously radical working-class politics, represented new political worlds that were not dominated by the traditional interests, and where the focus was change, reform and innovation.

The Growth of Newspapers

The way to a new politics was opened up by the growth of the press and the expansion of the franchise. Newspaper taxes had helped limit sales, though the total annual sale of copies of stamped papers rose from 48 million in 1837 to 85 million in 1851, a rise greater than the rate of population increase. The removal of the advertising tax in 1853 was followed by the end of stamp duty in 1855. There was concern about the radical religious and political views of the supporters of reform, as well as that competition for cheapness would lower the general character of the press. In response, the Prime Minister, Henry, 3rd Viscount Palmerston (1784–1865), declared his confidence in the people; although, in practice, his liberalism was of the condescending type and he was a noteworthy opponent of any extension of the franchise, Palmerston's years as Prime Minister (1855–8, 1859–65) saw no advance in parliamentary reform. Instead, foreign policy dominated his attention, as Palmerston robustly defended Britain's expanding international interests while avoiding compromising alliances with foreign powers.

The final repeal of the newspaper taxes, that of the paper duties, was carried through in 1861. The newspapers responded by cutting their prices, helping to lead to a major broadening out of public culture. The first provincial dailies in Birmingham, Liverpool, Manchester and Sheffield appeared in 1855, in Newcastle in 1857, and in Bristol in 1858. The *Saturday Evening Post* launched in Birmingham in 1857 was specifically designed to fulfil the needs 'of the great body of the working classes'. By 1885, forty-seven English towns had daily papers.

The press became the prime source outside the family of ideas, images and comparisons through which people could understand their lives. This process was accentuated by the tremendous mobility of mid-Victorian society as massive urbanization drew on extensive migration within the country. This mobility challenged, indeed frequently undermined and dissolved (in a process that provided a basic theme in novels) earlier patterns of communal and family control or at least influence, not that these patterns had been without strain.

A newly expanded urban world that owed relatively little to traditional social patterns of behaviour searched for new ways to communicate, and the press provided the news, comment and advertising material that were required. The fast tempo of the daily press with the resulting rapid changeability of news matched a swiftly altering society. The scale of demand for the press offered a prospect of profitability that encouraged investment.

The capitalization of both newspaper and periodical production increased greatly in the second half of the nineteenth century. As equipment and staffing costs rose, this process was in part driven by the needs of the industry, but the opportunities for profit were also important, and these attracted investment capital. For financial reasons, it was best to avoid radical political views as they might inhibit advertisers, but it is wise to temper any quasi-conspiratorial account of capitalism by noting the degree to which much of the working class apparently sought the entertainment and human interest that was offered them, rather than seeking campaigning commitment.

Commercialization was scarcely new, and was not necessarily incompatible with the role of newspapers as vehicles for opinion. There is a parallel with the impact on television of advertisements (and of television advertisements) after the Television Act of 1954: commercial television transmissions began in the following year. It might have been possible for a regulated society drawing on Second World War practices of state control, notably conscription, to contain consumerism, but once television advertising was available, then it became difficult to prevent development of what was truly a consumer society. A century earlier, in the case of newspapers, legislative changes had combined with technology and economic expansion to create a major discontinuity in public culture, one that looked forward to the expansion of the franchise.

Expanding Franchise

The passage of the Great or First Reform Act in 1832 was a key step in this expansion. From the late 1820s, as both cause and result, the essence of British politics became that of a dynamic, evolving system that tapped into people's desires and engaged in debate about future direction. The Liberal Party which developed from the earlier Whigs was a major beneficiary, notably in the person of William Gladstone, under whom Liberalism became a movement enjoying mass support. A formidable and multi-faceted individual of great determination and integrity, Gladstone was a classical scholar and theological

controversialist, a hewer of trees and a pious rescuer of prostitutes. Able to present himself more easily as the 'People's
William' because he came from a commercial and not an aristocratic background, his appeal ran from Parliament to the
public. He benefited from the extent to which much of the
working class felt that Liberalism expressed their ideals and
advanced their interests.

While respectful of established institutions, Gladstone had a
strong sympathy for progressive causes, and he was willing to
present his support for often modest proposals in bold
language. In a Commons debate of May 1864, on extending the
franchise, Gladstone rejected the existing situation in calling
for an inclusiveness that in fact at that stage was still limited in
its implementation:

> ... every man who is not presumably incapacitated by some
> consideration of personal unfitness or of political danger is
> morally entitled to come within the pale of the Constitution.
> Of course, in giving utterance to such a proposition, I do not
> recede from the protest I have previously made against
> sudden, or violent, or excessive, or intoxicating change; but I
> apply it with confidence to this effect, that fitness for the
> franchise, when it is shown to exist – as I say it is shown to
> exist in the case of a select portion of the working class – is
> not repelled on sufficient grounds from the portals of the
> Constitution by the allegation that things are well as they are.

The rival Tory Party was also transformed in the second half
of the century. Far from becoming a landed, reactionary rump
on the margins of politics, the Tories became the
Conservatives, a national party, representing significant
elements of the new urban middle classes as well as a large
working-class constituency. Having done badly in the mid-
nineteenth century after their division over the repeal of the
Corn Laws, the Conservatives, between Benjamin Disraeli's
victory in 1874 and John Major's in 1992, were easily the most

successful party when it came to winning elections, and thus saw themselves as the natural party of government.

Passed by a minority Conservative government, with Disraeli, the Chancellor of the Exchequer and the Conservative leader in the Commons, doing most of the parliamentary work, the Second Reform Act (1867) nearly doubled the existing electorate, giving the right to vote to about 60 per cent of adult males in boroughs. Hopeful of the effects of redistributing parliamentary seats, and correctly gambling on the idea that working-class Conservatism would arise from the expansion of the franchise and that 'One Nation' Conservatism could work, Disraeli needed Liberal votes to get the legislation through the Commons. Liberal amendments were responsible for all borough ratepayers gaining the vote, a measure that, in practice, enfranchised many manual workers. Indeed, right-wing Conservatives, among whom the future Prime Minister, Robert, 3rd Marquess of Salisbury, was prominent, complained about the radicalism of Disraeli's legislation.

In turn, Gladstone's Liberal government passed the Third Reform Act in 1884, which extended this franchise to the counties, so that about 63 per cent of the entire adult male population received the vote, although the percentage who could vote was closer to 40 per cent than 63 because so many people changed address, and because a voter needed eighteen months' continuous residence before he could vote.

Reform movements helped politicize those who now held electoral power. As in 1868, the Conservatives in 1885 were defeated in the first election held with the new franchise; many rural electors voted against their landlords. Democracy indeed challenged the existing social politics, and, in particular, the rural strongholds of Conservatism. Thus, in East Denbighshire, Sir Watkin Williams Wynn (1820–85), whose family had long dominated the area, was defeated. But the defeats were not only in the countryside. The Tories were routed in County Durham, winning only the City of Durham, a more conservative constituency. Working-class

Liberal-Labour candidates were more successful there, two of the Durham Miners' Association agents winning seats, although, as yet, Labour sympathy was mostly contained within Liberalism.

The Politics of Reform

Worried about the potential radicalism of the new, far larger electorate, and mindful of the challenge posed by the radical Chartist movement of the 1840s, politicians sought to respond. Yet, while politicians increasingly found they had to appeal to their voters' different interests and views, they also tried to shape the process by creating a new unity behind a better Britain. A self-conscious process of reform was a key element in both processes: reform as an attempt to forestall radicalism, and reform in order to ensure a better Britain, which was seen as likely to facilitate the first goal.

Reform meant government intervention, and this intervention linked the late nineteenth to the early twentieth century; and did so more clearly than the late nineteenth was linked to the less interventionist stance of government in the first quarter of the nineteenth century, 1800–25. This contrast is a reminder of the danger of thinking of centuries as distinct and distinctive units separated by a clear process of change. In the first quarter of the nineteenth century, there was economic transformation and social change without comparable political shifts, something which owed much to the ideological and political hostility to radicalism that stemmed from the hostile reaction to the French Revolution.

Yet, for most of the rest of the nineteenth century, the emphasis was on reform as both means for progress and goal. Governments from both sides of politics were committed to reform; the distinction was simply that of how much change was desirable and how far reform was also intended to ensure continuity. The governments of both the Liberal William Gladstone (1868–74, 1880–5, 1886 and 1892–4), and, albeit less centrally, the Conservative Benjamin Disraeli (1868, 1874–80) pushed for social improvement, a policy already prefigured in mid-century, notably when Henry, 3rd Viscount Palmerston, was Home Secretary from 1852 to 1855 in the Earl of Aberdeen's government. This government was a coalition of political groups born out of the failure of both Liberal and Conservative governments to sustain a parliamentary majority in 1852, and it proved unequal to the political strains posed by the difficulties Britain faced in the Crimean War (1854–6).

In turn, Palmerston became Prime Minister in 1855, and he played an important part in developing some of the themes of which the late-Victorian Liberalism associated with Gladstone was to be composed. Prime Minister for most of the period until his death in office in 1865, Palmerston led the Liberals to victories in the elections of 1857, 1859 and 1865. While he focused on foreign policy, Gladstone, as his Chancellor of the Exchequer from 1859, became an increasingly vigorous focus of radical hopes and a proponent of parliamentary reform (the extension of the franchise). Palmerston was succeeded by the principled John, 1st Earl Russell, who had been Prime Minister from 1846 to 1852, but he held office again only to 1866 as he was defeated over the issue of parliamentary reform. In 1867, Russell retired as party leader, to be succeeded by Gladstone.

Once he was Prime Minister, there was, under Gladstone, a particular effort to improve education and to do so by means of standardization and change. This effort owed much to the Methodist impact on Liberal thought and, as such, was an aspect of the importance not only of the Nonconformist conscience but of religion more generally. Nonconformists saw education as critical to their Bible-centred religious views. The 1870 Education Act divided the country into school districts under education boards, and stipulated a minimum level of educational provision in each district. Supervision by central government was a central part of the new system, one that altered the relationship between central and local government. The Endowed Schools Commission founded that year redistributed endowments and reformed governing bodies.

This was a key aspect of a more general trend by which the role of the parish in education and social welfare declined in favour of new governmental agencies. Municipal and county government were better able than the Church to implement the aspirations of society for reform and control, and in many towns the prestige and authority held by the vicar passed to the mayor. Moreover, as an attempt to establish improved criteria for government, open competition was introduced in the Civil Service in 1870, a significant step in the move from patronage to merit. In 1872, the secret ballot was introduced for elections, an act intended to end intimidation and deference in voting, not least the sway of employers. Disease was attacked alongside disorder. Urban and rural sanitary authorities responsible for the maintenance of sewers and highways in their districts were inaugurated in England and Wales by the 1872 Public Health Act, following the recommendations of the report of the Sanitary Commission (1871). Typhus virtually disappeared by the 1890s, typhoid was brought under partial control, and death rates from tuberculosis and scarlet fever decreased.

Under Disraeli in 1874–80, there was also much social reform, although his commitment was limited compared to that of Gladstone. Disraeli was to be associated with 'One Nation' Conservatism, but in fact argued for the value of the aristocracy, even though he came from a background that was very different. His antecedents were Jewish (although he was baptized as an Anglican at the age of twelve) and, for long, Disraeli was more associated with the London literary world than with that of the country house, and his major public speeches at Manchester and the Crystal Palace in 1872 were very much part of the world of public politics. Yet, Disraeli saw the landed elite as important to the identity of both party and nation, the aristocracy, however, being willing, in his prospectus, to lead in the interests of the nation, rather than those of its class. The duties of status and power were central to Disraeli's political views, as they were to Liberal supporters of reform. Disraeli himself ended up as an earl with a stately home.

Some of the Disraeli ministry's legislation was inherited from the Gladstone government, and most of it did not receive Disraeli's full attention or support. Nevertheless, whatever the practical impact, the key point was that a Conservative government also sought change rather than opposing or reversing it. By Continental standards, the Conservative Party was notably liberal, while its Liberal rival was particularly popular. Legislation on factories (1874), public health, artisans' dwellings, and pure food and drugs (1875), systematized and extended the regulation of important aspects of public health and social welfare. The Artisans' Dwellings Act of 1875 made urban renewal possible, while the Prison Act of 1877 established state control of prisons, a step intended to end abuses.

As an important sign of the authority of the state, the Definition of Time Act of 1880 made the use of Greenwich Mean Time compulsory throughout Britain. As an instance of the general process of reform, in 1876 the Unseaworthy Ships Act ensured that ships carried a Plimsoll line: a horizontal line, named after Samuel Plimsoll MP (1824–98), that marked the point beyond which a ship was overladen and could not sail legally.

The larger electorate encouraged developments in organization as well as policy, and, like culture and leisure, was increasingly institutional. Thus, the National Union of Scottish Conservative Associations was founded in 1882. Meanwhile, the process of reform, both political and social, continued with the Local Government Act (1888) creating directly elected county councils and county boroughs, as well as the London County Council. These new councils replaced the government of the localities by unelected justices of the peace and town corporations.

Moreover, the basis was being laid for a welfare state, notably with the major role of government in education and with legislation like the Workmen's Compensation Act (1897), which obliged employers to provide compensation for industrial accidents. Government was becoming increasingly involved in the lives of the people it represented. As the state grew, so too did expectation as to its further expansion. People looked increasingly for reform or government control to improve their lives.

Yet, a common quest for reform did not mean that politics was absent. Instead, to contemporaries, there were serious issues at stake. In particular, thanks to the divisive effect of Gladstone's support for Irish Home Rule (self-government) on the Liberals from 1886, the Conservatives were in office, with the support of Liberal Unionists, from 1886 to 1892 and 1895 to 1905. They were led by Robert, 3rd Marquess of Salisbury, and, from 1902, his nephew ('Bob's His Uncle'), Arthur Balfour (1848–1930). Despite Salisbury's preference for the seclusion of Hatfield House, his stately home, and his lack of interest in managing Parliament, the party sustained power with the popularity of its imperialist policies and the long-term expansion of the middle class, exemplified by the foundation in 1883 of the Primrose League, which stood for Church, Crown, empire, property and order, and proved an effective popular organization for the Conservatives. By 1891, the League had over a million members. Although committed to the Establishment, the Conservatives were keen to reach out and win the active backing of what they saw as the inherent conservatism of the populace. They followed a cautious policy on domestic reform, ceding workmen's compensation for injury, but not old-age pensions.

This emphasis on reform helped ensure that the politics of the period made Britain's economic transformation possible. There were major social pressures but no serious breakdown in social or political stability or, indeed, large-scale disruption. In part, this was a product of an earlier lack of resort to violence. In contrast to many other European states, there was no political revolution in Britain, either at the time of the French Revolutionary crisis at the close of the eighteenth century or in the mid-nineteenth century, when there were revolutions across the Continent. This does not mean that hardship and discontent were on a small scale, but simply that, in a comparative context, they, and their consequences, should not be exaggerated.

Ireland and Wales

Politics were different in Ireland, where there was a violent nationalist streak looking back to the unsuccessful 1798 revolution, a revolution that had been the prelude to parliamentary union between Ireland and Britain in 1801, as a result of which Irish elections were to the Westminster Parliament. Yet, most Irish nationalism was non-violent. The Dublin authorities fostered attempts to improve the lot of the population through reform and firm action aimed at limiting extra-parliamentary agitation. The extension of the franchise in 1867 and 1884 greatly increased the number of Catholic voters, and most of them supported Home Rule which would have left an Irish Parliament and government in control of all bar defence and foreign policy. The Home Government Association of 1870 was followed by the Home Rule League in 1873. Charles Parnell (1846–91) became leader of the MPs pressing for Home Rule in 1879, and this group became an organized and powerful parliamentary party, with eighty-five MPs in 1886, which helped ensure that Home Rule came to play a major role in the political agenda.

Home Rule brought together issues of national identity and religion in both Ireland and Britain. To an extent that is easy to underplay from the perspective of the far more secular 2000s, religion proved an important issue in politics and one that linked to key concerns of government. No fewer than 217 Bills on religious subjects were introduced in Parliament between 1880 and 1913. There was criticism of the very idea of an Established (state) Church, and this became an important political issue and a cause of division between the political parties. Church issues were linked to the control and funding of education, matters of great contention. Liberals pressed for disestablishment of the state Church from the 1860s. The

Church of Ireland, the Anglican (Protestant) Church, was the official Church in Ireland despite the majority of the population being Catholic. This Church was disestablished by Gladstone in 1869, a major step in Irish politics and in their relationship with Liberalism.

In Wales there were bitter political disputes over Church disestablishment throughout the rest of the century and beyond. Welsh Liberals were also strongly opposed to Church schools, and especially to measures to provide public assistance to them. Political activism took the form of local, extra-parliamentary action, indicating the extent to which politics was not simply a matter of parliamentary activity. The 1902 Act compelling finance from the rates for Church schools, passed by a Conservative government, led to the 'Welsh Revolt', as county councils refused to implement it. By the time the Conservative government fell in late 1905, there had been 65,000 prosecutions for non-payment. Much bitterness was caused by the 100 imprisonments and the 3,000 property auctions to pay the rates. The entire episode indicated the depth of anger that disputes linked to religion could generate, and the extent to which they were not restricted to Ireland.

Agitation in Wales and Ireland serves as a reminder of the number of political narratives at issue and of the extent to which nationalism was also a question within the British Isles. In both, as in Scotland, there were also factors strengthening links within Britain. To take Ireland, it is possible to write a brief survey that centres on hardship and discord: the aftermath of the potato famine of 1845–8 and the struggle for Irish political autonomy. Both, indeed, were of great importance. Yet, it is also important to recall that other themes can be advanced. Ireland remained within the empire, largely speaking English, there was no collapse into anarchy or civil war, and the Irish economy developed as part of the growing imperial economy. The closing decades of the nineteenth century brought economic and social change, commercialization, continued Anglicization, and the dismantling of landlord power; and, by 1914, Ireland had gained a large share of its economic independence. Thanks to legislation in 1860, 1870, 1881, 1885, 1891 and 1903, landlords were obliged to settle the land question largely on their tenants' terms: farmers increasingly owned their holdings.

The position of the Catholic Church markedly improved. For example, in the town of Kildare a convent was established, soon followed by a church and schools, and in 1889 a magnificent Catholic Gothic church whose spire dominated the town was opened.

Ireland was more closely linked to Britain than hitherto by economic interdependence and the rapid communications offered by railways and steamships, but its Catholic areas were at the same time becoming more socially and culturally distinct. The reform process that characterized Britain was also seen in Ireland. The Irish Local Government Act of 1898 brought to Ireland the system of elected local councils introduced in England by Acts of 1888 and 1894, such that local government was transferred to the control of the largely Catholic bulk of the population.

In Ireland, as in Britain, the major growth of the police further lessened the need to rely on the Army for domestic control, and this process was important in the transition from popular anti-militarism to a more positive view of military service. Although the Army was still called out to aid the civil power, there was less need for such action.

In Wales, convergence with England was seen with the increased use of the English language, notably, with immigration, in South Wales. Furthermore, the usage of English was encouraged by members of the emerging middle class. Gentry landowners were commonly English-speaking, but, more significantly, English was the language of commerce, and thus, as the Welsh economy was affected by economic growth and integration, of cattle dealers and drovers, merchants, shopkeepers and master mariners.

Yet, as the usage of English became more common, it also became more politically charged, a consequence in part of debates over the role and nature of public education. Furthermore, in the second half of the nineteenth century, language came to play a role in a powerful political critique directed against Conservative landowners and the Anglican Church and in favour of Liberalism and Nonconformity, both of which were presented as truly Welsh. There was a parallel with the Irish Home Rule movement and the late-nineteenth-century Gaelic cultural revival. Thus, T.E. Ellis (1859–99), elected as Liberal MP for Merioneth in 1886, declared, in his election address, his support for Home Rule for Ireland and Wales, for the disestablishment of the Church of England in Wales, a revision of the land laws, and better education facilities that were under the control of public, not Anglican, bodies. The *Cymru Fydd* ('Wales that is to be' or 'Young Wales') Home Rule movement, launched in 1886, was very influential but foundered in the mid-1890s on the antagonism between the south and north Welsh.

There was also a greater interest in Welsh cultural history and identity, a growth in Welsh poetry, the development of choral singing and, in 1858, two years after the Welsh national anthem was composed, the 'revival' of the eisteddfod. A range of new institutions, from University College Aberystwyth (1872) on, testified to a stronger sense of national identity, the institutionalization of which created bodies that had an interest in its furtherance and which provided a vital platform and focus for those seeking to assert Welsh identities. Both the National Library, funded partly from the 'penny contributions' of miners, and the National Museum were authorized by royal charter in 1907.

In political terms, the assertion of Welsh identity was largely represented by Liberalism, but, as later with Labour for both Wales and Scotland, this was as part of a British political consciousness. The key Welsh issues of the late nineteenth century – land reform, disestablishment and public education – could be presented in radical Liberal terms and thus incorporated into British politics. Agitation over rents and tithes led to riots, especially in 1887, but landlords were not shot: the Welsh wished to differentiate themselves from the more bitter contemporary agitation in Ireland.

Scotland

Scotland was affected by the same trends as England and Wales, especially industrialization and urbanization. There was, moreover, a strong identification with the British empire. Yet, the nineteenth century also saw the development of a sense of Scottishness centring on a new cultural identity that, however, did not involve any widespread demand for independence: kilts and literary consciousness, but no Home Rule Party. The National Association for the Vindication of Scottish Rights, launched in 1853, was not explicitly nationalist, but was followed by the Scottish Patriotic Association, the Scottish Home Rule Association (SHRA), and other bodies, which all played a role in the development of a stronger sense of political separateness. The SHRA regarded the exerting of pressure on the most sympathetic political party as the best political strategy. In place of the notion of North Britain, which was rejected by the late nineteenth century, that of Scotland returned, although it was an increasingly Anglicized Scotland. The Secretaryship for Scotland, abolished in 1746, was restored in 1885.

There was more specific opposition in the Highlands and Islands of Scotland, where potato famine in the late 1840s had led to emigration and to the clearances of cultivation and settlement from the land by landowners in order to make way for sheep-farming and deer-stalking. By 1884, 1.98 million acres (801,278 hectares), over 10 per cent of Scottish land, was reserved for deer and thus the hunting interests of a small minority. In the 1880s, crofting MPs, opposed to clearances, won five seats in northern Scotland, while the 'Battle of the Braes' against clearances in Skye grew more intense. This struggle was a central focus of an Irish-type resistance to clearing: the Land League, modelled on the Irish Land League, had 15,000 members by 1884. The crisis led to the Napier

Commission and the Crofters' Holding Act of 1886 which established crofting rights and ended the major phase of the clearances. Yet, far from being separate, Scotland was in the mainstream of British politics. The Liberals were powerful there, but so also were the Conservatives.

Party Politics

Rather than pressing for distinctive policies such as Irish Home Rule and Welsh disestablishment, the Conservatives did not seek to transform Britain, but they did wish to strengthen it. As later in response to Labour in the 1920s, 1930s, 1950s and 1980s, the Conservatives benefited from the increasing perceived radicalism of Gladstonian Liberalism which drove the satiated and newly anxious middle class, many themselves the beneficiaries of the meritocratic reforms of the first Gladstone ministry of 1868–74, into the Conservative camp. Taxes were a key issue. The spread in the power and activity of government had led to new commitments, for example by school boards, and these commitments pushed up the rates (local property taxes). Rising tax demands pressed on a society that was less buoyant and, crucially, less confident economically than that of the middle decades of the century, and this hit support for the Liberals.

The Conservatives, who were in power from 1874 to 1880, 1885 to 1886, 1886 to 1892, and 1895 to 1905, also benefited from more positive support, notably the ability to tap populist themes and to present their policies in nationalist terms. They put considerable emphasis on imperialism abroad (both spreading empire and imperial sentiment) and at home (in Ireland), hitting the Liberals on both heads. Indeed, proposals for Home Rule for Ireland, introduced by Gladstone, were defeated in 1886 and 1893 at Westminster; in part because they divided the Liberals as well as energizing the Conservatives. Far from being politically and socially rigid, the Conservatives also displayed an openness to social trends, as with a willingness to recruit Catholics and to mobilize female support.

The latter proved particularly useful after women gained the vote in 1918.

The relatively benign 1890s gave rise to a more troubling situation in the following decade, and there was no Edwardian calm to British politics, despite subsequent suggestions from the vantage point of the troubled post-war world. Instead, Edward VII's reign (1901–10) was a period of uncertainty and tension, such that these years, running on to the outbreak of the First World War in 1914, while often seen as a continuation of the late nineteenth century, can be regarded, conversely, as its dissolution, a dissolution that had gathered pace before the war.

The twentieth century opened with Britain already at war, albeit that the Boer War (1899–1902) was very different in scale to the First World War. Moreover, in the early 1900s, the National Debt was rising substantially, and politicians were unsure about how best to respond to growing industrial militancy, as well as to concern about national efficiency and pressures for social reform. War and domestic issues were linked in anxiety about Britain's strength relative to other powers, particularly Germany. Rudyard Kipling's (1865–1936) poem 'The Islanders' (1902) saw the British as weak and self-regarding, concerned with trinkets and 'the flannelled fools at the wicket or the muddied oafs at the goals'. Far from there being any general complacency, there was a widespread feeling that something had to be done, a feeling exacerbated by serious defeats in the early stages of the Boer War. Moreover, to pay for the war, the government raised taxes, including income tax from 8d. (3p) to 1s. 3d. (6p) in the pound, and borrowed £135 million.

What was to be done was less clear. Salisbury and the Conservatives, then called Unionists because of their support for the existing constitutional arrangements in Ireland, won in October 1900 what was called a 'khaki election' because it was held when the Boer War was arousing patriotic sentiments and going well, while the Liberals were publicly divided over the merits of the war. In contrast, most of the electorate had no such doubt about the expansion of empire. Only 184 Liberals were elected and no fewer than 163 government supporters were elected unopposed.

However, this victory could not, for long, conceal important weaknesses in the Conservative position, including the inability to respond successfully to the growing demands of organized labour. The elderly Salisbury also failed to take advantage of the general election in order to reorganize and strengthen the government, and very few middle-class politicians were brought into office. The Liberals moreover were helped by the still considerable strength of their Nonconformist constituency.

A political freneticism on the part of some reflected the sense that real issues were at stake. The first lightning rod was cast by Joseph Chamberlain, Colonial Secretary from 1895 to 1903, who, concerned about the pressure of international competition, sought to replace free trade by tariffs (import duties), with, in addition, a system of imperial preference to encourage trade within the empire. The revenue tariffs produced was to be spent on social welfare, thus easing social tension, without increasing taxes. To Chamberlain, this policy offered imperial revival, populism and an opportunity to strengthen the Conservative government, but, in fact, his policy divided and weakened the party.

The popularity of the tariff policy was compromised because it was presented as a taxation on food imports that would hit the urban working class by increasing the price of food. In an instructive instance of the importance of the public dimension, Chamberlain's campaigning gesture of 1903, when he held up two loaves of similar size to demonstrate that the tariffs he proposed would not have a great effect on consumers, was hijacked by opponents who contrasted the protectionist 'little loaf' with the current 'big loaf'. The cheap big loaf was the key representation in posters, postcards and parades; a readily grasped image suited to an age of democratic politics. The Free Trade campaigners and the Tariff Reformers both actively sought popular support through local campaigns across the country.

Furthermore, the tariff issue united the Liberals and increased their popularity, thus demonstrating the political limitations of tariff reform for the Conservatives. Never underestimating the credulity of their audience, Liberal speakers focused on the price of food and ignored the wider questions posed by the challenges to the British economy represented by free trade, especially the serious competition for British industry. As a result both of their stance on cheap food and of their willingness to seek the support of organized labour, the Liberals were far better placed than the Conservatives to give voice to popular pressure for social reform and, more generally, for change.

Unable to unite the party over tariff reform, or to offer solutions on questions such as social reform, Salisbury's successor, his nephew Arthur Balfour, resigned as Prime Minister on 4 December 1905. He hoped that, once in government, the Liberals would divide, providing the Conservatives with an opportunity to win the imminent general election, but instead the election, held in January 1906, led to a Liberal landslide, with the Liberals gaining 401 seats to the Conservatives' 157. The Liberals had recovered well from earlier divisions over Ireland and the Boer War.

Moreover, growing pressure for more radical policies had led political opinion to coalesce and polarize to a considerable extent along social and class lines, with the working class increasingly Liberal and the less numerous middle and upper classes Conservative. In 1891, Gladstone had called for a reduction in factory work-hours, free education, electoral reform, and the reform or abolition of the House of Lords. In 1903, the Liberals secretly allied with Labour, in part because they saw a shared class interest, the two parties agreeing not to fight each other in certain seats lest they help the Conservatives. This cooperation was helped by common hostility to tariffs and by Labour anger with the Conservative government's attitude towards trade unions. In the 1906 election, the majority of Liberal candidates included pledges for social reform in their election addresses.

The Conservatives were seen as overly linked to sectional interests – the employers, the agricultural interest, the Church of England and the brewers (who were unpopular with the Nonconformist temperance lobby) – and had not acquired any reputation for competence. They were blamed for the misman-agement of the Boer War and suffered from the sour taste the conflict had left. Furthermore, Balfour was unable to unite his party. He was also no populist and a poor campaigner. In the 1906 election, the Conservatives lost some of their urban working-class support, while the Liberals took the former Conservative strongholds of London and Lancashire, and also made important gains in rural and suburban parts of southern England, the Conservative heartland. Many of the latter gains were lost in the two general elections of 1910, but the Liberals then retained Lancashire and London, ensuring that they were the major party in all the leading industrial areas.

Politics was developing towards what was to be its class-orientated character for much of the twentieth century. The foundation of trade unions reflected the growing industrial-ization of the economy, the rise of larger concerns employing more people, and, by the end of the nineteenth century, a new, more adversarial and combative working-class consciousness. Moreover, the trade union lodge displaced the chapel as the main meeting place for men in many working-class communities. The Trades Union Congress (TUC), a federation of trade unions, began in 1868, unionism spreading from the skilled craft sector to the more numerous semi-skilled and unskilled workers whose interests had not initially been represented, and TUC support led, in 1900, to the formation of the Labour Representation Committee, the basis of the Labour Party. Some working-class militants looked to a Marxist tradition: the Social Democratic Federation pioneered the development of socialism in the 1880s and was Britain's first avowedly Marxist party. Most, however, looked to Labour. For example, the decision of the South Wales miners in 1906 to affiliate with the Labour Party marked the beginning of the end of Liberalism's hold over the Welsh urban working class.

Greater radicalism contributed to, and in part reflected and sustained, a sense of doubt, if not a crisis of confidence in society. The demand for reform was matched by a pressure for security in a competitive international environment, the two combining to produce an uneasiness about present and future that fed into debate about the condition of the people and calls for National Efficiency: competence in government, and a more vigorous and better-educated populace.

New Liberalism

Some prominent Liberals, especially the dynamic David Lloyd George, a Welsh solicitor who became Chancellor of the Exchequer from 1908 to 1915 (and Prime Minister from 1916 to 1922), sought to change the state of the people by undermining the power and possessions of the old landed elite and by providing assured social welfare. As with much else in politics, problems provided a key context. Indeed, the New Liberalism of the Liberal Reforms was more to do with propping up the tottering Poor Law than bringing about social reform and harmony.

In 1909, Lloyd George announced a 'People's Budget'. Proposing redistributive measures in order to give force to assumptions about the necessary nature of society if Britain was to improve, this budget raised direct taxation on higher incomes, and prepared the way for taxes on land. The Liberals lessened the concern about redistribution by planning no tax increases on annual earned income below £2,000, a figure that then excluded the middle class; but the notion of redistributive taxation was indeed a threat to this group, as was to be shown clearly under Labour in the 1970s. The House of Lords rejected the budget, only for two general elections in 1910 to return a minority Liberal government dependent on support from Labour and the Irish Nationalists. Aside from the passage of the budget, the Parliament Act of 1911 replaced the Lords' ability to veto Commons' legislation with the right only to delay it, an Act only passed as a result of the threat of creating many more peers to pack the Lords with Liberal supporters, the policy already followed in order to push through the 'Great' or First Reform Act, of 1832.

The entire dispute was accompanied by strident social criticism of the aristocracy. In 1911, H.G. Wells, in his novel *The New Machiavelli*, presented Richard Remington as narrator, a fictional politician who advocated a 'trained aristocracy', universal education, feminism, and a more perfect, and thus stronger, Britain.

In 1911, Lloyd George's National Insurance Act provided for unemployment assistance and for all males eligible for insurance to be registered with a doctor who was to receive a fee per patient, irrespective of the amount of medical attention required. Thus, with the key exclusion of children and most women from the health proposals, and of unskilled workers from the unemployment provisions, exclusions that reflected costs as well as notions of entitlement, there was already considerable provision of public welfare support prior to the establishment of the National Health Service in 1948. At the same time, the 1911 legislation reflected the determination to align private commitment to one's own future alongside state security.

The legislation of the Liberal government was designed to provide an environment for further regulation, as with the first Town Planning Act, passed in 1909. The context, however, was one of social and political division. In 1906, the Liberals passed a Trade Disputes Act that gave the trade unions immunity from actions for damages as a result of strike action, and thus rejected the attempts of the courts, through the Taff Vale case of 1901, to bring the unions within the law. The latter verdict had threatened to make strike action prohibitively expensive.

The Liberals thus appealed to the working class, although, despite the populist and collectivist strain in New Liberalism, the Liberals were unhappy with using the language of class, unenthusiastic about powerful trade unions, and did not adopt working-class candidates. Yet, there was also a powerful radical strain to New Liberalism. In late 1913, Lloyd George proposed state-funded rural house building and a minimum agricultural wage, and, when war began in 1914, it cut short initiatives by the Liberal government that were being planned for health, housing, education and a minimum wage. Balfour had claimed in 1894 that 'the best antidote to Socialism was practical social reform', but it was the Liberals who seemed most determined and able to implement this policy.

Welsh Church disestablishment was pushed through in 1914, although, with the intervention of war, it was not implemented until 1920. Irish Home Rule was also a key issue, although the Liberal government initially sidelined it. The determination of the Ulster Protestants, who were in a minority in Ireland, to resist Home Rule took the country to the brink of civil war in 1914. The formation of the Ulster Unionist Council (1905) and the Ulster Volunteer Force (1913) revealed the unwillingness of the Ulster Protestants to subordinate their sense of identity to Irish nationalism. They were assisted by the Conservatives, from 1912 the Conservative and Unionist Party, who did their best to resist the Home Rule Bill introduced by the Liberal government in 1912. The Bill, twice rejected by the House of Lords, was passed in an amended form in 1914, with the proviso that it was not to be implemented until after the war. The crisis defined the political forces in Ireland and gave a powerful impetus to the consciousness of the Ulster Protestants. The authority and power of the British state was challenged in a fashion that was far more potent and threatening than the Boer War.

Prior to the First World War, the Liberal Party, with its desire for the cooperation of capital and labour and its stress on class harmony for all except the aristocracy, still displayed few signs of decline at the hands of Labour, and showed much confidence in its future. Another general election was due by

1915, and, although the Conservatives were in better shape than they had been after the 1906 election, there seemed many reasons to assume that they would face a fourth election defeat, not least because they had fewer allies than the Liberals.

Period costume dramas on television and film, notably *The Shooting Party* and *Upstairs Downstairs*, suggest that it was an elysian (or, in contrast, far less than perfect) world that was to be swept away by war. These works offer an image of class, gender and political stereotypes, but one that dramatically underplays the dynamism of the period. In particular, there was a widespread conviction among politicians, writers and key sections in society that change was necessary and beneficial. The aristocracy indeed opposed the Liberal Party because it not only sought to preserve its political position, but also to resist what appeared to be an entire ethos of change centring on the policies of the extension of the power of the state, collectivism and the destruction of the Union with Ireland. The aristocracy saw a danger that democracy might entail the poor plundering the rich, or, in the eyes of its supporters, the social justice of redistribution. There was scant sense that the change also seen in other aspects of life, notably technology and the economy, would not affect social power and politics.

The First World War
The terrible and unexpected strains of the First World War resulted, in May 1915, in the establishment of a coalition government, with Liberal, Conservative and Labour Cabinet ministers. Conservative backing for the war led them to accept higher taxation and a massive expansion in state power, but the conduct of the war divided the Liberals. Herbert Asquith (1852–1928), who had been Prime Minister since 1908, proved less successful as a wartime leader than as a peacetime reformer, in large part because he lacked the single-minded determination and drive to rise to the challenges posed by industrial warfare. Governmental instability arose because the most

dynamic minister, Lloyd George, who had moved to the key
Ministry of Munitions in order to deal with the serious
shortage in shells of the Army, understandably lost confidence
in Asquith's ability to lead the country. Lloyd George wanted
to mobilize all the country's resources for war, and this attitude
and determination found more favour with the Conservatives
than with many Liberals.

There was powerful opposition, however, within the Liberal
Party to conscription (compulsory military service) which was
seen as opposed to the Liberal tradition of civil liberty.
Prominent Liberals, such as Reginald McKenna (1863–1943),
Lloyd George's replacement as Chancellor of the Exchequer,
resisted the measure. Nevertheless, Lloyd George and the
Conservatives were determined to see it through in order to
provide sufficient men for the trenches on the Western Front,
not least due to the heavy and unexpected casualties of the first
year of the war. A fudge, Lord Derby's semi-voluntary
scheme, introduced in October 1915, failed to produce sufficient recruits and, faced with Lloyd George's threat to resign,
Asquith gave way. The Military Service Act of January 1916
introduced conscription for single men, and, in response to a
sudden surge in weddings, it was extended to the married in
April.

Nevertheless, there was still widespread political dissatisfaction with the conduct of the war and particular pressure
from backbench Conservative opinion. Differences between
Conservatives and Liberals prevented coalition cohesion and
contributed to a sense of malaise. The management of the war
seemed inadequate. This situation led to pressure in November
1916 for a small war committee to direct the war effort.
Asquith saw this call as aimed against his premiership, but his
effort to preserve his position collapsed in the face of the
growing alignment of Lloyd George and the Conservatives.

In December 1916, Lloyd George took control of the war
effort. Less politically skilful than in the past, the over-
confident Asquith was displaced, and the government was

recast. Lloyd George became Prime Minister, and both Conservatives and Labour continued to offer support. Stubborn as well as weak, Asquith, however, refused to hold office in the new government and was supported in this by most of the Liberal ministers. Lloyd George therefore had divided the Liberals, even as he brought new vitality to the government, not least with the formation of a War Cabinet. As a result of this division, Conservative support for the government was much more important than when Asquith had been Prime Minister.

Politics was not banished for the remainder of the war. Important issues were raised, especially about the possibility of negotiations with Germany in 1917. This was an unsuccessful proposal that led to the resignation of its sponsor, Arthur Henderson (1863–1935), the first Labour Cabinet minister, from the War Cabinet, although Labour remained in the Coalition. By 1917, there was also a degree of trade union and Labour Party disquiet about the consequences of the conflict, notably food shortages and rising prices. There was also anger at wage controls, labour direction and profiteering; and at facets of social difference that appeared less acceptable in a period of total war.

In 1918, Lloyd George's war leadership was challenged by Asquith in a debate over the availability of troops for the Western Front, an issue on which Lloyd George had given the House of Commons misleading information. Lloyd George survived, in large part thanks to Conservative support, but the Liberals were now very bitterly divided.

The Coalition was continued after the war, with Labour, benefiting from the growth in its resources and organization in 1917–18, newly important as a result of the major extension of the franchise in 1918. In that year's general election, which was held under the new, greatly extended franchise (see p.105), Labour received more votes than the Liberals and won sixty seats. The traditional Liberal concerns with temperance, Church schools and Church disestablishment no longer

seemed of interest or relevant to most of the electorate. The
Liberals also lacked new or attractive policies and leaders, and
their pre-war social welfare platform now seemed better, and
certainly more popularly, represented by Labour.

However significant in the medium term, Labour support
rose, but the party did not win. The election, held on
14 December 1918, was known as the coupon election as
Asquithian MPs were denied the letter of endorsement (or
coupon) from Lloyd George and the Conservative leader,
Andrew Bonar Law (1858–1923). Held in the relief and
euphoria of victory, the election, the first since 1910, brought
the Coalition more than 500, and maybe up to 523 out of 707
MPs: the precise figure is unclear as not all the Coalition's
supporters received the coupon. The Conservatives won 382
seats. Having lost three general elections before the war (in
1906 and two in 1910), and then drifted to the right, and further
from electoral popularity, not least by supporting Ulster's
opposition to Irish Home Rule, the Conservatives had been
offered by the war an unexpected way back to the centre of
politics from where they were able to benefit from their skills
in flag-waving.

Irish Independence

Ireland proved a key issue for the post-war government.
Already, in 1916, there had been a nationalist rebellion against
British rule, at the same time that far larger numbers of Irish
men fought, as volunteers, for George V in the First World
War. Launched by the Irish Republican Brotherhood, this
rebellion, the Easter Rising, focused on Dublin. There was
supporting action in other parts of Ireland, but, due to divisions in the leadership, nothing of note, which helped ensure
that the rising in Dublin on Easter Monday (24 April) would
fail militarily. Instead, it became merely a bold and bloody
gesture. About 1,200 people rose and seized a number of sites,
but their actions suffered from bad planning, poor tactics and
the strength of the British response, which included the

uncompromising use of artillery. The insurgents were forced to surrender unconditionally on 29 April.

The rebellion, which revived long-standing fears of Ireland as a backdoor to Britain, was particularly unwelcome while Britain was involved in a difficult war and short of troops, but the firm British response served to radicalize Irish public opinion. Martial law was declared, and a series of trials, fifteen executions and numerous internments, provided martyrs for the nationalist cause, although, of course, far more Irishmen were dying as volunteers while fighting against the Germans, and the Easter Rising can be seen as stabbing them in the back.

Nevertheless, Irish nationalism received a powerful impulse. The Irish Volunteers were swiftly re-established and, by the end of 1917, had begun public drilling exercises. Political support for independence grew in 1918, when a government proposal to introduce conscription was very unpopular. This proposal seemed necessary because troop numbers were a key issue after Germany's victory over Russia. By the close of the war, the issue of conscription had undermined support for the Home Rulers, who had sought autonomy within the empire, but not independence. Instead, Sinn Fein, the Catholic nationalist movement, took the majority of the seats in the 1918 general election.

In 1919, the Irish Volunteers, soon to rename themselves the Irish Republican Army (IRA), began terrorist activity. Fired by nationalist zeal, they were opposed to conventional politics, which they correctly saw as likely to lead to compromise. The British refusal to accept independence precipitated a brutal civil war in 1919–21, in which terrorism and guerrilla warfare, including the assassination of police officers, destroyed the British ability to maintain control despite the use of unauthorized reprisals by British auxiliary forces. In tones that were to become familiar from counter-insurgency operations elsewhere, Lieutenant-General Sir Philip Chetwode (1869–1950), Deputy Chief of the Imperial General Staff, claimed that victory was possible, but only if the Army was given more power, including control of the police, and the full support of British public opinion:

> The full incidence of Martial Law will demand very severe measures and to begin with many executions. In the present state of ignorance of the population in England, I doubt very much that it would not result in a protest which would not only ruin our efforts, but would be most dangerous to the army. The latter have behaved magnificently throughout, but they feel from top to bottom that they are not supported by their countrymen, and should there be a strong protest against severe action it would be extremely difficult to hold them.

Public opinion would not have stood for it, while the government also deferred to American sensibilities, which were pro-Irish.

Instead of coercion, there was a British withdrawal from much of Ireland under the Anglo-Irish Treaty of 1921. This withdrawal was the result of a partition of the island between a new, self-governing Irish Free State, which, initially, stayed within the empire, independent but with a Governor General, and a mainly Protestant Northern Ireland, comprising most of the historic province of Ulster. This remained part of the UK, which now became the United Kingdom of Great Britain and Northern Ireland. The partition owed much to the violence that had followed Sinn Fein's electoral victory in 1918 and to the sectional interests both of the Catholic Church and Sinn Fein, which turned Irish nationalism into a Catholic sectarian movement, and of the Northern Irish Protestant loyalists who oppressed the Catholic minority in the north. This partition was to be remembered in sharply contrasting fashion by the Nationalist and Unionist communities and to be very differently treated by histories written in the 1960s, 1970s, 1980s and 1990s.

The partition was opposed by much of the IRA, the anti-Treaty forces known as the Irregulars, as they were unable to accept a settlement that provided anything short of a united

Ireland. The Irregulars mounted a terrorist campaign in Northern Ireland in 1921, and also fought the newly independent government in the south in 1922–3 in what was a more bloody conflict than that of 1919–21. The IRA, however, was beaten both north and south of the border, the new government of the Irish Free State proving firmer than the British government had been; and, thereafter, IRA terrorism remained only a minor irritant until the late 1960s.

The Lloyd George Government, 1918–22

The Anglo-Irish Treaty of 1921 was one of the many factors that lessened Conservative support for Lloyd George. Indeed, forty Conservative MPs voted against the Act. More generally, Lloyd George's attempt to give the Coalition coherence, by creating a new centre party that would accommodate the Conservatives with the social reformism of the Lloyd George Liberals, fell foul of the incompatible views of both sides. In particular, the Conservatives limited Lloyd George's freedom of action over peace terms with Germany, as well as with Ireland and labour relations, in each case pressing for greater firmness. They were also unenthusiastic about social reform policies that would lead to high taxes. Taxes had already risen greatly during the war and the number of income tax payers had been considerably increased, which raised public and political sensitivity to taxation, a key development.

Nevertheless, Lloyd George used the Conservatives' fear that if they broke with him that might pave the way to a Labour government in order to retain power and have some leeway over policy, and his premiership served to give the government an aura of progressivism. Indeed, National Insurance was extended in 1920 to include those not covered under the 1911 Act. This helped to make the system more expensive, which created the financial crises of the late 1920s and 1930s, leading to restrictions on the right to claim unemployment benefits. The 1931 crisis over unemployment benefit (see p.81) can thus be set against a background of the long-term problem of funding social insurance with more claimants and with less money coming into the system.

Most of the Conservatives were initially keen to maintain the Coalition in order to strengthen opposition to socialism. They were disturbed by Labour's success in the recent 1918 general election, by trade union militancy, which markedly increased after the war, and by the spectre of Communism sweeping Europe: having seized power in Russia in 1917, the Communists triumphed in the Russian Civil War, and then supported Communist movements elsewhere.

Post-war economic problems were serious and appeared linked to political radicalism. There were numerous strikes in 1919, including a railway strike, and these led to fears of a revolutionary working class seizing power through industrial militancy. Moreover, a worldwide depression in 1921–2 hit British exports. In 1921, unemployment rose markedly (to 1.8 million insured workers), as did industrial disputes, including an unsuccessful (coal) miners' strike. Lloyd George no longer seemed able to control social unrest or to ensure industrial peace. The government's popularity was further compromised in 1922 when a committee, under the chairmanship of the businessman Sir Eric Geddes (1875–1937), appointed to recommend cuts in the face of an anti-waste campaign in the Conservative heartlands, urged deflation, a classic instance of the economics that prevailed before the theories of John Maynard Keynes gained credence in mid-century. The 'Geddes Axe' included cuts in governmental expenditure on social services, education and housing (as well as defence), and, partly as a result, the government's social politics seemed clearly different from what Labour offered.

Yet Lloyd George was to fall because he lost Conservative support, and not because he increasingly alienated radicals. Much of the Conservative leadership, including the leader since March 1921, Austen Chamberlain (1863–1937), a son of Joseph Chamberlain, did not want to divide the anti-Labour vote by breaking with Lloyd George. Nevertheless, concern about

Lloyd George and his policies led many Conservatives in 1921 to decide that they would not fight a second election in alliance with him. Support ebbed further in 1922, as the disclosure of Lloyd George's sale of honours for party funds (at a scale greater than that allegedly under later prime ministers) led to a public scandal. He was no longer trusted, admired or felt necessary by the majority of the Conservative MPs.

The Party Politics of the 1920s

The year 1922, therefore, marked the post-war return of the party system. The Conservative revolt was staged by back-benchers, junior ministers and constituency activists, with a meeting of the parliamentary party at the Carlton Club on 19 October leading to the decision to abandon the Coalition, a meeting that gave its name to the Conservative backbench committee. In response, Lloyd George and Chamberlain resigned. Chamberlain's predecessor, Andrew Bonar Law, returned as party leader and formed a totally Conservative government. Far from having broken the mould of British politics, Lloyd George was consigned to the political wilderness. When he held power, he had been unwilling to support electoral reform, the proportional representation (allocation of parliamentary seats in accordance with the ratio of total votes cast) that would have helped the Liberals in the 1920s, and, once out of power, he certainly could not obtain such a change.

A more broadly based Labour had replaced the divided Liberals as the leading party of opposition. Labour was therefore the party that opposition to the Conservatives had to cohere round were it to be successful. Although there were important exceptions, for example in Liberal-dominated Cornwall, and in many agricultural areas, Labour had become the natural first-choice party of the working class, and, as such, was strong in all major conurbations and industrial areas. Labour benefited from the rise in class politics and from the growing prominence of class issues, such as industrial relations. Trade union membership had doubled from 4 million in

1914 to 8 million in 1920, and the party constitution of 1918 consolidated trade union domination of Labour. The new electorate was not interested in such pre-war Liberal Nonconformist causes as the disestablishment of the Church of England, the temperance movement and Church schools. The Labour Party also enjoyed a measure of support in rural areas among agricultural workers, although that was to ebb as the agricultural workforce declined, while the rural workforce anyway tended to be less unionized than their urban counterparts. Labour, moreover, profited greatly from the weakness of its radical challengers: Communism and the Independent Labour Party. Labour's dominance of the left was, thereafter, a key element in British politics and contrasted, for example, with the strength of the Communists in Italy and Spain.

The Liberals suffered from this shift in working-class support. Yet, many of the Labour voters were new voters enfranchised in 1918, and, rather than the Liberals losing support to Labour, they lost it more heavily to the Conservatives. The Liberals also suffered from their divisions, and, more lastingly, from the effect of the absence of proportional representation on a party whose support was evenly spread and perennially second to Labour or Conservatives at the constituency level.

The Conservatives formed a government in 1922, their first since 1905, and easily won the general election of 15 November 1922. However, their hold on power proved shortlived. Suffering from throat cancer, Bonar Law resigned as Prime Minister (and party leader) in May 1923, dying soon after. He was succeeded by Stanley Baldwin (1867–1947), a Midlands manufacturer who had become the Chancellor of the Exchequer, rather than by the Foreign Secretary, George, Marquess Curzon, an aristocrat who felt that he had the best claim to the post.

However, Baldwin's strong support for tariffs, which he felt necessary in order to improve the economy, was distrusted, unpopular and widely perceived in class terms as a measure that would help the few, not the many. Protectionism was presented by its opponents as likely to increase food prices. Whereas the Conservatives had won 344 seats in 1922, they gained only 258 in the general election held on 6 December 1923: Labour won 191 and the Liberals 158. The reunion of the Asquith and Lloyd George Liberals hit the Conservatives in the constituencies.

No party had a majority in the Commons. The Liberals refused to support the Baldwin government, which was voted out on its protectionist King's Speech by the new House of Commons in January 1924, thanks to cooperation between the Liberals and Labour, both of which were opposed to protectionism. Labour then took office as a minority party, without Liberal support, although, in effect, the Labour government depended on the Liberals. This was a contrast to the situation before the First World War when Labour had supported the Liberals.

The new government was led by Ramsay MacDonald (1866–1937), the illegitimate son of Scottish farmworkers. He was determined that Labour should replace the Liberals as the key anti-Conservative force, and this brief government was important because it showed that Labour could rule without causing any crisis in British society, still less sponsoring revolution. There were no serious upsets, and financial policy was particularly prudent, with the orthodoxy of Philip Snowden (1864–1937) making him an ideal Treasury-minded Chancellor of the Exchequer. Far from introducing a capital levy or wealth tax, Snowden was a supporter of tax cuts.

The Labour government also kept the unions at a distance, but a loss of Liberal backing over the treatment of a Communist agitator led to a fresh general election on 29 October 1924 that was won by the Conservatives under Baldwin. The supposed (in practice very limited) sympathy of Labour for the Soviet Union and Communism was an issue in the election, not least due to the publication on 25 October of an apparently compromising letter, allegedly by Grigory

Zinoviev, the President of the Communist International, giving instructions to British sympathizers to provoke a revolution.

This letter did not greatly hit the Labour vote, which was larger, in terms of both number and percentage of votes, than in earlier elections. The Liberals, however, did very badly, winning only forty seats. They were affected by serious financial problems in what was the third election in quick succession, and did not contest 207 seats, which helped the Conservatives to dominate the anti-Labour vote. The Liberals also lacked a viable strategy. Their role in putting Labour into power had alienated much of their middle-class support and also helped reunite the Conservatives. In turn, Liberal weaknesses cost Labour seats – Labour lost forty, which assisted the Conservatives, who appeared as the party best placed to protect property. During their months in opposition, the Conservatives had ended the division that had stemmed from the Carlton Club meeting, abandoned tariff reform, and improved their organization. In October 1924, they took 48.3 per cent of the votes and won 419 seats, gaining the largest majority (223 seats) for a single party since the Great Reform Act of 1832 had transformed politics.

In so far as one party could lay claim to the position, the Conservatives indeed were the national party. They were overwhelmingly the middle-class party, and benefited greatly from the expansion of this sector of society as the economy changed; but the Conservatives also received a large share of the working-class vote. Yet, the new, larger electorate was potentially volatile, and winning its support posed a considerable challenge to politicians, both Conservative and others, repeating, on a larger scale, the problems which had earlier confronted Disraeli and Gladstone.

A skilled tactician, Baldwin was to play a major role in making the Conservatives appear to much of the electorate to be conservative, but not reactionary, consensual, not divisive, and the natural party of government. Baldwin was also adroit at selling a new politics. The media were harnessed to create a political image for a mass electorate, with frequent radio broadcasts helping to cultivate the folksiness which Baldwin sought to project, while Conservative Party propaganda, often geared towards the new female electorate, emphasized the dangers of socialism to family life and property in general. Radio broadcasts had begun in 1922 and the British Broadcasting Corporation, a monopoly acting in the 'national interest' and financed by licence fees paid by radio owners, was established in 1926.

Baldwin offered in his speeches a vision of England in which Christian and ethical values, an appeal to the need for continuity, pastoral and paternalist themes, and a sense of national exceptionalism, were all fused. This vision was not intended to exclude the Scots, Welsh and people of Ulster, each of whom was presented as possessing a distinctive character and traditions, but also qualities that had been enriched by the English. In the 1920s, Baldwin frequently employed rural imagery as an important way to address the issue of the national character, not least in his stress on the country as representing eternal values and traditions. Such language was especially attractive to the propertied with their concern about left-wing subversion at the behest of international Communism.

Baldwin spoke of promoting peace between the two sides of industry and of striving to bring masters and men together in one industrial nation. However, his deflationary policy of returning the pound (sterling) to the gold standard (convertibility of sterling to gold at a fixed rate) in 1925, and his remark that 'Wages had to come down', did not contribute to industrial calm. The coal industry was the centre of strife. International competition, especially, but not only, from Germany and the US, an overvalued pound (sterling) as a result of the return to the gold standard at the pre-war exchange rate, and inadequate investment, all hit production, a fall which pressed on the living standards of the miners.

This situation led to a protracted national miners' strike in 1926, and, in turn, to the TUC calling a national strike in support of the miners: the General Strike of May 1926. Support for the strike varied greatly across the country, but the power of the state was a key element in its failure. The Lloyd George Coalition government of 1918–22 had put in place plans for the use of the Army and the police, and in 1926 these plans were utilized with a careless disregard for the law: both the Common Law and even law under the Emergency Powers Act. In the end, the state won because it was better organized, while the TUC was less committed than Baldwin and the government. The TUC did not wish to press the confrontation, and the General Strike was rapidly called off. Although presented in retrospect as a peaceful episode that indicated the strength in moderation of the British system and way of life, the General Strike was not a soft and gentle event.

The Conservatives won more votes in the election of 30 May 1929, the first contested on a fully democratic franchise, but Labour was, with 288 MPs, for the first time, the largest party in the Commons. The Conservatives suffered in 1929 because their modest and uninspiring measures and proposals did not inspire much popularity. Indeed, they fought on the platform of 'Safety First' (suggested by an advertising agency), but with little else to offer by way of policy. The return of sterling in 1925 to the gold standard had overvalued sterling, hit exports and helped deflate the economy. The reforms of the Poor Law and local government by Neville Chamberlain (1869–1940; son of Joseph), the Minister of Health, had brought scant popularity; and there was a widespread sense that it was time for a change. Labour seemed moderate, and the defeat of the General Strike helped lessen anxiety about socialism. Ramsay MacDonald, still the leader, did not arouse fear or anger.

In the election, the Conservatives suffered from loss of marginal seats in the industrial parts of Lancashire and the West Midlands, while, although the increase in the Liberal vote was insufficient to win many seats, it sufficiently hit the Conservatives to let Labour win many. MacDonald formed his second minority Labour government; with the Liberals providing support, but, with only fifty-nine MPs, from a far weaker base than in the case of the first government.

The Crisis of 1929–31

The Labour government, however, was to be badly hit by the serious world economic crisis that began in October 1929, the slump and the Depression, although the economic situation was already serious when Labour came to power. Baldwin had left an inheritance of unemployment at 1.16 million, a government deficit and high interest rates to protect the gold reserves, rates that hit economic activity. Moreover, the unemployment figures were a less than full account of unemployment and underemployment.

The impact of the dramatic fall in world trade after the Wall Street Crash of 1929 greatly exacerbated the situation, not least because much of the British economy depended on exports. Although bold solutions were proposed by radicals, the government, in 1930, relied on modest public works schemes to combat unemployment, and on an increase in taxation to fund unemployment benefits. Nevertheless, the Treasury warned that the latter threatened national bankruptcy. Most of the Cabinet, however, was unprepared to accept MacDonald's pressure for cuts in benefits, while, in the midst of a European banking crisis, he was urged in August 1931 by the Bank of England to act in order to avert an apparently imminent national bankruptcy.

Cuts in expenditure seemed necessary, not least because the Conservative and Liberal leaders were opposed to raising taxes, and Labour lacked the necessary majority to push them through. Unwilling to accept cuts, the divided Labour Cabinet resigned on 23 August 1931, leading, next day, to a cross-party National Government headed by MacDonald but largely composed of Conservatives supported by a few Liberal and Labour MPs, who became known as National Liberal and National Labour. A widespread fear of economic collapse and social and political disruption had combined to encourage the formation of such a government, which was designed to tackle the crisis and to push through the necessary changes without destabilizing society. On the left, MacDonald was seen as a traitor, leading to the poem:

Here Lies the Body of Ramsay Mac
A friend of all humanity
Too many pats on the back
Inflated Ramsay's vanity
...
Having been born a Socialist
He died a bloody Tory!

The decade 1922–31 suggested that coalition governments would be weak and unpopular. The Lloyd George Coalition had failed, as had the two Labour governments dependent on Liberal votes. The new government, in contrast, appeared to match the public mood. Indeed, the new National Government went on to win the general election of 27 October 1931 with a convincing victory, the Conservatives gaining 473 seats. Labour lost working-class votes as a result of the economic problems of 1929–31 and won only fifty-two seats, while the Conservatives benefited from the consolidation of propertied and business interests into one anti-socialist bloc.

This electoral verdict was a democratic process, as was the willingness of the opposition not to resort to action on the streets. This avoidance of extremism in the crisis of 1931 (and subsequently) was to be important to the character of British politics over the following decade; and, moreover, to the extent to which Britain remained a free and liberal society. There was to be no equivalent in Britain to the rise in extremist power seen with Hitler's ascent in Germany, which culminated in his becoming Chancellor in 1933. Nor was the economic strain as heavy as in 1930s America, with, as a result, no British New Deal to transform, as well as divide, society. The success of the National Government made it appear likely that Britain would preserve its political and social system. In 1931, the greatest empire in history still seemed stable, strong and with a secure future.

3

CHANGING PEOPLE

'Progress is the great animating principle of being. The world, time, our country have advanced and are advancing.'

The Western Luminary, 2 January 1855

The War Against Disease

In the 1850s, there was little doubt that the living circumstances of much of the population were bleak. Population density rose as urban numbers grew, leading to serious overcrowding. The Bradford Sanitary Committee visited over 300 houses in 1845 and found an average of three people sleeping per bed. Indicators such as height, physical well-being and real earnings suggest that living standards, while rising in aggregate, were not increasing as fast as growth in leading industrial sectors might have suggested. The visitations of disease were particularly bleak and in a fashion that today is largely only recaptured in imaginative fiction and newspaper headlines. There were major epidemics of cholera, a bacterial infection largely transmitted by water contaminated by the excreta of victims, in Britain in 1854 and 1866, in part due to inadequate sewerage systems and the impure nature of the water supply. In an outbreak in Newcastle in 1853, 1,500 out of the city's 90,000 people died in five weeks.

Typhoid, another water-borne infection, was also serious. Prince Albert was killed by it in 1861, while Edward, Prince of Wales (1841–1910; later Edward VII) nearly died from it a decade later. Dysentery, diarrhoea, diphtheria, whooping cough, scarlet fever, measles and enteric fever were significant problems and frequently fatal. The death or illness of bread-winners wrecked family economies, producing or exacerbating poverty and related social problems.

Disease was not only the problem of the crowded big cities, 10,000 Londoners dying of cholera in 1854 and 6,000 in 1866. A report on the Sussex town of Battle drawn up in 1850 noted:

> There is no provision for the removal of any offensive or noxious refuse from the houses and gardens of the poorer classes; all the decomposing and putrescent animal and vegetable matter which is brought out of the house is thrown into a pool, around which is engendered an atmos-phere favourable to the production of febrile epidemics.

Yet, there was also substantial change, notably as part of the abandonment of earlier practices of limited and local regu-lation in favour of a more self-conscious commitment to change. The report above is indicative, as it was written by Edward Cresy (1792–1858), a superintending inspector under the General Board of Health. The latter had been created by the Public Health Act of 1848 which established an adminis-trative structure to improve sanitation and to ensure clean water. This Act was effectively swept on to the statute books as a result of cholera, which does not discriminate between social groups. As a result the middle class pushed for the legislation.

The new Act was not a matter solely of changes at the centre, nor of what would more recently be called spin. Instead, local boards of health were created, and they took action. For example, the one established in Leicester in 1849 was instrumental in the creation of a sewerage system and in tackling slaughterhouses and smoke pollution. Similarly, Cresy's critical report on Derby led its Whig councillors to embark on a programme of works, including public baths and wash houses. Yet the powers the Act gave were limited and left much to often reluctant authorities to do. Despite its limitations and the opposition that it encountered, the legislation was a definite advance in awareness of, and organization for, public health, but, once the cholera pandemic fizzled out, interest in the Act fell.

Scientific advances were also important. Dr John Snow (1813–58) carried out research in London that led him to conclude, in his *On the Mode and Communication of Cholera* (1849), that the disease was transmitted not via 'miasma' or bad air, as was generally believed, but through drinking water contaminated by sewage, a problem that highlighted the state of the Thames. This research was supplemented, in a second edition published in 1855, by an analysis of the 1853–4 epidemic, and led to the closure of the public water pump in Broad Street (south of Oxford Street, in the West End), where a sewer was leaking into the well. After this closure, the number of new cases of cholera fell. Snow also showed that the majority of the victims had drunk water provided by the Southwark and Vauxhall company which extracted water from near sewer outflows.

A vivid comment was provided by the *Punch* cartoon, *Father Thames Introducing His Offspring To The Fair City Of London*, of 3 July 1858, a response to the 'Great Stink' of that summer. In this facetious design for a fresco for the new Houses of Parliament, to replace those burned down in 1834, a filthy Thames, polluted by factories, sewage and steamships, presents figures representing diphtheria, scrofula and cholera to London. In *The Times* in 1855, Michael Faraday, a prominent scientist, had already described the river between

London and Hungerford bridges as a 'fermenting sewer', a description that was accurate in both parts, and that contrasts with the return of fish to the modern Thames. The Houses of Parliament were also affected by smoke from the many factories in Lambeth on the other side of the river.

With its population rising from just over 1 million in 1810 to over 7 million by 1911, London presented the most serious problem of public health in Britain but, from 1859, under the direction of the determined and effective Joseph Bazalgette (1819–91), Chief Engineer to the Metropolitan Commission of Sewers (a body established in 1847), a drainage system was constructed. As a result of the 'Great Stink', Parliament, in August 1858, extended the powers of the Metropolitan Board of Works at the expense of the Office of Works and permitted the Board to raise £3 million.

Fully completed in 1875, albeit at a sum greater than the original estimate but one financed by borrowing, the drainage system contained 82 miles (132 kilometres) of intercepting sewers. These took sewage from earlier pipes that had drained into the Thames, and transported it, instead, to new downstream works and storage tanks from which the effluent could be pumped into the river when the tide was flowing into the North Sea. A large number of pumping stations provided the power. The big one at Abbey Mills, built in 1865–8, was an astonishing instance of the determination to disguise function, with the station's role concealed under Moorish towers and a Slavic dome. Storm-relief sewers followed in the 1880s. In part, the storm-relief system used London's rivers other than the Thames, completing the process by which they had been directed underground; the concealment of the rivers made their use for the sewerage system acceptable. Water provision also altered. The 1852 Metropolitan Water Act obliged the London water companies to move their supply sources to above the tidal reach of the Thames.

The improvement in the water supply produced a large fall in mortality figures. By 1874, the death rate per 1,000 had fallen, from a mid-eighteenth-century figure of 48 for London, to 18, compared to 29 for Leeds and 32 for Liverpool and Newcastle. As a sign of gradual but patchy improvement, the impact of the 1866 cholera epidemic was moderate in the western areas, where the drainage and sewerage system had already been improved, but was still deadly further east. The growing population also posed a serious problem for water supplies. Early in the century the emphasis had been on shallow surface waters, but by mid-century there was a major use of boreholes sunk into the chalk aquifers under the London clay. From the 1860s, the Geological Survey produced information on falling water levels in these aquifers.

Across Britain, major attempts to provide clean drinking water for all brought together engineering skill, organizational ability and public action. Thus, on Tyneside, a key centre of urbanization and industrialization, reservoir storage capacity rose to 215 million gallons (977 million litres) in 1848, 530 million (2,409 million litres) in 1854, over 1,200 million (5,455 million litres) in 1871, and over 3,000 million (13,638 million litres) by the end of the 1880s; increases that greatly exceeded the rise in population. There were two developments at work – more people and more hygiene, and the latter won. Filter beds were installed in Tyneside in 1863, and stricter filtering controls were imposed in 1870.

Water supply was also a key aspect of new relationships of power and influence between and within regions. Thus, distant upland areas were tapped by reservoirs for Newcastle, including from 1905 the Catcleugh Reservoir in Redesdale, with pipelines providing the links. The River Tyne, itself the site of shipbuilding and other industries, and a focus of trade, was dredged from 1863 by the typical combination of a reforming body – the Tyne Improvement Commissioners, an able engineer – J.F. Ure (1820–83), and new technology – the world's most powerful bucket dredgers. To help navigation, the Souter Lighthouse was opened nearby in 1871; it was the first in the world to be powered by alternating electric current.

The process of improvement was widespread: Manchester began to get water from Longdendale in the early 1850s, and gained parliamentary approval in 1877 for the drowning of the Thirlmere Valley; Brighton obtained adequate water in the 1860s, and an intercepting sewer in 1874; and Carlisle a reservoir at Castle Carrock in 1909. Moreover, the new infrastructure had an impact on health. For example, the average annual death rate per 1,000 people from typhoid in the Welsh slate-mining centre of Ffestiniog fell from 12.9 in 1865–74 to 1.3 in 1880–90, thanks to piped water and a better sewerage system.

Yet it is important not to exaggerate the degree and pace of improvement. Poor housing, low incomes and crowded hospitals remained a threat to public health. In 1866, 43 per cent of Newcastle's population was still living in dwellings of only one or two rooms; in 1885, 30.6 per cent. In 1911, 12.8 per cent of Scotland's dwellings still had only one room, and in 1918, 45 per cent of Scotland's population still lived at a housing density of more than two people per room. Disease, moreover, continued to hit hard. Gastro-intestinal disorders linked to inadequate water and sewerage systems were responsible for Bradford's very high infant morality rates in the late nineteenth century, and for comparable problems in crowded parts of Newcastle and elsewhere.

More generally, the supply of fresh cow's milk became badly infected in the 1880s and 1890s, leading to a serious increase in diarrhoea in inner cities in hot weather and a rise in infant mortality in the 1890s, especially as the practice of breast-feeding decreased. The extent to which applied knowledge and government action were seen as important is apparent from the three Royal Commissions that focused on the transmission of tuberculosis to humans via milk.

Death rates, especially due to the infectious diseases of early childhood, such as measles and scarlet fever, were higher in urban areas, so the redistribution of the population through migration to the cities delayed the decline in national mortality.

Yet, serious public health problems also existed in small towns and rural areas. Rural poverty, the impact of the agricultural depression, opposition to the interference of central government, and the preference for traditional practices (including inaction), could be a potent mix. Reports revealed that the Somerset town of Bruton had inadequate sewerage disposal and a lack of clean water in the 1870s and 1880s, but a reluctance to spend money ensured that plans to alleviate the situation were delayed; although the sewerage system was finally improved, Bruton did not construct a water supply system in the Victorian period.

Furthermore, industrial activity and developments led to increased or new sources of pollution. In Sunderland, where shipbuilding brought good jobs and a large percentage of workers owned their houses, life took place under a thick layer of coal dust, which was definitely detrimental to health. The sky was smoke-blackened. More generally, gas-works produced coal-gas tar which drained into rivers, polluting them.

Public Health, Poverty and Reform

Working conditions were frequently grim. Industries such as steel were 'sweated' and created a workforce whose leisure centred on the company pub where men could rehydrate, sometimes with four quarts (4.5 litres) a day paid for by the employer. In addition, poor ventilation, a problem in mines, helped the build-up of gas, leading to explosions. The average annual death rate from fatal accidents per 1,000 workers underground in 1875–93 was 2.09 for coal miners, 2.34 for Cleveland ironworkers and 3.23 for Ffestiniog slate miners. In 1878, 189 men and boys were killed by an underground gas explosion at Wood Pit in Haydock, Lancashire.

Mining was physically punishing as well as dangerous. The records of Welsh troops discharged on medical grounds in the First World War indicated the strains of pre-war work: colliers were found to be suffering from hernias and poorly mended broken bones. Miners' health was also affected by dust particles. Other production processes were also dangerous. The manufacture of matches from yellow phosphorous, a task employing many women, contributed to jaundice, psoriasis, chronic diarrhoea and phosphorous rotted jaw. Trawling for fish was another dangerous occupation with many deaths.

Legislation regulating conditions of employment still left work both long and arduous. The Acts of 1847 and 1850 reduced the hours women and thirteen- to eighteen-year-olds could work in the textile industry, but only to ten hours daily. In 1907, however, there were still 5,000 children under thirteen working half-time in the Bradford worsted industry.

Furthermore, the decision to tackle public health essentially through engineering projects directed by administrators ensured that alternative responses, such as measures to alleviate poverty, were sidetracked. The focus was on sewerage systems and clean water, and not on securing the supply of food and work or income at levels sufficient to lessen the impact of disease. If the bulk of the working population faced difficult circumstances, the situation was even worse for those who were more 'marginal' to the economy or to society's moral framework. Henry Stuart, who reported on East Anglian poor relief in 1834, found three main groups of inmates in the often miserable parish workhouses: the old and infirm, orphaned and illegitimate children, and unmarried pregnant women; the last a group that was generally treated harshly, far more so than the men responsible. Aside from scandals in individual work-houses, the situation in many was bleak. In Wimborne, beds had to be shared, meat was provided only once a week, there were no vegetables other than potatoes until 1849, husbands and wives were segregated, and unmarried mothers had to wear distinctive clothes. In general, expenditure was severely controlled, discipline was harsh, and the stigma attached to dependent poverty grew.

The Poor Law Amendment Act of 1834 had introduced national guidelines in place of the former, more varied, parish-based system, but the uniform workhouse system that it sought to create and that lasted into the twentieth century was not generous to its inmates. Outdoor relief was abolished for the able-bodied, who instead were obliged to enter the workhouse where they were to be treated no better than the conditions that could be expected outside in order to deter all bar the very destitute from being a charge on the community. Bastardy and indigent marriage and parenthood were to be discouraged. The system was overseen by the Poor Law Commissioners in London. The legislation was strongly resisted by the Anti-Poor Law movement, and outdoor relief continued into the 1870s.

The prioritization of public health accorded with the importance given it by the reforming middle classes and their priorities helped ensure that there were steadily greater attempts to create a legislative framework for reform. In place of a reliance on self-help and the efforts of local communities, there was a stress on institutional provision and national standards. The Factory Acts of 1860 and 1874 regulated conditions of employment, the Metaliferous Mines Acts of 1872 and 1875 sought better working conditions underground, including by improving ventilation, and the Miners Regulation Act of 1908 limited the number of hours that miners could spend underground.

Attempts were also made to improve and regulate society, especially the cities, which seemed particularly troubling, with their rapid growth and lack of established social controls. The County and Borough Police Act of 1856 made the formation of paid police forces obligatory. Policing sought to bring order and decorum to the streets. Moreover, in 1854, pubs in England were forced to close at midnight on Saturday and, except for Sunday lunch and evening, not to reopen until 4 a.m. on Monday. Complete Sunday closing was enforced in Scotland from 1853 and in Wales from 1881. Drinking was also affected by the 1869 Wine and Beerhouse Act and the 1872 Licensing Act. As pubs were central to working-class communal experience, and alcohol lessened inhibitions, these charges were very much part of a more controlled society; although self-regulation was also a key theme.

Social Assumptions

It was no longer a case of change affecting society, politics, the economy and culture. Instead, change became integral to their structures, and, in part, their ethos. Social criticism became more common. Under the heading 'The Lord Lieutenant and the North Devon Railway', *Trewman's Exeter Flying Post* of 3 January 1856 reported at length a clash between the mores of aristocratic society and the notion of public responsibility:

> Express trains will not do the bidding of Lords Lieutenant. Railways are not managed as are coaches; – the times of arrival and departure, as advertised, are kept as regularly as possible; and a railway superintendent would as soon think of keeping a train back to accommodate a peer of the realm as he would of sending off a train too soon to baulk a director. Lord Fortescue, however, seems to think that in his case exceptions ought to be made to the rule which governs all railway companies. It was his misfortune to be in the down express from Bristol last Saturday afternoon week, which did not happen to reach Taunton until after the time it was due at Exeter. The North Devon train is advertised to leave the station at 3.30, – half an hour after the arrival of the express. The superintendent having ascertained by telegraph that the express was much behind its time, started the North Devon train at 3.45.

Fortescue complained about the failure to delay the latter, despite the large number of passengers on it, leading the paper to ask, 'Does Lord Fortescue mean to say that these should have been detained an hour and a half to suit his Lordship's convenience?' Thus, the broad acres around the ancestral Fortescue seat at Castle Hill in north Devon provided scant guarantee against the reality and criticism of a new world. There was also potent criticism in the fictional world. In his novel *Bleak House* (1852–3), Charles Dickens not only indicated the coldness of law and Church, but also society, in the haughty personages of Sir Leicester Dedlock – 'his family is as old as the hills and infinitely more respectable' – and his wife, who are revealed as concealing a guilty secret. Such accounts served to identify and criticize an entire class.

Yet, although the world of the 1850s had democratic aspects, it was very much a nation that was to be guided by moral conduct. Paternalistic and evangelical concern about Christian welfare lay behind much pressure for reform, rather than egalitarianism. These values were noted in the 11 July 1855 issue of Chudleigh's *Weekly Express* which praised the situation under which 'the children of our poorer brethren here receive a sound religious and moral education'. Education was certainly seen as a key goal. Under the heading 'Popular Education', the *Western Times* of 25 January 1851 declared:

> We have only space to refer to the satisfactory report of the meeting held at the Guildhall, to establish public libraries. We should prefer seeing a more direct effort to promote the education of the destitute youth and children of the city, but we receive the conclusions of the meeting as an admission of the public *duty* to provide a means of education for that class of society whose means do not enable it to educate its offspring.

Paternalism was linked to social order, so that in the late nineteenth century those who killed a social superior were punished more severely than the opposite, while working-class killers were more likely to be executed than their social 'betters'.

Change challenged all institutions and was unsettling for much of the population. The varied manifestations of this unease included hostility to immigrants, which was more of an issue towards the close of the century, and a wider disquiet about the state of the nation, not least the extent of urban poverty and the social problems associated with it. This concern encouraged social analysis, led to calls for public action and promoted charitable missions.

The plight of poor children moved crusading philanthropists such as Thomas Barnardo (1845–1905) who, in 1867, founded the East End [of London] Juvenile Mission, the basis of what later became 'Dr Barnardo's Homes' for destitute children. From 1882, he sent some children to Canada for resettlement. Similarly, in 1869, the Reverend Thomas Stephenson (1839–1912) established near Waterloo Road, London, a refuge for destitute children, the basis of the National Children's Home. In Whitechapel, in the East End, in 1865, William Booth (1829–1912) and his wife Catherine launched the 'Christian Mission to the Heathen of our Own Country' and, thirteen years later, this became the Salvation Army. Initially focused on spiritual salvation, the Salvation Army's mission also became directed at social reform. Wilson Carlile (1847–1942), an Anglican curate in Kensington, matched this by launching the Church Army in 1882, again linking evangelism and social welfare. Temperance was a key theme of the moral rearmers. Emma Cons (1838–1912), who owned the Old Vic (formerly the Royal Coburg Theatre and then the Royal Victoria) from 1881 until 1912, provided decent and moral entertainment on temperance lines.

The motives of crusading philanthropists have been queried in recent decades, but, however much philanthropy could serve the interests of the donors' spiritual well-being, curiosity and even personal aggrandizement, there was a drive both to offer relieving improvement and, in understanding the plight of the poor, to provide a more nuanced appreciation of the social environment. Yet, the moral panics about the plight of the poor that crusading philanthropy and journalism inspired, were, to a degree, replicated by unease about the willingness of philanthropists to compromise class and gender assumptions and roles in their charitable work. Their focus was on the East End, which became more orderly as a result of the major effort for public improvement.

The Pressure for Improvement

Educational expansion and reform were part of this process of public improvement. They also reflected the range and energy of Victorian philanthropy. Mason Science College, which eventually became part of the University of Birmingham established in 1900, was founded in 1880 by Sir Josiah Mason (1795–1881), a self-educated manufacturer of split-rings and steel pen-nibs. He spent part of his fortune on local orphans as well as on his new foundation, which was designed to be especially useful for local industries. Men such as Martin set the self-conscious tone of much of urban Victorian Britain. Their views and wealth were a tremendous stimulus to the process of improvement.

As government became more activist and regulatory, so the goal of politics increasingly became seizing the opportunity to push though policy, as much as office-holding for personal profit and prestige; ideology rather than interest. Linked to this, the nature of power within society was now discussed to a greater extent than a century earlier. The expanding middle class, which, unlike its counterpart in the late twentieth century, worked for the private rather than the public sector, expected power and status. In pursuit of its interests and views, the Victorian middle class, like its later counterpart, was dubious of established institutions and practices that did not seem reformist or useful. Deference was eroded and reconceptualized, as middle-class views and wealth stimulated a demand for, and a process of, civic and moral improvement that was central to the movement for reform, with government action increasingly seen as a substitute for the resort to religious faith. This movement was directed as much against the habits of the poor as those of the Establishment and inherited privilege. Rational organization, meritocratic conduct and moral purpose were the goals.

It would be misleading to see change as arising only due to reforming Liberal and, from 1924, Labour governments. Instead, as earlier in the late nineteenth century, and again, in part, as an aspect of the interplay between remedies linked to the state, voluntary bodies and individuals, there was a widespread and continuous commitment to reform. Thus, the Midwives Act of 1902, passed by a Conservative government, and the Maternity and Child Welfare Act of 1918, passed by the Coalition, improved infant and maternal health care and encouraged a sense of public responsibility. The Midwives Act improved the registration and quality of midwives, and this measure has been linked to a fairly steep decline in infant mortality after a peak in 1900.

By 1914, a basic national network of infant and child welfare centres had been created. Health-visiting was expanding. Educational authorities had been made responsible for the medical inspection of schoolchildren. Isolation, tuberculosis, smallpox and maternity hospitals and sanatoria were established by local authorities, elements of the process by which social welfare was linked to a growing institutionalization of society, which also led to the construction of schools, workhouses and asylums.

Medical Advances

Far from unconstrained capitalism, this was increasingly a regulated society. In his novel *When the Sleeper Awakes* (1899), H.G. Wells felt able to look forward 200 years to a world where disease had been vanquished, and there was enough food, a misleading utopia but one that cast light on what seemed possible at the time. Improved diet, thanks in part to a significant fall in food prices, had already played an important role in the decline in mortality rates, which in Newcastle fell from 30.1 to 19.1 per thousand between 1872 and 1900. Medical advances, not least the replacement of the 'miasma' theory of disease by that of 'germs', helped, although mortality contrasts between registration districts persisted and there was a noticeable, although not invariable, relationship between life expectancy and population density, and thus poverty.

Medical knowledge and care improved in the early decades of the century. For example, the use, from the mid-1920s, of insulin, discovered in 1922, enabled diabetics to live. The increased distribution in the inter-war years (1918–39) of vitamins, which had been discovered earlier in the century, as well as the establishment of antenatal screening, were important in health, as were improvements to the milk supply through the introduction of milk depots and the provision of free pasteurized milk.

Inter-war medical advances included immunization against diphtheria and tetanus, improved blood transfusion techniques (which owed much to the experience of the First World War), the use of gamma globulin against measles, and the first sulphonamide drugs which, although later outclassed by antibiotics, had a major impact, especially on streptococcal infections, and were widely seen as miracle drugs. The Poor Law infirmaries and, from 1929, the municipal hospitals, offered free care; and the specialist hospitals had long offered care at a price that artisan and lower-middle-class families could well afford.

Yet, there were still major problems with public health, poor housing and medical provision in the inter-war years, even before the major crisis caused by the Depression of the 1930s. Much of the population did not benefit fully from medical advances, and health indicators continued to be closely related to socio-economic factors. Tuberculosis remained serious, especially among the urban poor, although death rates had a steady downward trend from about 1870. Hospital provision varied greatly across the country.

The balance of judgement is significant, because advocates of post-1945 social programmes, such as the NHS, used their view of the earlier situation as a basis for assessment. In practice, while no years are of course typical, those from 1931 to 1945, first the slump and Depression and then the Second

World War, were scarcely typical. Instead, looking back to the
1920s, it is possible to point to a long-standing process of
improvement. This process was a matter of general trends in
health as well as the results of specific legislation.

The Position of Women

A similar conclusion can be advanced for the position of
women. Modern standards of equality were still distant, even
after women gained the vote in 1918, in part because the
general notion of equality was still largely one of respect for
separate functions and developments. Women's special role
was for long defined as that of running the home and family,
and was used to justify their exclusion from other spheres. The
ideology of separate spheres, in part stemming from a
substantial body of medical and philosophical literature on the
supposedly natural differences between men and women, was
well established from the late eighteenth century.

The rise during Queen Victoria's reign (1837–1901) of
science as a source of authority provided new life for such
ideas. Older views of the intellectual superiority of men over
women were given new vigour by men such as George
Romanes (1848–94), who claimed that the greater brain size of
men proved the point. In other ways, science, more specifically
medicine, encouraged the idea of women as inferior by arguing
that they were naturally hormonally unstable and potentially
hysterical.

At a more day-to-day level, women were less well treated in
a myriad of ways, with these distinctions publicly endorsed in
official, semi-official and private functions. In both public and
private, women ate less well. For the celebration of Queen
Victoria's Golden Jubilee in 1887, the women and children of
the town of Ashby de la Zouch sat down in the marketplace to
a tea of sandwiches, bread and butter, and cake; while the men
had earlier had a meal of roast beef, mutton, potatoes, plum
pudding and beer, which had been prepared by women, as
meals in general were.

The world of work was also heavily biased against women, and more so than today. Women mostly moved into the low-skill, low-pay, arduous 'sweated' sector, and were generally worse treated than men, a practice in which the trade unions cooperated with the management. Both condemned the women woollen workers of Batley and Dewsbury for organizing themselves in a 1875 dispute. Definitions of skills, which affected pay, were controlled by men and favoured them; skilled women, such as the weavers of Preston or Bolton, were poorly recognized. In contrast, women in the pottery industry were able to maintain status and pay despite male opposition.

A common form of work, indeed the largest category of female employment in Wales in 1911 (and in many other places), was domestic service. Household tasks, such as cleaning and drying clothes, involved much effort. It was possible in the hierarchy of service to gain promotion, but, in general, domestic service was unskilled and not a career. Wages were poor and pay was largely in kind, which made life very hard for those who wished to marry and leave service. The working conditions, however, were generally better and less hazardous than in the factories, where repetitive work for many hours was expected. Servants rarely, if ever, went without food.

The absence of an effective social welfare system, and the low wages paid to most women, ensured that prostitution was the fate of many, and part-time prostitution was related to economic conditions. At Liverpool, where about 30,000 sailors were ashore at any one time, there were 538 brothels in 1846, and in 1857 there were at least 200 regular prostitutes under twelve. As was typical of the values of the age, women, not men, were blamed for the spread of venereal diseases which was seen as a threat not only to individual health but also to family purity and values, and to the health of society. Under the Contagious Diseases Acts of 1864, 1866 and 1869, passed because of concern about the health of the armed forces, in garrison towns and ports women suspected of being prostitutes, but not men who also might have spread disease, were subjected to physical examination and detention, if infected. After an extended campaign, in which women acquired experience of acting as political leaders, in the Ladies' National Association for the Repeal of the Contagious Diseases Acts, the Acts were repealed in 1886.

Social pressures and health problems interacted. There was an emphasis by both men and women on maternity, but very much within marriage; the marital prospects of unmarried mothers were low. Frequent childbirth was exhausting and many women died giving birth, ensuring that children were often brought up by stepmothers. Joseph Chamberlain's first two wives died in childbirth, leaving him with responsibility for six children. Female pelvises were often distorted by rickets during malnourished childhoods, while there was no adequate training in midwifery. As a result, obstetric haemorrhages were poorly managed and often fatal. The situation greatly improved after the 1902 Midwives Act. Whether single or married, women suffered from the generally limited and primitive nature of contraceptive practices. Many single women resorted to abortion, which was treated as a crime and therefore was a 'back street' practice without regulation. This situation contributed to the extent to which abortion was greatly hazardous to health and frequently led to the woman's death.

Women were also affected by the strength of hierarchy and deference, not least in the number and treatment of servants. In his novel *He Knew He Was Right* (1868–9), Anthony Trollope (1815–82) depicted the debilitating pressure of personal service. The snobbish, religious and reactionary spinster Jemima Stanbury

> kept three maid-servants. ... But it was not every young woman who could live with her. A rigidity as to hours, as to religious exercises, and as to dress, was exacted, under which many poor girls altogether broke down; but they who could

stand this rigidity came to know that their places were very valuable.

Wilkie Collins, often a novelist of social issues, criticized the marriage laws in his novel *Man and Wife* (1870). Sexual hypocrisy, not least linked to the seduction of women, was also a theme of novels, as in Collins' *The New Magdalen* (1873) and George Eliot's *Adam Bede* (1859). Arthur Wing Pinero wrote social dramas that focused on the difficult position of women, notably *The Second Mrs Tanqueray* (1893), *The Notorious Mrs Ebbsmith* (1895) and *The Benefit of the Doubt* (1895). In the powerful first of these, Paula Tanqueray commits suicide because of the social stigma created by the engagement of her seducer to her step-daughter and her opposition to the match. Pinero also dealt with seduction in his controversial play *The Profligate* (1889).

Rising pressure towards the end of the century for women to receive a fairer deal, and for women's interests to be regarded as a separate question not to be answered by reference to the past, challenged conventional assumptions. The idea of the 'new woman' developed in the late nineteenth century as established gender roles were challenged.

Yet, the practical impact of the idea is easily overstated, even for middle-class, let alone working-class, women. A potentially important change was the institution of divorce proceedings in England in 1857; in Scotland divorce was already legal and there were many divorces. Before the 1857 Act, divorce required a private Act of Parliament in England, a very difficult process open only to the wealthy, or a separation achieved through the ecclesiastical courts, which did not allow remarriage. Even after the Act, divorce still remained costly, and therefore not a possibility for the poor. As a result, former practices of 'self-divorce', such as the 'wife selling' described in Thomas Hardy's novel *The Mayor of Casterbridge* (1886), continued. Cohabitation was another option, although offering most women no economic security. Women suffered because marital desertions were generally a matter of men leaving, with the women bearing the burden of supporting the children: poverty made some men heedless of the potent and oft-repeated Victorian cult of the family and patriarchy.

Higher education for women began at both Cambridge and Oxford, although they were not permitted to take degrees for many years. At Aberdeen University, it was formally agreed in 1892 that women be admitted to all faculties, but none studied law or divinity, they were not offered equivalent teaching in medicine, and there was unequal access to the bursary competition. Women students took no positions of influence and the student newspaper, *Alma Mater*, was hostile, presenting them as unfeminine or flighty and foolish: the men clearly found it difficult to adjust to female students, although their numbers and influence increased, especially during the First World War. More generally, until the 1940s, female teachers had to leave the profession when they married.

Moreover, the degree to which the journalist and novelist Eliza Linton (1822–98) could write, in works for women such as *The Girl of the Period and Other Essays* (1883), against the 'new woman' is an indication of the fears that were aroused. Far from being readily discredited, the separate spheres ideology displayed both resilience and adaptability, and was to continue to do so during the twentieth century. One of the major voluntary legacies of the Victorian age, the Mothers' Union, an Anglican women's organization founded in 1876 by Mary Sumner (1828–1921), a vicar's wife, rapidly spread from being a parish body designed to support 'the sanctity of marriage' and a Christian family environment, to be first a diocesan organization (1885) and then a national one, with a central council, in 1895. By 1939, the Mothers' Union had 538,000 members. Such developments are overly neglected as a result of the focus on the suffragette movement.

The extensions of the franchise in the nineteenth century brought scant benefit to women. Female ratepayers had the vote for local government from 1869, but lacked the same role in national politics. From the early 1900s, a vociferous suffragette movement demanded the vote in parliamentary elections. The militant tactics of the Women's Social and Political Union founded by Emmeline (1858–1928) and Christabel Pankhurst (1880–1958) in 1903 were designed to force public attention, although other feminist leaders, such as Millicent Fawcett (1847–1929), the leader of the National Union of Women's Suffrage Societies, advocated democratic, non-violent tactics. A different impression of the movement is created depending on which leader is emphasized. Suffrage Bills in 1910 and 1911 failed, in part due to a lack of government support, and suffragette violence attracted much publicity but proved counterproductive. So did the suffragettes' Electoral Fighting Fund to support Labour candidates.

The First World War transformed the situation, as it also changed much else. Female employment shot up, and new roles, many in industry, were performed by women, including the manufacture of munitions. Women also received higher wages, although they remained lower than men's, and in factories women were controlled by male foremen.

At the same time, the war led to an important change in social attitudes, including those towards women. As a result, in 1918 it was possible to extend the vote to women of thirty and over, as long as they were householders or wives of householders, occupants of property worth £5 annually, or graduates of British universities; for men the age was changed to twenty-one, but, in practice, with no such restrictions. It has been suggested that war work, and the extent to which women were shown to be capable of significant tasks, gained women the vote, although most of those who did such work were propertyless and under thirty and were thus not enfranchised in 1918. It has also been argued that (some) women got the vote in a defensive step to lessen the potentially radical consequences of universal male suffrage. Whatever the reason, and both probably played a role, the number of women who gained the vote in 1918 was larger than that proposed in most Bills supported by the suffragettes prior to the war.

Society was changing, and in 1928 women achieved equal suffrage, and thus comprised a majority of the electorate. The changing position of women was not restricted to work and the vote. New opportunities were related to increased mobility and independence, and included a decline in control and influence over young women by their elders, male and female. As a consequence, there was a new sexual climate. Chaperonage became less comprehensive and effective, and styles of courtship became much freer. As an aspect of the disruption of the war and of the freer sexual climate that it led to, the percentage of illegitimate births rose to 6 in 1918.

Furthermore, there was a greater interest in the informed public discussion of sex. The British Society for the Study of Sex Psychology was founded in 1914, and, with Marie Stopes' (1880–1958) influential *Married Love* published in 1918, there was an emphasis on mutual desire as a basis for sex, and thus for marriage.

Moreover, society was less deferential in the 1920s than hitherto, and there was more of a cult of youth and novelty, although not as great as was to be the case in the 1960s. With relatively low rates of juvenile unemployment, the young were able to choose jobs, and did not need to be as deferential at work as hitherto. With far higher disposable income than in the 1900s, the young also had their own leisure choices, especially the cinema and dance halls. There were 11,000 dance halls in Britain by the mid-1920s, a form of entertainment that had begun only after the First World War and one that reflected and encouraged the appeal of popular music, which was greatly influenced by American developments. It was no longer a case of the young following the leisure preferences of their parents.

Having gained the vote, the women's movement continued to be active, pressing for the removal of bars on female activity and for equality through society. Under the leadership of Eleanor Rathbone (1872–1946), the National Union of Societies for Equal Citizenship sought by parliamentary lobbying, rather than the Pankhursts' militant tactics, to gain legislative goals, such as welfare benefits for married women. Women were allowed to enter the legal profession and become JPs in 1918. Socially, women benefited from less discrimination than before the war, and there was less segregation, with the sexes mixing more freely, both before and after marriage.

Yet, women continued to suffer discrimination in most fields: the jobs they were expected to do and the tasks allocated to them in these jobs. Thus, women police were introduced during the First World War, but, for long, they were largely required to deal with women and children, rather than with the bulk of crime. Women teachers had to resign when they married. Moreover, many women workers were still 'sweated' workers, working in harsh conditions and for little pay, for example in textile manufacturing. Furthermore, the new ideology of domesticity that emerged in the inter-war period affected attitudes towards women workers.

Religion

A key element of change was provided by the declining public role of religion. To a Victorian, it would have been surprising to discuss sport or leisure, medicine or gender, before religion, but the latter was less prominent in public life than had been the case a century earlier. As Britain became a more industrial and urban society, it also became a more secular one. Religion lost its central role in everyday life and memory, and church attendance began to decline: developments that were to become more marked during the twentieth century.

The 1820s saw the dismantling of much of the legal privilege of Establishment (official status as the state Church) for the Anglican Church in England, Wales and Ireland, and the Presbyterian church in Scotland (the Church of Scotland). Thereafter, these churches experienced challenges from a number of directions: from social and economic change, from other faiths, from government, from intellectual challenges, and from growing disbelief. The first led to major population changes, particularly the expansion of the industrial cities, which stretched existing church provision. In many cases, there were insufficient church buildings, or the mission of the churches did not strike a response with people who were adapting to a rapidly altering society.

Nevertheless, industrialization was also linked to religious revival in some areas. Indeed, there was a powerful movement of reform, with committed clerics seeking to make Christian teaching more accessible. 'Slum priests' took the Church's message to the urban poor. More generally, Anglican church interiors were rebuilt in order to replace box pews, which belonged to families, with rows of identical, open pews, most of which were rent-free and open to all.

Britain remained very much a Christian country, although, since Catholic emancipation in 1829, it had largely ceased to be a confessional state as far as the law was concerned. Jewish immigration from Eastern Europe became important in the late nineteenth century, leading to an upsurge in anti-Semitism, but the Jews largely settled in major urban centres, especially London, the vast bulk of the population remained Christian, and most subscribed at the very least to the formal requirements of Christian living.

The Church of England encountered particular difficulties in winning adherents in those parts of the country that were developing fastest. The rise of Dissent (Protestant Nonconformity) in numbers and respectability was a problem, especially in Wales and northern England. The re-emergence of 'public' Catholicism, with the re-establishment of the Catholic hierarchy in England in 1850, and in Scotland in 1878, caused tension which was accentuated by massive Irish immigration. There were anti-Catholic riots in Stockport in 1852, and violence on Merseyside in 1850–1. Between 1850 and 1910, 1,173 Catholic churches were opened in England and Wales, the largest number in London and Lancashire. 'Unbelief' also gained respectability through the development of Darwinism: Charles Darwin's (1809–82) theory of evolution made a major impact on public discussion not only of science but also of religion and society.

The changing role of government also challenged the Established Churches. The role of the parish in education and social welfare declined in favour of new government agencies such as school boards. Municipal and county government was better able than the Churches to channel and implement the aspirations of society for reform and control.

The Religious Census of 1851 suggested that there was a crisis of faith, with falling church attendance. The Census of Religious Worship was the first (and last) attempt by government to record all places in England and Wales where public worship was held, the frequency of their services, the extent of their accommodation, and the number of people in them. In all, 34,467 places of worship were identified and the census revealed nearly 11 million attendances at church on census Sunday, 30 March (60.8 per cent of the population), of which 48.6 per cent were in Anglican churches and 51.4 per cent in others, a return that led to Anglican anger. The Anglicans did best in the rural south and in small towns, while Catholics and Nonconformists were most successful in the cities. Working-class attendance was lower than clerics would have liked, John Davies (1788–1858), Rector of St Clement's, Worcester, reporting that his working-class parishioners 'seldom ever attend Sunday Morning Service. The Saturday Market and the late payment of wages on the evening of that day contribute probably in no small degree to produce this remark.' Drink thus kept devotion at bay.

Yet, the census also indicated the role of local circumstances and the greatly contrasting character of religious activity. Indeed, there was re-Christianization as well as secularization. Religious validation continued to be important for the key turning points in life, such as birth (baptism), marriage and death; and making a good and Christian death was an important aspect of the latter.

Moreover, the major Christian Churches, especially the

Church of England, the Catholic Church and the Methodists, still had much life in them. They were energetically building new churches in an effort to reach out to new congregations, especially in the expanding cities. Furthermore, in Scotland there was a huge building programme by United Presbyterian and Free kirks alongside Church of Scotland places of worship. In addition, the strong drive for missionary work in the outside world was matched by a powerful sense of the need for such efforts in Britain, notably in the slums. Aside from the commitment to Christian mission, there was a marked attempt to improve the institutional framework of the Churches, an attempt that also captured the interest in reform. For example, there was extensive improvement to existing church buildings, and far more effort was devoted to training clerics than hitherto. Attention was also devoted to organization. New dioceses were created. In Cornwall, where a diocese was created at Truro in 1877, more than fifty new churches were built between 1870 and 1900. Chelmsford was selected in 1913 for the new cathedral for Essex. Derby became a diocese in 1914.

Religion was also important in British culture. Religious scenes were often reproduced in the engravings that decorated many walls, from the loftiest to the most humble dwellings. Moreover, the various religious groupings were keen to develop church music. Leading composers such as Sir Hubert Parry (1848–1918), who wrote the chorus 'Jerusalem' (1916) to words by William Blake, and Sir Charles Villiers Stanford (1852–1924) both played a major role in the British choral tradition, while the output of Sir Arthur Sullivan (1842–1900) included 'Onward Christian Soldiers' (1871) and the oratorio *The Light of the World* (1873), and Sir Edward Elgar wrote *The Dream of Gerontius* (1900).

The heavy casualties of the First World War sapped confidence in divine purpose (and, paradoxically, encouraged spiritualism) while the widespread disruption brought on by the war affected established religious practices, including churchgoing, throughout Britain. There seems to have been a recovery in at least nominal church attendance thereafter, but in the inter-war years the Churches continued to find it difficult to reach out successfully to the bulk of the industrial working class. Much of this group was indifferent to, or alienated from, all Churches.

The Catholics were most successful, their numbers rising from 2.2 million in 1910 to 3.0 million in 1940. In contrast, in the inter-war period, the numbers of Methodists, Baptists, Congregationalists and Welsh Presbyterians all fell, as did the number of Scottish Episcopalians. The decline of the chapel as the centre of community life in Wales was particularly marked after 1918, and served to alter significantly the nature of Welsh society, so that Wales became more secular. The Church of England, meanwhile, continued its institutional expansion, founding a diocese in Portsmouth in 1926, and had scant change in membership, but, given the rise of population, this was an important proportional decline in support.

The most influential clergyman of the inter-war years, William Temple (1881–1944), Bishop of Manchester 1921–9, Archbishop of York 1929–42, and of Canterbury 1942–4, sought to reverse the decline of organized religion, and to make England an Anglican nation again, and thus justify the Church of England's claim to speak for it. Temple offered a synthesis of Christianity with modern culture, in works such as *Mens Creatrix* (1917), *Christus Veritas* (1924) and *Christianity and Social Order* (1942). At times, Temple, who viewed welfare as representing Christian social values, was seen as left-wing, a label he would have denied. In the event, although Temple strengthened the Church, he failed to give England a more clearly Christian character. Furthermore, Temple's inspiration of the already developing role of the Church as a voice of social criticism and concern led to it being seen increasingly in a secular light. This was despite major efforts to keep religion central to society and to public life.

Church-based societies became less important, both for the young and for their elders. In addition, poverty helped lead many to question Church teachings; although a large number of the poor did find meaning and support in faith. Moreover, religious ideas were important in popular moral codes, and in public traditions, even for those who lacked faith. The Established Churches, however, were more successful in catering to a middle-class constituency, not least because of the important role they allowed for middle-class socializing and for female voluntary service, than they were in catering for the poor.

Social Tension

Society was changing, therefore, but not to the extent that is suggested by the disruption of the First World War nor the radical ideas of the period. Despite the rise of the Labour Party, Britain was still a hierarchical society with much deference. New institutions and developments were moulded to take note of existing social divisions. Rail passengers were classified by class and each had very different conditions on the trains and in the stations. The class-based analysis of society advanced by Karl Marx (1818–83), who lived and wrote in London from 1849, remained pertinent.

Yet, the structure and ethos of society were being affected by the rise of individual and collective merit as a defining characteristic at the expense of heredity. Under the process of Victorian reform, institutions, notably the Civil Service, the professions, the universities, the public schools, the Army and the Navy, both expanded greatly and developed a more meritocratic ethos. This change was very significant in the creation of a new establishment to replace the aristocracy. The challenge was most overt from the Liberals and Labour. Lloyd George wooed Labour and the trade unions and successfully sought to move the Liberals to the left. He declared in a speech in Newcastle that 'a fully equipped duke costs as much to keep up as two Dreadnoughts [battleships]', and that the House of Lords comprised 'five hundred men, ordinary men, chosen accidentally from among the unemployed'; a different tone to that of his predecessors.

This was the language of class struggle, and the latter was in evidence, notably in strike waves, such as that of 1910–12. Sabotage by striking miners in 1910 against collieries, strike-breakers and trains was resisted and led to much violence. In 1911, the first general rail strike led to sabotage at Llanelli, and also to the deployment of troops, who killed two strikers in Liverpool; in 1911 police killed one in Tonypandy. Nearly 41 million working days were lost through strikes in 1912 alone. Those of dockers and seamen in Glasgow in 1911 contributed to the idea of 'Red Clydeside', an idea which was to return after the war.

Although strikes arose from particular disputes in individual industries, they also benefited from a growing sense of class consciousness felt by much of the working class, an attitude that was reinforced by the coercive response to the strikes. This sense encouraged the growth of the Labour Party, the attraction of the radical programme of New Liberalism, and Liberal–Labour cooperation. The growing socialism of the unions was a victory for the more militant elements among the working population, their militancy in part stemming from immersion in the radical doctrines of syndicalism, with their call for direct action by the workers, although syndicalism was limited geographically and occupationally.

Yet, alongside social division and the role of social classes, there were factors making for social cohesion as well as other sources of identity. Lloyd George's legislation was designed to contain social problems. In part, his reforms were a response to the failure of the Poor Law as a result of the burdens posed by the large-scale need for social assistance. The Royal Commission on the Poor Law that sat between 1905 and 1909 produced majority and minority reports, each of which would have cost a great deal. As a result, Lloyd George decided to leave the Poor Law as it was, but to reduce the burden on it by providing old age pensions, national insurance and employment exchanges.

Moreover, a whole range of institutions and practices helped to link people of different backgrounds and to lessen social tensions. These included churches and sport, patriotic groups and youth bodies such as the Boy Scouts, which may have included 34 per cent of all males born between 1901 and 1920. This movement deliberately sought to lessen class division.

Such bodies and practices were not themselves free of tension and could themselves be the sites, and even cause, of social division and even antagonism. Nevertheless, the determined effort by many such institutions to offer a different basis for identity and activity to that of class division was important. Furthermore, the variety of bases for identity affected the political world. For example, Christian Socialism was important and many prominent Labour figures, such as Arthur Henderson and George Lansbury (1859–1940), were committed Christians.

Indeed, religious, regional and occupational divisions were as important as class issues. In 1914, over 75 per cent of the working population were not members of trade unions, and divisions existed within the workforce, between skilled and unskilled, between Protestants and Irish immigrants, and between, and within, regional economies. Thus, in the cotton finishing industry, elite foremen engravers had little in common with poorly paid bleachers. Such divisions remained apparent in the 1920s, and, as before, were displayed in, and sustained by, new developments. This was true, for example, of the expanding world of material goods, which reflected social contrasts, both between the middle and working class and within the latter.

Conclusions

I do not mean that it was all rather self-conscious and arty, like those awful parties in London at which women with unpleasant breath advocate free love and nudism.

The misogynist, philistine and sneering tone of *Case for Three Detectives* (1936) by Leo Bruce (Rupert Croft-Cooke;

1903–80) is a reminder that, alongside the reforms and changes described in the last chapter, many of the social assumptions of the period proved resistant to change. Looked at more blandly, continuity in change was an important aspect of the British in the period 1851 to 1931 and not only in religion. For example, the same was true in population changes. Most of the major rise in population was from native growth rather than immigration, a situation dramatically different to that in the 2000s; although there was immigration from outside the British Isles, notably of Jews, while a 1919 riot at Glasgow harbour directed at black residents was the first in a series in British ports that reflected anger by white workers about competition from black workers.

The degree of continuity helped ensure that the period was often to be recalled and recovered in terms of the stereotypes of deep-seated social divisions, as well as of such factors as sexual repression. While these elements were indeed all present, the situation was far more complex. The different narratives of these years, both individual and group, were not only opposed to each other. In practice, they also interacted in a complex patchwork of social alignments, a patchwork in which the variety in personal circumstances was matched to a hitherto unprecedented extent by those in social assumptions, not least over the role of women and the place of religion. Yet, as Chapters 6 and 8 will show, these assumptions were to change far more in the late twentieth century.

4

IMPERIAL STRENGTH

The history of Britain in this period owes much of its importance to the state's leading position in the world. This was most obviously a matter of imperial extent, naval power and success in war, but the 'soft' nature of British power, in terms of the influence of the British constitution and system of government, was also very significant. In the nineteenth century, Britain's commitment to parliamentary government, the rule of law, individual liberties and free trade enjoyed great repute, which, in turn, confirmed their importance to its domestic audience. Moreover, the development of the empire away from an emphasis on control of colonies, and towards, for some, a degree of self-government, helped enhance the global impact of the British model, because the self-governing Dominions, such as Australia, were, at least initially, expressions of a Greater Britain.

'Rise and Fall' is the standard imperial narrative, with an established account of Victorian rise, followed by a growing perception of difficulties from the late nineteenth century (due to relative decline as other states rose to power), and then crisis. The First World War, in particular, serves in this account as both consequence and cause of crisis. This narrative has considerable force, but it also underplays the extent to which Britain, nevertheless, enjoyed an empire of unprecedented size after that war. Moreover, helped by victory in the First World War, and by the defeat (Germany, Russia, Austria) or isolationism (US) of pre-war powers, Britain was very much still the leading imperial state in the 1920s.

This is why the span covered in Part 1 is, deliberately, to 1931, rather than ending in 1901, 1914 or 1918. Japan's successful invasion of Manchuria, China's leading industrial region, in 1931 was the first major challenge to the liberal international order (as well as a measure that revealed the consequences of the earlier collapse of the Anglo-Japanese alliance); and the conflicts of 1931–45 were to leave Britain not only a far weaker state and empire, but also one overshadowed by other world powers, especially the US, which had a powerful anti-imperialist ideology.

Imperialism

The span from 1851 to 1945, let alone 1931, was not a long one, and, until the 1960s, the memories of individuals, families and communities, as well as the resonances of imperial literature and propaganda, could readily recover a sense of power and consequence that it is difficult to appreciate now when Britain lacks this sense of confidence. Yet, to fail to understand the imperial experience and the sense of imperial mission prior to the 1940s is to neglect much of the political atmosphere of the age. Empire was in large part a matter of power politics, military interests, elite careers and an ideology of mission that appealed in particular to the propertied and the proselytizing. Sectional interests, such as traders, export industries, missionaries, the Army, politicians and the monarchy, each had their own imperial narrative and culture.

Self-interest alone, however, does not explain imperial expansion. Most clearly in the final decades of the nineteenth century, empire had relevance and meaning throughout much of British society, as was reflected in the jingoistic strains of popular culture: adventure stories, the ballads of the music hall, and the images depicted on advertisements for mass-produced goods, many of which indeed were manufactured from products imported from the empire such as palm oil, rubber and tea.

Empire also affected senses of identity, including notions of masculinity. Soldier heroes, such as General Charles Gordon (1833–85) and Field Marshals Garnet Wolseley (1833–1913), Frederick Roberts (1832–1914) and Earl Kitchener (1850–1916), fed a tradition of exemplary imperial masculinity, which was a combination of Anglo-Saxon authority, superiority and martial prowess, with Protestant religious zeal and moral righteousness. Winston Churchill used his military service in India and the Sudan, including at the key victory of Omdurman (1898), as well as his escape when captured as a war correspondent during the Boer War, to advantage in beginning his political career.

Launching the Boy Scout movement in 1908 (the Girl Guides followed in 1909), Robert Baden-Powell (1857–1941) exploited his own reputation as a hero during the resistance to the Boer siege of Mafeking in the Boer War, celebrated by the press, and also the more general model of masculinity allegedly provided by the self-sufficiency and vigour of life on the frontiers of empire. This model was given form in adventure novels such as those of G.A. Henty (1832–1902), including *With Kitchener in the Soudan* (1903), an account of recent operations there. These novels were still in the local library for me to read as a child in the 1960s, as were the Biggles adventure stories of Captain W.E. Johns (1893–1968), which were also redolent of imperial purpose and confidence.

From the late nineteenth century, the image of national resolution and endeavour was sustained by the extensive news of imperial conflict carried by the press, news provided by the development of telegraphy. The sieges of British positions in the Indian Mutiny (1857–9) and the Boer War offered drama for the entire country, although that did not imply that imperialism was popular with all of the working class, and, indeed, many workers appear to have been pretty apathetic. The crowds that applauded the relief of Mafeking from Boer siege in 1900 were mainly clerks and medical students, rather than labourers.

Nevertheless, it would be mistaken to treat empire as an expression of class interest, a view that was to be adopted then and subsequently by many left-wing critics. Instead, support for imperial activities crossed social divides. Thus, the Protestant churches of Britain devoted their resources to missionary activity outside Europe, particularly, though not only, within the empire, and not to proselytism on the Continent. Moreover, to criticize attitudes to empire, as if Britain could have been abstracted from the contemporary situation elsewhere, is unhelpful and is also, as with much subsequent criticism of the Victorian period, profoundly ahistorical. Furthermore, within the constraints of the attitudes of the age, the British were more liberal than other major European powers. The contrast between the British treatment of the Zulu and the genocidal German response to resistance by the Herero in Namibia, was, and is, readily apparent.

There was also an economic dimension to this imperialism, one that entailed a liberal commitment to free trade as well as the pursuit of power politics. Britain traded abroad far more than the Continental countries, and far more widely, and a sense of maritime destiny was linked to adventure and pride. In his *Just So Stories* (1902), Kipling wrote 'weekly from Southampton,| Great steamers white and gold,| Go rolling down to Rio|'. Britain's major industrial sectors – textiles and metal products – were dependent on exports and their markets were both imperial and non-imperial, with India and Germany respectively being key markets.

This dependency was related to other aspects of Britain's distinctiveness: the degree to which the country was outward-looking and internationalist; the interest in peace (which was believed to create the best conditions for trade); and the opposition to a large, expensive Army and to compulsory military service, both of which were seen by many as products of authoritarianism and as likely to sustain a state power judged unacceptable to the political libertarianism of British society. The US shared this opposition to conscription, which, however, was the norm on the Continent.

There were significant similarities with the US, but the British attitude towards America was ambivalent, and vice versa. While Oscar Wilde toured the US in 1882–3, many prominent Victorians wrote about the country, including Dickens, Sir Charles Wentworth Dilke (1843–1911), Trollope and the Liberal politician and intellectual James Bryce (1838–1922), all of whom were taken by its energy and drive, yet often shocked by its 'vulgar' (populist) politics. Later, J.B. Priestley was also to be engaged by the energy but to deplore what he saw as the emptiness of American culture.

In the Victorian period, a standard means of criticizing a politician was to accuse him of the 'Americanization' of British politics, and Gladstone and Joseph Chamberlain both suffered accordingly. Moreover, the American Civil War (1861–5) divided British public opinion. The Confederacy (south) sought to win diplomatic recognition from Britain, but fears that recognition would lead to war with the Union (north) prevented the step. There were also disputes with the US over clashing imperial interests, for example in the Pacific over Hawaii and Samoa in the 1890s, and cultural and economic rivalries, as over copyright law in the 1850s. On the other hand, differences over the Canadian border were handled without conflict, there was massive investment in the US, particularly in railways, the transfer of British technology, and important cultural and social links.

Empire meanwhile changed the details of British life in many respects, not least the diet. Tea from India, taken with milk, replaced China tea and became the basic drink for both polite men and women, in turn encouraging the import of sugar from the West Indies. Gin was mixed with quinine-rich tonic water, a drink developed to provide resistance to malaria in India. Indian words also entered the language, and games such as badminton and polo were introduced from India.

Territorial expansion provided raw materials for British industry, such as tin from Malaya, as well as markets and employment and, combined with evangelicalism, encouraged a sense of Britain as at the cutting edge of civilization. The economic value of colonies increased as steamships and railways aided economic integration, while the cultural and ideological factors focused on the attraction of empire were such that imperialism became normative. This drew on a sense of mission, as well as triumphalism, racialism and cultural arrogance, all supporting a belief that the West was unbeatable and was bringing civilization to a benighted world – not least by ending what were seen as uncivilized as well as un-Christian practices, such as widow-burning and ritual banditry (thuggee) in India. Yet, Queen Victoria's Proclamation to the People of India of 1858 repudiated any right or desire to impose Christianity on her subjects and promised all, irrespective of religion, the rights of law, although this did not stop missionary activity. On her state visits to Ireland in 1861 and 1900, the queen met the heads of the Catholic hierarchy. This was a long way from the conspicuous Protestantist Reformation monarchy.

The net result was a national commitment to imperial rule and experience that encouraged persistence in spreading and sustaining trans-oceanic control in the face of adversity and often grave difficulties. Britain's role was part of the wider story of European imperialism; but it was far greater than that of any other state, because of the limited part she played in European power politics, her unprecedented naval and commercial strength, and the already extensive character of the empire when the period started.

The Wars of the 1850s
The two major conflicts of the 1850s underlined potential challenges to the British empire. The crushing Russian naval victory

over the Turkish off Sinope in the Black Sea in 1853 exacerbated long-standing concerns about the weakness of the Turkish empire and about possible Russian domination in the Black Sea and the Balkans. Employing the geopolitical ideas of the day, British commentators saw the prospect of Russian advances as a threat to the overland route to India, although they considerably exaggerated this threat. The British government greatly distrusted Napoleon III of France and his intentions, but joined with France in seeking to limit Russian expansion.

The war focused on naval and amphibious action against the Russians. Allied naval operations in the Baltic threatened St Petersburg, while a full-scale amphibious expedition was sent to the Crimea in order to capture the naval base of Sevastopol, which seemed a way to protect Turkey from naval attack. However, landing on 14 September 1854, the Allies began the campaign late without having properly assessed the difficulty of the task, and they lacked the necessary manpower. The siege of Sevastopol was not fully effective as road links to the north of the port remained open – a consequence of the lack of sufficient Allied troops to mount a comprehensive blockade. The Allies also had to face both particularly bad weather, which hit supply links across the Black Sea, as well as attempts by the Russian army in the Crimea to disrupt the siege.

The Russians mounted unsuccessful attacks on the ports through which the Allies were landing all their supplies, and this was the cause of the battles of Balaclava and Inkerman. There was some serious flawed Allied generalship, most famously the unsuccessful Charge of the British Light Brigade at Balaclava into the face of Russian artillery on 25 October 1854. Moreover, Lord Raglan's (1788–1855) frequent and mistaken description of the French allies as 'the enemy' was an example of decrepitude. The diseased squalor in the entrenchments outside Sevastopol was less dramatic than poor generalship, but even more deadly.

Victory was eventually won with the capture of Sevastopol, but at a heavy cost. As a result, the Crimean War offers an instructive parallel with the First World War, both of which are generally seen in terms of folly, futility and horror. The terrible conditions of the troops in the Crimean War, especially a lack of adequate food, clean water, medical attention, shelter and clothing, helped lead to very heavy losses from disease, and the administrative deficiencies were bitterly criticized in Parliament and the press. During the war as a whole, about 3,000 British troops were killed in action, but 19,000 died of disease, exposure or infected wounds, leading to great prominence being given to Florence Nightingale's organization of nursing for sick troops. As in the First World War, only a brief conflict was anticipated, and there were no adequate preparations, not least in strategic and tactical doctrine. In practice, the multiple weaknesses of Russia as a military power were important to British success, while, underwritten by the strength of the economy, the British Army made improvements. In 1855, better transport, medical provisions and logistics helped the Army's health.

The Treaty of Paris of 1856 achieved Allied war goals by severely limiting Russian naval forces on the Black Sea, but Russia was able to resume expansion at the expense of the Turks in the 1870s. The British deficiencies highlighted by the war, and the accompanying furore, led to a measure of reform, notably in Army administration, that, in part, reflected impulses already present before the conflict.

The Indian Mutiny of 1857–9 was triggered by the British demand that their Indian soldiers use cartridges greased in animal tallow for their new Enfield rifles, a measure that was widely unacceptable for religious reasons; although there was a concerted plan for mutiny before this issue arose. The Indian troops at Meerut mutinied on 10 May 1857, and the next day mutineers took over Delhi, proclaiming the Mughal Bahadur Shah sovereign. Fortunately for the British, much of the Indian Army remained loyal, including the Madras Army in the south and most of the Bombay area. The Punjab remained under control, and the rulers of Hyderabad, Kashmir and Nepal provided assistance. However, most of the Bengal Army in the Ganges Valley mutinied. British failures to regain control – Delhi was not retaken swiftly and on 29 June an attack on mutineers near Chinhat was defeated – helped the Mutiny to gather momentum.

Yet, the movement of troops and cannon from outside the rebellious area helped the British regain the initiative. On 14 September 1857, Delhi was stormed and, although there were heavy British losses in street-fighting, the city was cleared by 20 September. In November, the garrison at Lucknow was relieved and then the British made a safe withdrawal from it. The following spring, the British were able to overrun the rebellious area. On 21 March 1858, Lucknow was recaptured, and in May and June the key region of Awadh (Oudh) was cleared, while Sir Hugh Rose regained control of central India.

The rising was suppressed by British and loyal Indian troops, especially Gurkhas and Sikhs, in the largest deployment of British forces since the Napoleonic Wars ended at Waterloo in 1815 and before the Boer War of 1899–1902. No major Indian prince joined the rising, which also had no foreign support. Moreover, sheer fighting determination was important to British success. Writing to his parents from Cawnpore, a centre of the rebellion, Lieutenant Hugh Pearce Pearson of the 84th Foot noted that the rebels did not dare 'charge our little squares with their clouds of cavalry', a description which apparently paints a clear picture of the supe-riority of British fighting methods, but he continued 'They had most magnificent gunners'. These two remarks indicate the danger of selective quotation.

The Mutiny led, in 1858 by the India Act, to the end of rule by the East India Company and, instead, to the direct adminis-tration by the British government of that part of India that was not left under dependent local princes, a system that continued until the country gained independence in 1947. As a result of the Mutiny, the British also became more cautious in their treatment of Indian opinion, not least in their willingness to consider unwelcome reforms. This was more significant because the empire focused on India, which was its most populous part and the basis of much of its power, especially its ability to act as a force on land.

Caution owed something to the bitterness and racial violence of the struggle, and the long-standing images of cruelty it provoked. For the British, this was the case with mutineers massacring women, children and prisoners at Cawnpore in 1857. In contrast, Colin Campbell's (1792–1863) ability to lead a column to the relief of Lucknow later that year became a totemic occasion of Victorian soldiering and served as a model for subsequent actions, while Henry Havelock (1795–1857) and other commanders demonstrated successful Christian militarism.

However, there were alternative images of cruelty, with British troops killing captured mutineers, most dramatically by strapping them across the muzzles of cannon which were then fired. Pearson wrote in August 1857 that the British forces had taken very heavy casualties, adding,

> … village fighting … desperate … we took two sepoy prisoners the other day and they were blown away from the guns: the stink of fresh flesh was sickening in the extreme, but I have seen so many disgusting sights and so much bloodshed that I have grown quite callous.

In modern India, the Mutiny has been reinterpreted, somewhat anachronistically, as India's first war of independence or nationalism, and is now widely referred to as the 'Rebellion'.

The challenges of the 1850s prefigured those the empire was to face from 1939, but the latter were more serious, in strategic and security terms, not least with the German assault on the British Isles, and also in so far as the stability and continuity of imperial rule were concerned: the empire was largely gone within three decades of the outbreak of the Second World War. In contrast, the British empire overcame the challenges of the 1850s and expanded thereafter.

After the Crimean War, Britain did not fight another European power until the First World War broke out in 1914. There was repeated concern about the danger of conflict with France and Russia, and fears of invasion from France led to the construction of defensive positions, such as the Needles Old Battery on the Isle of Wight, as well as to the central emphasis on maintaining the world's leading navy. In the event, however, competition with other European powers stopped short of war, and only encouraged the drive to empire. As yet, Germany, Italy, Japan and the US were not mounting a serious naval or imperial challenge.

1860–99

There were still limits to British power. Given the strength of its possible opponents and the limits to what could be achieved by the Royal Navy when up against a Continental power, it would have been unwise to intervene in the American Civil War or the German unification driven by Prussia that had led, in 1866, to the annexation of Hanover (which was ruled by Queen Victoria's first cousin); but the strength of other powers did not yet pose a serious challenge to British interests. There was repeated concern about Russia's advance into Central Asia and the apparent threat it posed to the security of India, but the international situation appeared relatively benign and, with its rapidly growing economy, Britain could act as a major power without too great an impact on its public finances or society.

This situation helped ensure that the Navy in the 1870s displayed scant improvement in organization, technology or doctrine, while the Army did not seek to emulate German capabilities, for example with annual manoeuvres or a planning department. Britain indeed was a great power on the cheap, a situation that was not sustainable, but one that looked towards the later cheap hawkery of seeking a major role but being unwilling to accept the consequences, a situation very much seen over the last decade.

Once the Mutiny was suppressed, India returned to its

former role as a key support for British power elsewhere, including China, where the Second Opium War began in 1857. In 1860, Beijing was captured, the role of Sikh cavalry supported by Armstrong artillery showing the combination of imperial manpower and home industry in the spread of British power.

In the 1860s and 1870s, the pace of expansion increased. None of the conflicts in which Britain was involved was a war of survival (for Britain) and none transformed British society, but their cumulative impact for Britain was important, and their individual impact on other societies was formative. Native resistance was overcome in New Zealand, although the Maoris used well-sited trench and *pa* (fort) systems that were difficult to bombard or storm, and inflicted serious defeats on the British. The availability of British colonial and allied Maori units, and the consequences of road and fort construction, ensured an eventual settlement on British terms.

In Africa, Lagos was annexed in 1861, and, although an expedition against one of the more powerful African people, the Asante, was wrecked by disease in 1864, in 1873–4 a fresh expedition under Garnet Wolseley was more successful. He benefited from the assistance of other African peoples, especially the Fante, but his superior firepower – Gatling machine guns, breach-loading rifles, and seven-pounder artillery – was crucial.

Another major African kingdom, Abyssinia (Ethiopia), was brought low in 1868. In a methodically planned campaign, an expedition entered the Red Sea, landed and marched from the coast into the mountains – a formidable logistical task – defeated the Abyssinians at Arogee, stormed the fortress of Magdala, and rescued the imprisoned British hostages who were the cause of the crisis, before withdrawing. The campaign helped boost confidence in the military and reflected the growing strategic importance of the region for British power. This was to be further enhanced by the opening of the British-run Suez Canal in 1869, which greatly cut the steaming distance to India and the Far East. The Abyssinian campaign drew on the resources of the empire in India, an example of the reinforcing nature of the empire at this time.

Meanwhile, the organization of the Army was being transformed as a result of the Cardwell reforms. As Secretary of State for the Colonies (1864–6), Edward Cardwell (1813–86) withdrew regular troops from colonies that were not willing to pay for them, a key move towards colonial self-defence, and as Secretary of State for War (1869–74) he pushed through the ending of the purchase of commissions, instead insisting on appointment and promotion by merit and selection. This, however, did not transform the social composition of the officer corps, which remained an admixture of landed elite and professional groups, with particular commitment derived from the extent to which many officers were themselves the sons of officers, a frequent pattern in a society in which far more people followed their parents in employment and place of residence than is the case today. Cardwell's failure to increase pay ensured that officers still had to be men of means, however.

Yet, there were other reforms. Flogging in peacetime was abolished in 1869, while provisions were made for better military education and the retirement of officers. More generally, with their stress on professionalism, the Cardwell reforms meant the end of an *ancien régime* that no longer seemed appropriate in an age of widespread change. For example, the opening of the Suez Canal in 1869 transformed the geopolitics of British power, encouraging interest in the eastern Mediterranean and the Middle East as a forward defence zone for India; while the spread of steam power and ironclad warships ensured that Nelson's navy no longer set the model for naval conflict.

There were defeats along the way to imperial expansion, especially at Isandlwana (1879) and Maiwand (1880) at the hands of the Zulus and Afghans respectively, but the British were usually successful in battle, notably over the Zulus in 1879, in particular at Ulundi. Victory at Tel el Kebir (1882) left Britain dominant in Egypt, while the fate of Sudan was settled at Omdurman in 1898, when artillery, machine guns and rifle fire devastated the attacking Mahdists, with 31,000 casualties for the latter and only 430 for the Anglo-Egyptian force. Technology and resources were not only at stake on the battlefield. In 1896, the British force invading the Sudan built a railway straight across the Sahara Desert, from Wadi Halfa to Abu Hamed. Extended to Atbara in 1898, it played a major role in the supply of the British forces.

Much British imperial expansion, especially in 1880–1914, arose directly from the response to the real or apparent plans of other powers, particularly France and Russia. However, the search for markets for British industry was also important. Thus, both economic and political security were at stake and, as a result, the imperialist surge of activity at the close of the century has been seen as marking the beginning of a long decline from the zenith of British power, of imperial position starting to fray under pressure at the same time as it continued to expand.

The nature of empire also changed. Sovereignty and territorial control became crucial goals. They replaced the pursuit of influence and of island and port possessions which had been the characteristic features of much, although by no means all, British expansion earlier in the nineteenth century. Suspicion of Russian designs on the Turkish empire, and of French schemes in north Africa, led the British to move into Cyprus (1878) and Egypt (1882); concern about French ambitions in South-East Asia resulted in the conquest of Mandalay (1885) and the annexation of Upper Burma (1886); while Russia's advance across Central Asia led to attempts to strengthen and move forward the 'North-West Frontier' of British India and also to the development of British influence in southern Iran and the Persian Gulf, through which the British routed the telegraph to India. French and German expansion in Africa led Britain to take counter-measures, in Gambia, Sierra Leone, the Gold Coast (Ghana), Nigeria and Uganda, all moves in the 'Scramble for Africa' by the European powers.

Specific clashes over colonial influence with other European powers increasingly interacted from the late 1870s with a more general sense of imperial insecurity as confidence was put under pressure by the growing strength of other states. More clearly, in the 1880s, there was public and governmental concern about naval vulnerability and, in 1889, this concern led to the Naval Defence Act, which sought a two-power standard: superiority over the next two largest naval powers combined. The importance of naval dominance was taken for granted. It was a prerequisite of an ideal of national self-sufficiency that peaked in the late nineteenth century.

The Boer War

By 1900, the British had an empire covering a fifth of the world's land surface and including 400 million people. This was an empire of power and technology that was articulated by the application of British knowledge. The infrastructure of power was impressive. Britain had constructed 20,000 miles of railways in India by 1900, while a British-controlled submarine cable to India was in place from 1870.

Yet, this primacy faced problems. Britain was also involved in a difficult trans-oceanic conflict, the Boer War with the Afrikaner (Boer; whites of Dutch descent) republics of the Orange Free State and the Transvaal in southern Africa. Regional hegemony was a key issue. British leaders found it difficult to accept Boer views and were willing to risk war in order to achieve a transfer of some power in the region. The Boer War is often seen as a classic instance of 'capitalist-driven' empire building. However, Alfred Milner (1854–1925), the aggressive Governor of Cape Colony, was essentially driven by political considerations and his own ambition. The British ministers were greatly influenced by the fear that if, given the gold and diamond discoveries, the Boers became the most powerful force in southern Africa, it might not be long before they were working with Britain's imperial rivals, especially the Germans in South-West Africa, and threatening its strategic interests at the Cape. The Prime Minister, Salisbury, remarked that Britain had to be supreme.

Ministers in London thought the Boers were bluffing and would not put up much of a fight if war followed; while the failure of the British to send sufficient reinforcements persuaded the Boers to think it was the British who were bluffing. The Boer republics declared war after Britain had isolated them internationally and had done everything possible to provoke them. Initially, the outnumbered and poorly led British were outfought by the Boers' effective combination of the strategic offensive and a successful use of defensive positions, as well as by their superior marksmanship with smokeless, long-range Mauser magazine rifles.

Boer capabilities revealed serious deficiencies in British tactics and training, not least a continued preference for frontal attacks and volley firing; a lack of emphasis on the use of cover and the understanding of the consequences of smokeless powder; and, more generally, a lack of appreciation of enhanced defensive firepower. In 'Black Week', in December 1899, British forces suffered heavy casualties in a series of battles, including Magersfontein and Colenso, with frontal attacks foolishly preferred to the uncertainties of flank movement.

More effective generalship by Roberts and Kitchener transformed the situation in 1900. Moreover, the Army proved adaptable, both tactically and organizationally, as when, responding to Boer tactics, there was use of mounted infantry to a great extent. Britain's larger force was applied methodically in the overrunning of the Boer heartland in the Transvaal: its capital, Pretoria, was captured on 5 June 1900. The British then turned to the more difficult task of countering Boer raiders. Boer guerrilla operations proved a formidable, but ultimately unsuccessful, challenge, not least because of the British combination of methodical force with flexible mobility.

The ability of Britain to allocate about £200 million and to deploy 400,000 troops was a testimony to the strength of its economic and imperial systems. Yet, income tax had to be doubled to pay for the war, which also greatly pushed up government borrowing. The Conservative policy of low taxation with financial retrenchment had to be abandoned under the pressure of imperial expansion.

An anticipation of recent warfare was provided by domestic and international sensitivity to the treatment of Boer civilians, notably moving them from their farms and incarcerating them in camps, in order to prevent them from providing a base and support for guerrilla attacks. To later critics, lacking a sense of comparative perspective, these concentration camps were an early anticipation of subsequent horrors. In fact, the detention camps were not intended as death camps, although the disease that spread there proved fatal to many of the inmates. After the war, British victory was anchored when the Union of South Africa was formed in 1910 in a settlement that gave considerable power to the Afrikaners. This was very much a 'white' solution, and one that greatly disappointed the hopes held by some black leaders.

Queen Victoria's Empire

Meanwhile, Empire Day had been launched in 1896 on 24 May, Queen Victoria's birthday. While, in 1871, having defeated France, Wilhelm I, King of Prussia, became Emperor of Germany, Queen Victoria, five years later, as a result of the Royal Titles Act, became Empress of India – an empire that was to last until the subcontinent was granted independence seventy-one years later, with the title being inherited by her four successors. Streets, towns, geographical features and whole tracts of land were named or renamed in her honour, including the Australian state of Victoria, the city of Victoria on Vancouver Island in Canada, Victoria Falls on the Zambezi, and Lake Victoria in East Africa.

Imperial status was also part of the re-creation of Queen Victoria in the late 1870s. She was coaxed from reclusive widowhood to a new public role by Benjamin Disraeli, who, as

Prime Minister, combined imperial policies with social reform
and who sought, in doing so, to foster a sense of national unity
and continuity. He realized that monarchy was a potent way to
lead the public and control the consequences of the spread of
the franchise, a view gently mocked in Gilbert and Sullivan's
comic operetta, the *Pirates of Penzance* (1879), in which the
pirates, victorious over the maladroit police, rapidly surrender
at the close when summoned to do so in the name of the queen.
At once an opportunistic and skilful political tactician, who
was also an acute and imaginative thinker, Disraeli was able to
create a political culture around the themes of national identity,
national pride and social cohesion, and to focus popular
support for the Conservatives on these themes as an alternative
to the Liberal moral certainty in which Gladstone flourished.
Disraeli carefully manipulated the queen into accepting his
view and playing the role he had allocated her.

The government of Queen Victoria's empire was very
varied. In some colonies, notably in much of Africa, there was
straightforward imperial rule by representatives of the British
state, whereas in India there was a careful attempt to incor-
porate existing hierarchies, interests and rituals. There, the
princely dynasties were wooed, from the 1870s, by the creation
of an Anglicized princely hierarchy that gave them roles and
honours, such as the orders of the Star of India and the Indian
Empire, in accordance with British models and interests – a
process that was also to be followed in Malaya and in parts of
Africa. This process led to a stress on status, not race, that is
easy to criticize, not least because the resulting emphasis on
inherited privilege served as a brake on inculcating values of
economic, social and political development. Nevertheless, this
policy was also a response to the large amount of India that had
been left under princely rule, while, in practice, the search for
support in India and elsewhere was not restricted to the social
elite, but was a multi-layered one, extending to the co-option
or creation of professional and administrative groups able to
meet local as well as imperial needs. Moreover, princes were

downgraded to knights in these orders, a subtle demotion that suited British interests.

In the long-established colonies of white settlement, self-government was extended from the mid-nineteenth century, with the growth of what was called 'responsible government'. This meant that, in a major measure of liberalization, colonial governors were to be politically responsible to locally elected legislatures, rather than to London, a process that reflected the comparable parliamentary arrangement in Victorian Britain.

Dominion status, self-government under the Crown, took this process further, offering a peaceful, evolutionary route to independence. Canada became a Dominion in 1867, Australia in 1901, New Zealand in 1907 and South Africa in 1910. Although the Colonial Laws Validity Act of 1865 had declared invalid any colonial legislation that clashed with that from Westminster, the Act was only rarely invoked. This was a federalism that worked. Meetings of prime ministers from 1887 helped give the Dominions a voice in imperial policy and also offered a means of coherence. During the Boer War, the empire, particularly Australia, Canada, Cape Colony and New Zealand, sent troops, which helped foster Dominion nationalism within the empire, rather than having this nationalism act as a separatist force.

Yet, at the same time, alongside these changes designed to benefit from the situation of flux in the empire, cracks were appearing in the imperial edifice. Due, in part, to the diffusion within it of British notions of community, identity and political action, there was a measure of opposition to imperial control, with the Indian National Congress formed in 1885 and the Egyptian National Party in 1897. Yet, opposition in the colonies and in the informal empire was still limited in scope, certainly in comparison to the situation after the First World War; and there was also a considerable measure of compliance with British rule. In Ireland, the preferred option was 'Home Rule' under the Crown, not republican independence, which, at the time, was the preference of only a minority. Meanwhile, Scots benefited greatly from the empire, while the degree to which they retained considerable independence within the United Kingdom – including their own established Church and legal and educational systems – also militated against political nationalism.

Britain, France and Germany, 1898–1914

France was the traditional national and imperial foe, and colonial rivalries provided fresh fuel to keep fear and animosity alive, with the two powers coming close to war over Sudan in 1898 in the Fashoda Crisis as each sought to establish a position on the Upper Nile. Yet Britain and France went to war as allies in 1914. Chance played a central role in this: a major European war broke out at a moment very different to those of heightened Anglo-French and Anglo-Russian colonial tension in the late nineteenth century. Instead, fear of German intentions, and particularly of its naval ambitions, encouraged closer British relations with France from 1904. The Anglo-French *entente* of 1904 led to military talks in part because defeat in the Russo-Japanese war of 1904–5 weakened Russia (France's ally) as a balancing element within Europe, thereby exposing France to German diplomatic pressure, and creating British alarm about German intentions, as in the First Moroccan Crisis of 1905–6 (a Franco-German confrontation triggered by German opposition to French expansion in Morocco). This crisis, provoked by Germany, was followed by Anglo-French staff talks aimed at dealing with a German threat. In 1907, British military manoeuvres were conducted for the first time on the basis that Germany, not France, was the enemy, while, also that year, fears of Germany contributed to an Anglo-Russian *entente* which eased tensions between the two powers, notably competing ambitions and contrasting anxieties in south Asia. Germany, with its great economic strength and its search for a 'place in the sun', was increasingly seen in Britain as the principal threat.

The economic statistics were all too present to British commentators, not least because Germany's economic power enabled it to pursue a 'naval race' for battleship strength with Britain from 1906. The annual average output of coal and lignite in million tons in 1870–4 was 121 (123 million tonnes) for Britain and 40.4 (41) for Germany, but by 1910–14 the figures were 270 (274) to 243 (247). For pig-iron, the annual figures changed from 7.8 (7.9) and 2.65 (2.7) in 1880 to 10 (10.2) and 14.6 (14.8) in 1910; for steel from 3.5 (3.6) and 2.16 (2.2) in 1890 to 6.4 (6.5) and 13.5 (13.7) in 1910. In 1900, the German population was 56.4 million, but that of Britain excluding Ireland only 37 million, and including it still only 41.5 million.

In December 1899, the rising journalist J.L. Garvin (1868–1947) decided that Germany and not, as he had previously thought, France and Russia, was the greatest threat to Britain. Rejecting the view of Joseph Chamberlain, Secretary of State for the Colonies, that Britain and Germany were natural allies, their peoples of a similar racial 'character', Garvin saw 'the Anglo-Saxons' as the obstacle to Germany's naval and commercial policy.

British resources and political will were subsequently tested in a major naval race between the two powers, in which the British, in 1906, launched HMS *Dreadnought*, the first of a new class of battleships and one that reflected the vitality of British industry, at least in shipbuilding. Imaginative literature reflected, and contributed to, the sense of crisis. A projected German invasion was central to *The Riddle of the Sands* (1903), a novel by Erskine Childers (1870–1922) which was first planned in 1897, when indeed the Germans discussed such a project.

Yet, political opinion was divided. There were British politicians who sought to maintain good relations with Germany. Moreover, the *ententes* with France and Russia were not alliances, and Britain failed to make its position clear, thus encouraging Germany to hope that Britain would not act in the event of war (which was also Hitler's mistaken belief when he invaded Poland in 1939). In 1914, the British certainly failed to make effective use of their fleet as a deterrent, restraining Germany from hostile acts.

The First World War, 1914–18

The British government was divided over war in 1914, and the German invasion of Belgium (a neutral state guaranteed by Britain) on 3 August was crucial to the decision to enter the war on 4 August as it gave a moral imperative to the outbreak of hostilities. However, the major reason for the British government to act was to defend France from German attack as well as concern over losing it as a vital element in the balance of power. There was fear about what might happen in Europe and to overseas interests if Germany won the war.

This conflict was to be the worst that Britain had ever waged. It was widely, but erroneously, assumed that the war, although costly in lives, would be short. Furthermore, the First World War was crucially different from Britain's experience of conflict since the Napoleonic Wars because of its seemingly intractable character, the threat to the British home base, the probability that Britain might lose, with very serious consequences, and the massive quantity of manpower and resources that the war required and destroyed; and if each of these, instead, echoed the experience of the Napoleonic Wars, that was an experience unknown to those alive in 1914. In addition, Britain took a far greater role in the land conflict in the First World War than it had done in the Napoleonic Wars, and, in doing so, broke with previous British assumptions about the country's natural strategy, as well as responding essentially to German warmaking instead of employing Britain's strengths, notably its naval power, to best effect.

Germany's plan to deliver a knock-out blow against France in 1914 failed, but left the Germans in control of much of Belgium and part of France. This put Britain and France under the necessity to mount offensives in order to prevent a peace settlement that left Germany with gains. Another impetus to attack was provided by the wish to reduce German pressure on their ally Russia and to prevent it from being knocked out of the war. Furthermore, there was a conviction that only through mounting an offensive would it be possible for the Allies to gain the initiative and, conversely, deny it to the Germans, and that both these were prerequisites for victory. Attacking to restart a war of manoeuvre was the goal, and it was not generally appreciated that stalemate and trench warfare reflected the nature of the war once both sides had committed large numbers and lacked the ability to accomplish a break-through.

The First World War is generally remembered in terms of the trench warfare of the Western Front in France and Belgium, where very large numbers fought and many died in battles such as Loos (1915), the Somme (1916) and Passchendaele (1917). The concentration of large forces in a relatively small area, and the defensive strength of trench positions, especially thanks to machine guns, with their range and rapidity of fire, and to quick-firing artillery, but also helped by barbed wire and concrete fortifications, ensured that, until the collapse of the German position in the last weeks of the war, the situation on the Western Front was essentially deadlocked. Yet both sides believed that attritional conflict could be successful if they could take the initiative, and thus choose both the terrain and a battlefield where they had amassed artillery. In the event, the appalling British casualties owed much to the tactical, operational and strategic difficulties of overcoming the defence, and to Germany's military and economic resources. British battlefield deaths amounted to 58 per cent from artillery and mortar shells, and just below 39 per cent from machine gun and rifle bullets.

In attacking German positions, it proved very difficult to translate local superiority in numbers into decisive success. It was possible, albeit at heavy cost, to break through trench lines, but hard to exploit such successes. Motor vehicles and aircraft were not effectively harnessed to help the offensive until 1918. Furthermore, once troops had advanced, it was difficult to recognize, reinforce and exploit success; until radio communications improved in late 1917, control and communications were limited. Unrolling telephone wire under fire demonstrated the fragility of the response to the challenges of the new warfare. Without major gains of territory, the war, and notably its frontal attacks, have been seen as the epitome of military futility and incompetence, a view traceable from bitter war poets who served in the trenches, such as Wilfred Owen (1893–1918) and Siegfried Sassoon (1886–1967), and to the savage subsequent indictment of critical dramas, such as Joan Littlewood's (1914–2002) play *Oh What a Lovely War!* (1963) and the *Blackadder* television series (1989).

The conflict was indeed horrific, a terrible experience for both an age and a generation. A British quartermaster sergeant in the Somme offensive of 1916 noted in his diary:

> ... the whole place smells stale with the slaughter which has been going on for the past fourteen days – the smell of the dead and lachrymatory gas. The place is a very Hell with the whistling and crashing of shells, bursting shrapnel and the rattle of machine guns. The woods we had taken had not yet been cleared and there were pockets of Germans with machine guns still holding out and doing some damage. A sergeant sinks to the ground beside me with a bullet wound neatly drilled through his shoulder. Lucky man. It is not likely to prove fatal. It is too clean and it means a few months in Blighty [Britain] for him.

The experience of the many who served is kept alive by the strong current interest in family history, much of which focuses on the world wars. Linked to the horror is added the claim that British troops were poorly led and that the war itself was pointless. This account, however, is mistaken, as the war was not without important military and political results. In the end, Germany, the aggressor in Western Europe, was defeated on the battlefield and forced to surrender. The impasse of trench warfare was broken in 1918, with the British, who ably integrated artillery with infantry advances, playing a far larger role than they were to do in 1945. In marked contrast to the

Second World War, Russia was knocked out of the war by the Germans in 1917–18, while the US, which entered the war only in 1917, played a far smaller role in Germany's defeat than was to be the case in 1945.

Later attention tended to focus on explaining victory through the novelty of massed attacks by tanks, a key British development, but, in practice, they were less significant in 1918 than effective artillery–infantry coordination, in particular well-aimed heavy indirect fire, ably coordinated with rushes by infantry who avoided moving forward in vulnerable lines. Built up for the task, the Army had 440 heavy artillery batteries in November 1918, compared to six in 1914. Indeed, Britain's role in winning the war represented one of its most significant military successes, and one achieved without the mutinies seen in the French and Russian armies.

British naval superiority was also important to victory. The British retained control of their home waters, checking the German high sea fleet at the Battle of Jutland in 1916, and, after very heavy losses, eventually thwarting the German submarine (U-boat) assault, in part through the introduction of convoys for British merchantmen. Thanks to this naval superiority, the British were therefore able to avoid invasion, to retain trade links that permitted the mobilization of British and Allied resources around the world, and to blockade Germany. The blockade hit the German economy hard and also reduced German living standards, contributing to a war weariness that helped lead to the collapse of the German state in late 1918 once German forces had been defeated on the Western Front.

In addition, thanks in large part to the support of imperial and Dominion forces, notably from India and Australia, the German colonies in Africa and the Pacific were overrun, the Suez Canal and oil supplies in the Persian Gulf both protected from Germany's ally the Ottoman Empire (the basis of modern Turkey), and the Turks eventually driven from Palestine, Syria and Mesopotamia in 1917–18. However, the attempt to knock Turkey out of the war in 1915 by advancing on Constantinople (Istanbul) with a fleet and amphibious forces had been defeated at Gallipoli. The war also saw the earliest air attacks on Britain, first by Zeppelins (airships) and then by aircraft, albeit without the damage caused in the Second World War.

The ability to mobilize and apply resources, especially men and munitions, was crucial to the war effort, and led to an expansion of the regulatory powers of the government. The Defence of the Realm Act of 1914 greatly extended the powers of the administration, for example in censoring opinion. The government also took over control of the railways (1914), the coal mines (1917) and the flour mills (1918). A powerful Ministry of Munitions, which transformed the production of battlefield materials and resources, was created in 1915. David Lloyd George left the Treasury to become its first minister and made his name as a wartime leader in this role. Responding to the need to produce more artillery shells, Lloyd George bypassed established procedures by enlisting entrepreneurs in the cause of production. Moreover, a political purpose was served, as Lloyd George used his ministry to demonstrate his belief that capital and labour could combine to patriotic purpose.

Benefiting from a sense that the war was not being prosecuted effectively, Lloyd George replaced Asquith as Prime Minister in December 1916 and created a new coalition that encompassed Conservatives and Labour, although many Liberals followed the former leader and Prime Minister, Herbert Asquith, into opposition. A War Cabinet backed by a Secretariat streamlined policymaking and also played an important role in elevating the Prime Minister's role. New ministries were created for labour and shipping, and a food production department was established in 1917, in an attempt to reduce the dependence on trans-Atlantic imports. Also to that end, food rationing was introduced. The face of the country altered. County agricultural committees oversaw a 30 per cent rise in national cereal production as pastureland was ploughed up.

Not only the fields were conscripted. After initially relying on volunteering, which yielded 2.5 million men between August 1914 and December 1915, universal military service was also seen as crucial to the war effort. Conscription was introduced in 1916, helping to push the size of the armed forces up to 4.5 million in 1917–18, one in three of the male labour force. Such numbers, which were necessary to cover the heavy casualties, required a resolute populace, and attempts to rally public opinion by launching propaganda campaigns included the formation of the Department (from 1918 Ministry) of Information, while, reflecting the propaganda role of film, the War Office created a Cinematograph Committee to aid film production.

Germany was defeated on the front line, not 'stabbed in the back' by domestic opposition, as German nationalists later claimed; but, although the conviction that the war was a noble struggle remained widely held to the end, euphoria in Britain was limited. The numerous war memorials erected after the conflict were eloquent testimonials to the heavy cost, which included the loss of a tenth of male Scots between sixteen and fifty. The war also exhausted the economy, public finances and society. These factors helped ensure that British policymakers sought to avoid any similar conflict, an attitude that affected their response to Hitler in the 1930s.

The Empire 1918–31
Nevertheless, victory in 1918 carried Britain to the apex of empire. Britain played a leading role in the peace conferences held in Paris that resulted in the Paris peace settlements, notably the Treaty of Versailles. Britain gained parts of the German and Ottoman empires, including Palestine, Transjordan and Iraq from the latter, and Tanganyika (most of modern Tanzania) from the former. Britain's position in Palestine was pregnant with future possibilities as in 1917 the government had issued the Balfour Declaration promising to support the establishment there of a homeland for the Jewish

people. Australia, New Zealand and South Africa also gained German colonies. Moreover, British influence increased in both Persia (Iran) and Turkey, while British forces, operating against the Communists in the Russian Civil War that followed their revolution in 1917, moved into the Caucasus, Central Asia, and the White Sea region, and were deployed in the Baltic and the Black Sea.

Such ambitions, however, could not be sustained and the high tide of empire was to ebb very fast. The strain of the war was heavy enough, and it left a burdensome debt, but, in addition, the expansion of imperial rule and of Britain's international commitments involved intractable problems. Armed intervention in Russia was a failure and was abandoned in 1919. It had been opposed by British left-wingers sympathetic to the Communists and by conscripts eager for demobilization, but failed, essentially, because of the intractability of the task, an intractability not appreciated by supporters such as Churchill.

In the Middle East, prefiguring British problems in the 2000s, revolts in Egypt (1919) and Iraq (1920–1) led to Britain granting their independence in 1922 and 1924 respectively; although it maintained considerable influence in both, in what was to be a successful exercise in informal empire. Moreover, the Third Afghan War in 1919 underlined the difficult situation on the 'North-West Frontier' of India. British influence collapsed in Persia in 1921, and, in the Chanak Crisis of 1922, the British backed down in their confrontation with nationalist forces in Turkey, the last being a crucial factor in Lloyd George's fall. Furthermore, most of Ireland was lost as a result of nationalist opposition, which had led to a guerrilla insurrection, and this loss in 1922 was a major blow to imperial self-confidence: the empire began at home.

There was a lack of resources and will to sustain schemes for imperial expansion. These were expensive: it had cost £40 million to suppress the Iraq rising, and the garrison there cost £25 million a year. Retrenchment and having to judge between commitments were increasingly the order of the day. It had always been so, but the very extension of empire made the issue more serious.

The global and imperial context for Britain was more difficult than it had been in the 1850s. Soviet Communism was a threat to the entire idea of imperial rule, as was the American support for national self-determination, although, as yet, neither was a real challenge to the practice of control. However, by 1931, nationalist pressure in India for a new political dispensation was growing. The Amritsar massacre of 13 April 1919, when General Dyer ordered (Gurkha) troops during a serious public order crisis to fire on a demonstrating crowd, killing 379, had dented British authority in India by suggesting that it had an inherently repressive nature.

Yet, the British were not without resources. That same year, a Government of India Act established the principle of dyarchy, that is responsible self-government in certain areas. Moreover, imperial federation was a more influential idea than straightforward rule. The development of the notion of a Commonwealth – unity in independence – proved useful in maintaining the support of the Dominions. An imperial conference in 1926 defined the Commonwealth as 'the group of self-governing communities composed of Great Britain and the Dominions'. This formed the basis of the Statute of Westminster (1931), which determined that Commonwealth countries could now amend or repeal 'any existing or future act of the United Kingdom Parliament ... in so far as the same is part of the law of this dominion'.

To some imperialists, these and other changes were welcome as a sign of new ways to sustain imperial links, and, by the late 1920s, the empire appeared far more powerful and far less under threat than was to be the case a decade later. Others were less enthusiastic. For Churchill, out of government office from 1929, liberal policies on India were more than a tactical step, instead being a signpost on the route to the end of empire, a disastrous prospect; a view also taken by diehards such as John,

Viscount Sumner (1859–1934), President of the India Defence League, who had to face what he saw as successive betrayals over Ireland, Egypt and India. Churchill and Sumner, however, offered an apocalyptic vision that appeared out of place to many. The Viceroy of India described Churchill in 1929 as an 'Imperialist in the 1890–1900 sense of the word', and that world now appeared less relevant.

These changes occurred not only in the colonies but also in Britain itself. They were part of an altering culture of power and ideological drive, one that affected Britain before the inroads of the Second World War were to cause a crisis of national and imperial survival. As an instructive indication of new assumptions, American influence in British life and culture was growing. In July 1939, Philip Kerr, 11th Marquess of Lothian, en route to take up the embassy in Washington, spoke of 'the extent to which we in Britain have become Americanized, in the best sense of that word, in the last twenty-five years – not merely in the mechanization of our private lives but in our social and democratic life'. The sway of America was also increasing in part of the British empire, notably in Canada, and in the areas of British influence, especially South America. Yet, in 1931, the consequences of these changes in Britain and the empire were unclear, and the impact of the Second World War was to bear much of the responsibility for the collapse of empire.

PART TWO:

1931–2010

5

CHANGING COUNTRY

A 'quiet social revolution', was how V.F. Soothill (1887–1956), the Medical Officer for Norwich, described the spread of suburbia in 1935. More bluntly, the novelist D.H. Lawrence (1885–1930) had earlier referred to 'little red rat-traps', while the poet John Betjeman condescendingly thought Swindon's houses 'brick-built breeding boxes of new souls'. To begin this part, as with Part 1, with the changing country is to be reminded again of the scale and importance of the human impact on the landscape. This choice also underlines the extent to which this human impact has had a lasting character, unlike many (though certainly not all) of the more ephemeral issues and events in economic and political history, and notably the doings of politicians that tend to dominate accounts of the past.

A principal driver of change in Britain has been the major growth in its population, matched as it has been by rapidly rising expectations of lifestyle, as affluence has become the norm and consumerism its means. Individuals have come to express themselves, rather than simply live, through the creation of their own material worlds, their stuff, which is at once individualistic and, as a result of pressures from advertising and pricing, conformist. In the shape of demands for mobility (cars) and space (houses), this lifestyle has ensured the transfer of land from agriculture and the wild to roads and housing, with immense consequences for wildlife and for the human experience of the country.

The 1930s

If the changes seen in, and from, the 1930s were far from new – notably the large-scale expansion of housing and roads – the pressure of development only increased thereafter, as the population rose to unprecedented figures, rising with each successive year. Moreover, the context was different; first, as a result of greater public concern about environmental issues and, secondly, as a consequence of a more assertive regulatory environment, especially on housing. The focus was very much on urban Britain. Agriculture attracted government attention, especially during the Second World War when about 6 million acres (2.4 million hectares) were moved from grassland to plough, but, other than in wartime, was generally a low priority. There was an assumption that food could be imported, and the rural interest was far weaker than in the nineteenth century. County councils ceased to be dominated by landowners and farmers, while the Conservative Party was no longer as close to agriculture as had hitherto been the case and by the late 1960s was very much a businessman's rather than a landowners' party in its senior ranks and was led by Edward Heath (1916–2005) rather than the Earl of Home (1903–95). Protectionism was largely discussed in the 1930s as a means to protect industry and imperial links, and not British farming. More generally, land ownership became a less totemic issue in terms of national identity and, instead, was seen largely as a resource for development, which, increasingly, meant housing.

The pressure for new housing reflected not only the rise in population and the desire for a better lifestyle, but also the multiple shifts in economic fortune. Shift, however, seems a neutral word when employed to describe some of the harsh and difficult changes that occurred. People not only moved off the land, but also migrated from declining industrial regions. Areas, such as north-east England and south Wales, that were collectively the nineteenth-century 'workshop of the world', became in large part industrial museums and regions of social dereliction, designated as problems requiring regional assistance, as under the Special Areas Act of 1934. In fact, this Act provided only limited assistance, leading to criticism by a group of radical young Conservatives, such as Harold Macmillan (1894–1986), who advocated 'One Nation' Conservatism, and, more loudly, by Labour politicians, notably Aneurin Bevan (1897–1960).

During the slump of the 1930s, the urban fabric in depressed industrial regions was devastated, as communities were squeezed and businesses shut. Unemployment in Sunderland, a major centre of nineteenth-century industry, rose to 75 per cent of shipbuilders and half of the working population, and was associated with serious hardship and higher rates of ill-health. Jarrow, another shipbuilding town in north-east England (in this case on the Tyne), also had unemployment levels of over 70 per cent, following the closure of Palmers Yard, the main employer in the town – a plight clearly described in *The Town that was Murdered* (1939) by the MP Ellen Wilkinson (1891–1947), 'Red Ellen', and one that led to the Jarrow March, of unemployed workers, to London in 1936.

More generally, unemployment and poverty sapped much of the population, leading to malnutrition and poor housing. Many people lacked adequate food, clothes, housing and sanitation, and they were frequently cold and wet. Public health was badly hit and tuberculosis became a more serious problem.

People moved from towns affected to areas of greater economic opportunity, mostly in the Midlands and south-east England. There was migration within industries, as when Scottish coal miners moved to Nottinghamshire pits, and between them, as with the large-scale movement of workers from South Wales to the new industrial centres in the Thames Valley, especially Dagenham, Hounslow and Slough. The Welsh collieries, which employed 272,000 men at the beginning of 1920, had only 126,000 miners by 1934. Internal migrants left fossilized townscapes and helped create new sprawling suburbs where they moved.

Aside from the new-build on greenfield sites, there was a major assault on slum (crowded and substandard) housing. The 'Greenwood' Housing Act of 1930 gave local authorities powers and subsidies to clear or improve such housing. Thus, the responsibility of central government for the availability and quality of housing was established in the inter-war period. Much was achieved thanks to the availability of labour, materials and low interest rates. In 1931–9, local authorities cleared 250,000 slum properties and built over 700,000 houses. Most house building, however, was private and in the new suburbs, for example along the Northern Line in London from Golders Green to Edgware.

House building was linked to a marked shift in the world of things, as industry focused on consumer demand. A National Grid for electricity, to be developed under the control of the Central Electricity Board, had been established under the Electricity Supply Act of 1926, and household electricity supplies expanded greatly, replacing coal, gas, candles and human effort as the major source of domestic power. Electricity was seen as clean and convenient, and as a way to improve the environment, so that power, heat and light came to be increasingly dependent on it. Refrigeration, which relied on electricity, had a major impact on food storage and longevity, and thus on the range of food available in households with fridges. It was unnecessary to have cold pantries separate from the kitchen.

The housing boom meant that there were many houses that had to be equipped, and the percentage of homes wired for electricity rose from 31.8 in 1932 to 65.4 in 1938. This rise had a major impact on the consumption of power and on the sales of electric cookers, irons, fridges, water heaters and vacuum cleaners. This demand helped industrial expansion, notably in the south and Midlands, which, particularly the former, were also the areas of greatest house building.

Such expenditure reflected, and helped to define, class differences. Whereas radios, vacuum cleaners and electric irons were widely owned, in part thanks to the spread of hire purchase, with payments spread out over a long period, electric fridges, cookers and washing-machines were largely restricted to the middle class. These differences were linked to an aspect of the major social divide between those who employed others (increasingly, however, an occasional daily help, rather than the less numerous full-time domestic servants) and the employed.

The poor were also unable to participate fully in the new leisure society. Most lacked radios, and thus were unable to listen to the BBC, and they could not afford the cinema, let alone holidays in the new Butlin's holiday camps, such as the large ones outside Minehead and Skegness. Nevertheless, by 1939, 71 per cent of British households had radio licences and, that year, Birmingham alone had 110 cinemas, and Britain close to 5,000. In 1934, out of a population of 46 million, 18.5 million went to the cinema on a weekly basis.

Concern about the rate of the spread of suburbia and the threat to the environment, combined with a growing willingness to accept government control, led to legislation. A Town and Country Planning Act of 1932 was followed by the Restriction of Ribbon Development Act of 1935, which attempted to prevent unsightly and uncontrolled development along new or improved roads, and the Green Belt (London and Home Counties) Act of 1938.

Housing

The Second World War lent pace to the pressure for change and regulation, notably because there was serious wartime damage to the housing stock due to German bombing, especially in London, as well as a very low rate of wartime construction. Expectations of a better life after the war were also encouraged by the Labour Party, which came to power in 1945. These expectations resulted not only in large-scale house building, notably in the 1950s, but also in the belief in more comprehensive planning that led to the Town and Country Planning Acts of 1944 and 1947, and the New Towns Act of 1946.

The New Towns were intended to be 'balanced communities for working and living'. Especially prominent round London, they were designed to complement the Green Belt and to provide housing for the displaced, bombed-out, residents of the metropolis. Stevenage was rapidly followed by Harlow, Hemel Hempstead, Crawley, Bracknell, Basildon, Hatfield and Welwyn Garden City. The London Green Belt was finally secured with an Act of 1959. There were other New Towns elsewhere, including Skelmersdale for Liverpool, and Cumbernauld, East Kilbride, Glenrothes, Irvine and Livingston in Scotland. In Wales, Cwmbran, designated in 1949, was an overspill town, while Newtown (1967) was an attempt to encourage economic activity in mid-Wales.

In addition to New Towns, there was large-scale rebuilding in the cities. The Conservatives saw the shortage of houses as an electoral opportunity, and, in the election of 1951, which they won under Churchill, made much of a promise to build 300,000 houses a year. Helped by a higher allocation of government resources, cooperation with house builders, and reducing the housing standards for council houses, the Conservatives, who remained in power until 1964, achieved their target in 1953, and this success permitted extensive rehousing in the 1950s. The key political figure, Harold Macmillan, Minister of Housing and Local Government from 1951 to 1954, was to earn much credit for this and he became Prime Minister in 1957. The 1950s' buildings, many of which were low-rise and fairly generous with space, should be distinguished from the system-built tower blocks largely built in the 1960s, although the latter were also seen from the 1950s.

Many of the new houses provided people with their first bathrooms and inside toilets. The dynamics of family space, and the nature of privacy, changed as a result. The consequences can be seen in 20 Forthlin Road, a National Trust property that is very different to their usual stately homes. This Liverpool house is on the Mather Avenue estate, which was built by the council in 1949–52, and it had an inside toilet. It was the home of the McCartney family, who had earlier lived in a prefabricated bungalow intended as a temporary home, and Paul McCartney and John Lennon wrote songs in the living room.

Within existing cities, concern about urban sprawl, and the practical constraints of Green Belts, encouraged higher-density housing, which contributed to high-rise development. Prefabricated methods of construction ensured that multi-storey blocks of flats could be built rapidly and inexpensively, and local councils, such as Glasgow, Liverpool and Newcastle in the 1950s and 1960s, took pride in their number, size and visibility. Glasgow Corporation began to rebuild the Gorbals as a high-rise district in 1951 and, by the early 1970s, one home in every three being built in Scotland was in a block of six storeys or more.

New estates, such as Park Hill in Sheffield, an estate of concrete inner-city tower blocks built in 1957, were designed as entire communities, with elevated walkways called 'streets in the sky'. Most, however, were failures, not only because they were poorly built, but also because they did not contribute to social cohesion. Kirkby on Merseyside, for example, was associated with unemployment, crime and vandalism, and, by the 1970s, Park Hill was in part a concrete slum. The decision of English Heritage in 1998 to list it as an architectural masterpiece was widely deplored by the tenants.

There was also a brutal rebuilding of many city centres, for example Birmingham, Gateshead, Manchester, Plymouth and Newcastle, as well as parts of central London. The availability of low-cost concrete was important in encouraging the new brutalism: redbrick and stone were discarded, as were the styles associated with them, notably neo-Georgian. Professional planners played a major role alongside architects in this process, which sought both to cope with traffic congestion and to provide modern images for cities. Yet, together, developers, planners and city councils, convinced that the past should be discarded, and in some cases, notably Newcastle, with shared financial interests, embarked on widespread devastation and poor-quality rebuilding. In Newcastle, most of Eldon Square made way for a shopping centre. The Town and Country Planning Act of 1969 was less valuable in offering protection to the townscape than the economic downturn that followed the massive 1973 oil price hike.

Planning was not the sole sphere for legislation. There was also political contention over attempts to control the ownership of land in order to ensure that planning was a more proactive process. The Attlee government (1945–51) nationalized the value added by the development of land, but the Conservatives repealed the legislation. Labour then considered the bringing of all rent-controlled housing under the control of local councils before establishing, under the Wilson governments (1964–70, 1974–6), a Land Commission in order to ensure the availability of sufficient building land. This measure proved a failure.

Environmentalism

Green Belt and Clean Air legislation represented major advances in the principle of national responsibility and the practice of government intervention, while the establishment in 1949 of the National Parks Commission and of Areas of Outstanding Beauty was also important. Yet, despite greater interest in planning from the 1940s, such moves were not part of a coherent strategy, and the Clean Air Act of 1956, in particular, was a response to a specific crisis created by a very bad smog in London in 1952. The nightmarish quality of a smog was captured in Patricia Wentworth's (1878–1961) novel *Ladies' Bane* (1954), which was set in London:

> It was rather like a slow motion picture. There was the fog of course. Nothing could really move in a fog like this. The buses would be stopped – and the cars – and the people who

were abroad would crawl like beetles and wish to be at home again – and the watches and clocks would all slow down and time too.

Smog also encouraged respiratory illnesses, especially bronchitis. In response, there was legislation for particular cities, legislation that dramatically changed their feel, sight and sound. The first smokeless zone legislation was introduced in the Manchester Corporation Act of 1946, and smoke emissions in Newcastle were controlled from 1958.

Greater public awareness of environmental degradation as well as the fashionability of environmental concern led, from the 1960s, to more consistent and insistent government intervention. The Countryside Commission was founded in 1968 (a year after the Scottish Countryside Commission), and the Department of the Environment was established in 1970. The decline in the industrial base also contributed to a change in the character of pollution. Moreover, the conversion to smokeless fuel led to an atmosphere that was no longer acidic nor heavy with sooty smuts and helped ensure that cities such as Leeds and Newcastle became cleaner and brighter. Yet, other particulates and chemicals became more significant in the environment, in part as a consequence of more traffic, and concern grew about the levels of gases such as carbon monoxide, ozone, sulphur dioxide, hydrocarbons and nitrogen dioxide.

In 2009, the European Commission began legal action that could end in a fine against Britain over its poor air quality. Pollution in London is particularly bad and frequently breaches limits recommended by the World Health Organization. Road transport has been the major culprit.

By the end of the twentieth century, the environment was more clearly a political issue than it had been at the outset. What, in 1987, became the Green Party was founded in 1975, and in 1989 it won 15 per cent of the vote in the elections to the European Parliament. This was exceptional, but environmental consciousness and activism became more pronounced, as environmental science became both alarming and fashionable. Friends of the Earth and Greenpeace enjoyed much support in the 1990s, while the mainstream political parties then and in the 2000s presented themselves, with different degrees of success, as being the 'pro-environment party'. For example, in his efforts to modernize the Conservative Party and broaden its appeal, its leader, David Cameron (1966–), stressed his green credentials in 2008.

Environmental consciousness took a number of forms. In particular, public concern about the fate of wildlife became more pronounced from the 1960s, and it also had a powerful impact in children's literature, with works such as Richard Adams' (1920–) novel about rabbits, *Watership Down* (1972). Indeed, wildlife was badly affected by human action, notably more intensive agricultural methods such as mechanization, the large-scale use of pesticides, in particular organophosphates, and the destruction of hedgerows. The last affected birds, which found fewer places in which to build their nests, small mammals and other animals, as well as insects such as bumblebees. There were also fewer of the wildflowers from which the latter sip their nectar. By 2009, two bumblebee species had died out, seven were threatened and only six were buoyant, a situation which was a threat to plants that need them for pollination.

The diminution (and even disappearance) of the dawn chorus in several parts of the country and the decline in the number of butterfly species have been particularly poignant indicators of loss due to changes in land use. In 2009, a survey of rivers indicated that the majority did not meet European Union standards for cleanliness, with serious consequences for wildlife such as otters. There was a major release of cyanide from a water sewage treatment plant into the River Trent in October 2009.

At the same time, there have also been indications of improvement, notably with the return of fish to some rivers, especially the Thames, where the first salmon for a century was caught in 1974; improvement that owes much to de-industrialization. In September 2009, it was announced that lampreys, fish intolerant of pollution, had been spotted in the Sussex Ouse for the first time in decades. As a reminder of the ambiguities of developments, the smell of jobs (i.e. from factories) was gone from towns where factories had been closed.

Less benign change in wildlife was the marked increase in the numbers of urban rats, squirrels, seagulls and foxes, attracted by the volume of rubbish. Indeed, with the decline in inshore fishing, seagulls moved inland. Moreover, assumptions about appropriate attitudes towards animals ensured that the repertoire of means hitherto available for action against vermin was markedly restricted, with limitations on the poisons that could be used.

The destruction of hedgerows led, from the 1950s, to the replacement, especially in East Anglia, of the earlier patchwork of small fields bordered with dense hedges by large expanses of arable land. These expanses were more convenient for agricultural machinery, which was increasingly large-scale, for example combine harvesters, helping ensure that fewer workers were required to produce the same quantity of food. Partly as a result, where the countryside is not the base for commuting or retirement communities, it has become depopulated, or, at least, agricultural employment has declined dramatically. Mechanization also hit wildlife.

There was also a major change to the woodlands of Britain. The abrupt disappearance of long-established, semi-natural, forest contrasted with earlier patterns of generally stable management, with its emphasis on regular cutting or coppicing. Although forestry led to an extension of woodland in upland areas, often in regimented, gloomy plantings, there are now fewer trees in heavily farmed lowland areas. Not all the decline, however, can be attributed to agricultural change, as Dutch elm disease, caused by a fungus, hit elms hard from the 1960s.

Terrains were also altered by human action. Rivers were deepened and straightened, a process seen from the eighteenth century, and coastlines were altered. More dramatically, escarpments were cleft to provide routes for motorways, notably the M40 through the Chilterns at Stokenchurch and the M3 through St Catherine's Hill near Winchester. Estuaries such as the Hull and Severn (twice) were bridged; and islands were linked to the mainland, with both the Skye road bridge and the Channel Tunnel. The latter compromised Britain's status as an island.

More generally, economic growth, greater affluence and a greater number of people put pressure on the environment. More waste and pollution resulted from these developments. Coastal waters were heavily polluted by sewerage outflows, while industrial pollution was responsible for acid rain, which damaged some of the country's woodland, and hit both rivers and lakes. Increased use of water carried forward the long-established practice of drowning valleys, especially in the Pennines and Wales, for reservoirs. Newcastle was served from the very large Kielder Reservoir on the north Tyne, completed at a cost of £150 million in 1982 and filled in 1983.

More material goods meant a greater use of energy, despite marked increases in energy efficiency. As a result, larger amounts of carbon dioxide were dispersed into the atmosphere above Britain, while the supply of sufficient electricity and other power sources became a serious issue. Furthermore, the consumer society produced greater and greater quantities of rubbish, much of it non-biodegradable and some of it toxic. Babies' nappies were no longer cleaned by immersion in boiling water; instead, disposable nappies became a major component of rubbish.

Rubbish disposal increasingly became a problem for both local government and business, not least due to greater public sensitivity about the means and location of dumping, and about the supposed dangers arising from incineration. Both proved a classic issue of NIMBYism, as 'Not in *My* Back Yard' seemed a routine response to pressures for development.

In addition, noise and light pollution became issues and, in fact, more serious and widespread. Maps of both indicated their spread, and quiet, in particular, became a rarer quantity, in rural as well as in urban areas.

These environmental pressures stemmed from significant changes in national life. In particular, the unprecedented rise in average real earnings – by over two and a half times between 1945 and 1995 – had a serious impact on the environment. For example, the percentage of households with a washing-machine rose from 66 in 1972 to 88 in 1991, and this led to increased use of water as well as fewer laundrettes. Advertisements for washing powder, another environmental problem, played a major role on television.

While one set of environmental pressures related to the strains posed to the environment by human activity, another was posed by the availability of the resources necessary for this activity. The two were closely related, notably with the water supply, as the pressures of greater use hit water levels and underlying aquifers. Power supply is another major problem, and one greatly exacerbated by environmental concerns and NIMBYism.

The crisis also owes much to a failure to maintain adequate investment in infrastructure, a failure that contrasts not only with the Victorian investment in railways and sewers and the inter-war investment in electricity capacity and roads, but also with post-1945 investment in nuclear power stations, motorways and the infrastructure for natural gas. From the 1970s there was insufficient investment, due, in part, to economic downturns but also to the emphasis on personal consumerism and to state expenditure on social welfare. A reliance on market solutions was also a cause of problems, not least because the regulatory framework (for both prices and environmental impact) limited market factors and discouraged investment, while the necessity in such cases for returns largely in the long term was not generally welcome to investors who did not wish to wait a long time.

The net effect was that power stations were not built to keep up with estimated peak demand, and, moreover, were not built to take note of the obsolescence of existing power plants. In particular, there has been a failure to build new nuclear reactors, despite the degree to which they do not use up fossil fuels, while coal-power stations, which in 2008 supplied 31 per cent of British electricity, are hit by European Union rules on emissions. Moreover, promised national cuts in carbon emissions, to 80 per cent of 1990 levels by 2050, pose a real challenge to keeping the lights on. Confidence in renewables, notably offshore wind turbines but also tidal power and solar heating, plays a major role in government planning, but these face difficulties in provision (for example the effectiveness of wind turbines on calm days) and in attracting the necessary investment.

In 2008, the largest source of electricity supply (46 per cent) was natural gas, but there are problems in ensuring a stable supply. North Sea gas supplies peaked in 1999 and have fallen rapidly since. As a result, reliance on gas means exposure to the political interests of Russia, Europe's main supplier.

Energy supply thus brought issues of environmentalism, consumer interest and government policy into conflict. The policy from Margaret Thatcher (Prime Minister 1979–90) on was a liberal one of encouraging free market competition by private companies to provide investment and capacity, but that does not seem to have worked. In the winter of 2005–6, there were shortages of natural gas, leading to short-term working by factories and to threats to the domestic network, and in 2008 power station failures led to extensive blackouts due to a lack of sufficient spare capacity. These issues scarcely feature in conventional histories of Britain, but they are of importance, not least because the provision of infrastructure is significant to the relationship between different generations.

Transport

The car provides a key instance of the environmental pressures stemming from greater use. The number of cars, 110,000 in 1919, had risen to nearly 2 million by September 1938, by which time there were also 500,000 road goods vehicles and 53,000 buses and coaches. By 1939, estimated annual expenditure on private road transport was £135 million. Motoring was encouraged by a fall in its cost, especially in the 1930s when cars became cheaper in real terms.

Moreover, the rise in motor transport was also supported by government policy, with far more money being put into developing the road system than was being spent on the rail infrastructure. The government built roads but did not help the railways. In addition, the government insisted that the rail companies had to publish freight rates, which meant that the road hauliers could undercut them. The rail companies also could not refuse to carry uneconomic freight, whereas the road hauliers could.

In the 1920s and 1930s, arterial roads were constructed, for example the Great West Road in London and the East Lancashire Road. The Trunk Roads Programme was devised in 1929, both to provide employment and to ensure that road improvement schemes were pressed forward. Central government agreed to provide much of the cost. Although there was no centralized planning or overruling of local views and property rights akin to that of the German *autobahns* in the 1930s, and, indeed, no motorways, nevertheless, from the 1930s, trunk roads with dual carriageways became more common and new arterial roads, such as the Southend Arterial Road, proved effective long-distance routes. What was then the longest underwater tunnel in the world, the road link under the Mersey between Liverpool and Birkenhead, opened in 1934. Major road bridges, such as the Tyne Bridge between Newcastle and Gateshead (1928), matched earlier railway bridges which had been among the most dramatic engineering achievements of the Victorian age. Within towns, the role of road transport was seen as the more flexible buses competed actively with trams.

The new roads led to new smells and sounds, and affected the visual context of life, both in towns and in the countryside.

Roads created new demands for road signs, lamp posts, manhole covers and traffic lights, as well as for the large 'road houses' (service stations) where motorists could obtain refreshments and petrol. A world of services grew up around the car, and this world was a changing one. Thus, the maps and guides produced for motorists in the 1930s, for example the Shell Guides, were eventually replaced by satnav systems, with location-finding and route-planning handled in a very different fashion.

Roads led to new boundaries and commands, to zebra crossings and belisha beacons, the latter named after a Minister of Transport, Leslie Hore-Belisha (1893–1957). His period in office (1934–7) also saw the introduction of driving tests, urban speed limits and one-way systems. Nowadays, we are well aware of the damage and disruption brought by road transport, not least the resulting pollution; but, for much of the century, the freedom offered made cars seductive. In the inter-war years, those who could not afford cars were in the over-whelming majority, but vehicle ownership became a goal or model for many, creating a pent-up aspiration and ensuring that future affluence would lead to the purchase of motor cars.

This concern for affluence helped account for many features of 1930s society, culture and politics, not least support for the National Government that came to power in 1931, but also contributed to a restlessness with existing arrangements. This restlessness has attracted less scholarly attention than subsequent wartime (1939–45) desires for a fairer society, but the desire for more material goods and for a sense of possession and for possessions was one reason why Labour proved unable to sustain its post-1945 hold on office and why, instead, the Conservatives held power from 1951 to 1964.

The cinema helped to foster this romance with cars and other possessions: films, both the British ones and their influential American counterparts, created and disseminated lifestyles and images. Enormous cinemas, such as the vast Ritz at Gosport, made going to the films more glamorous. The cinema had become more popular with the middle class from the late 1920s, and this was linked to investment in these large and luxurious cinemas, especially in middle-class suburbs. Aside from acting as foci within towns, cinemas also gave a new vitality to the appeal of towns to their rural hinterlands. Country dwellers went to urban cinemas, such as the Grand in Banbury, to see the wider world, both through films and in news reels. Films also played a social role that was subsequently to be taken by television, but with important differences: the cinema was a communal experience, whereas the television was a family one. By 1934, there was one cinema seat for every ten people in South Wales, although this ratio can be seen as an index of how dreadful life outside the cinema was.

After a fall in car ownership during the Second World War, when national and personal resources were perforce concentrated on war, its rise accelerated rapidly, especially after petrol rationing ended in 1950. Private car ownership rose from 1.49 million in 1945 to 3 million in 1960 and 12.7 million in 1970. Private road transport shot up from 47 million miles (76 million kilometres) in 1954 to 217 million miles (350 million kilometres) in 1974, and an increase from 39 to 79 per cent of the total passenger journeys covered. This gain was made at the expense of bus, coach and rail transport. The percentage of goods traffic moved by road rose from 37 in 1952 to 58.3 in 1964 as lorries benefited from the programme of major road-building. A motorway system was created, beginning with the M6 Preston bypass, opened in 1958. The M1 was punched through the Midlands from Watford to Birmingham in 1959. Motorway bridges were opened across the Severn in 1966 and 1997.

The impact of the car on the country included more atmospheric pollution due to vehicle exhausts, as well as the destruction and blight linked to road-building. The structure of city life changed, not least because of this destruction brought by road-building, while roads became barriers within townscapes. The devastation was covered by the novelist P.D. James (1920–) in her novel *A Certain Justice* (1997), which describes the building in the late 1960s of Westway, the elevated section of dual carriageway that carries traffic on the A40 closer to central London:

> Westway had been a comfortable enclave of the respective, reliable, law-abiding lower middle class who owned their houses and took a pride in clean lace curtains and carefully tended front gardens ... Soon there would be nothing but tarmac and the ceaseless roar and screech of traffic thundering westward out of London.

Similarly, Wolverhampton's ring road was opened in stages between 1961 and 1986, clearing away established landmarks and residential districts, while Carlisle's, opened in 1974, cut the castle off from the city and was followed by the replacement of a long-established area by a shopping centre. Multi-storey car parks came to disfigure many townscapes from the 1960s, including those of historic towns such as Bath, Durham, Exeter and Newcastle.

The abrupt change in the landscape was shown with the building of motorways past historic buildings. The M1 speeds past Hardwick Hall and the M54 past Moseley Old Hall. The M4 was driven through the Osterley estate in west London in 1965, the M5 through the Killerton estate, and the six-lane Plympton bypass was cut through the park at Saltram in 1970, largely obliterating the eighteenth-century carriage drive. Conversely, pressure for bypasses grew and the towns that gained them, for example Honiton in 1966 and Ashburton in 1974, became more attractive places to live.

There were also changes in transport in the cities, where trams were replaced by diesel-engined buses. Many cities, including Glasgow, Leeds and Liverpool, were still investing strongly in tram systems in the late 1940s, but in the 1950s they were swiftly discarded. Newcastle's last tram ran in 1950 and London's in 1952, and by 1960 the sole surviving electric tramway in England was essentially a tourist attraction between Blackpool and Fleetwood. Aberdeen's last trams ran in 1958, and by 1962 even the extensive Glasgow system, the last in Scotland, had ceased. London's last trolley-bus followed in 1962, and, in 1963, Newcastle Corporation decided to replace trolley-buses by motor buses. The price of electricity and the maintenance cost of the wires hit trolley-buses, while motor buses benefited from greater manoeuvrability and low petrol prices. These changes in transport meant different daily sights and sounds for millions, both travellers and others, and were important to the altering fabric of life.

Meanwhile, the pace of car use increased, whichever criteria were employed, with car ownership rising from 224 per 1,000 people in 1971 to 380 per 1,000 in 1994. Commuting by car increased while the motorways became a network. Greater personal mobility for the bulk, but by no means all, of the population enabled and was a necessary consequence of lower-density housing, different employment patterns, and declining subsidies for public transport.

There were links between rising car use and significant changes in society, not least commercial development in the shape of out-of-town shopping centres and business parks. In addition, the percentage of people walking or travelling by bus fell markedly, an aspect of the declining use of 'public space'. This was also linked to an increase in obesity and unfitness among children, an increase that gave rise to belated public concern and governmental action in the 2000s as the public health consequences of this were more fully appreciated. Moreover, the use of cars interacted with fears about children being out by themselves. Nevertheless, cars were a democratizing mechanism, making work and leisure more accessible, indeed one of the most democratic elements in twentieth-century Britain.

Greater mobility for most, but not all, of the population, however, exacerbated social segregation. Car ownership brought a sense, maybe an illusion, of freedom, and an access to opportunities and options for many, but not all. The division of the population into communities defined by differing levels of wealth, expectations, opportunity and age was scarcely novel, but it became more apparent and pronounced during the late nineteenth and twentieth centuries; and an obvious aspect of what was termed the underclass, in both town and countryside, was their relative lack of mobility.

Consumerism and Environmental Change

Consumerism focused not only on mobility, but also on leisure, comfort, and the automatic and instant availability of the heat, water and food that previous generations had found difficult to obtain and ensure. Environmental pressure was an obvious result. Had the population remained at, say, 46 million, then each individual could have increased his 'carbon footprint' without the impact on the environment of the present-day 61 million. Thus, population increase is the prime factor in Britain's environmental crisis, a point that public debate tends to avoid. Moreover, the effect of over-crowding on the quality of life is considerable. Demand on water supplies stemmed not only from the rising population, but also from greater comfort and wealth in the shape of more frequent baths or showers, and a greater ownership of dish-washers and washing-machines. Other trends contributed to the same result. More cars meant more car washes, while a greater interest in leisure led to more effort being devoted to gardening, another call on water supplies, a trend encouraged by television programmes on the subject in the 2000s. Fashions were also significant, notably that in the 2000s for garden 'water features', generally man-made ponds and springs powered by electric motors.

The problems created by far larger quantities of rubbish are a pointed and less attractive consequence of the rise of consumerism and of population numbers. Home ownership also played a major role in consumerism. Whereas, in 1914, some 10 per cent of the English housing stock was owner-occupied, by 2000 the percentage was 70, and of a far larger stock. A key decade was the 1980s, when the Thatcher government sold, rather than built, council houses and also encouraged the ready availability of credit for mortgages. In Scotland, where wage levels are lower and the control by local authorities stronger, the percentage of owner-occupied houses is smaller. Ownership was linked to expenditure on decoration and furnishing, with owner-occupiers spending far more than those who rent.

By the 2000s, environmental concerns became more prominent as a result of global warming. Anxiety about major changes in climate and, through the melting of the ice caps, about a significant rise in sea levels, affected both public debate and governmental policy, and Britain played a major role in the negotiations leading to the 1997 Kyoto Protocol on climate change and the 2009 Copenhagen conference, as well as in the development of carbon trading. Rising sea levels are a particular threat to Britain, an island, and notably so in southern and eastern England.

Severe weather episodes contributed to public concern. Thus, widespread flooding in inland areas in 2000 and 2008 after persistent heavy rain indicated the extent to which building on floodplains (for example near Tewkesbury and York), drainage policies and agricultural practices had combined to make large areas vulnerable; while anxiety in 2006 over higher temperatures and the availability of water reflected worry over global warming and rising population numbers. In 2009, the latter was related to anxiety about the future availability of food. Whereas that had not played a role in public discussion for decades, it became more central. In this case, one form of environmental consciousness clashed with another, notably concern about the likely consequences of the genetic modifications of crops deemed necessary to raise their productivity. Such clashes are likely to become more common.

The impact of climate change was wide-ranging. For example, the rising sea temperatures on Britain's Atlantic coast

were linked to the increase in the number of Atlantic hurri-
canes, and thus of the climate's pressure on the westerly parts
of Britain. Tourism, agriculture and public morale are affected,
with, for example, the grain and hay rotting in wet fields, while
roads and railways are greatly affected by landslides. In the
North Sea, the average temperature has increased 1°C over the
last forty years, an increase sufficient to lead to the departure
for cooler waters of plankton, whose number in the North Sea
has fallen by 60 per cent in this period, and thus to a decline in
the cod that feed on them. The knock-on impact on the food
chain is wide-ranging, with fewer cod ensuring the survival of
more crabs and jellyfish, on which cod feed, and with more
crabs in turn hitting plaice and sole stocks as they eat their
young.

Climate change is scarcely unique to Britain, but there is a
tendency to underplay it in accounts of national history. This is
mistaken, for the degree to which Britain is changing as an
environment for humans, other species and plants is crucial to
its history, both to the experience, opportunities and problems
of life, and to the potent images and ideas held of the country
and of life there.

Images of the Country
The strength and endurance of the relationship between the
ruralist tradition and Englishness derives from the fact that this
tradition is not just conservative but has been able to accommodate and place the apparently irreconcilable ideals of the
romantic right (country house, parish church, squire, parson
and deferential society) and the romantic left (folk society, the
village, rural crafts and honest peasantry): that there are in
short several ruralist traditions which co-exist. Although there
are strong loyalties to particular cities, there is no comparable
sense of place for an alternative urban tradition drawing on all
cities, not least because of the remorseless process of new
building and destruction that has affected so much of the urban
environment.

Yet, rural England (and Britain) have been under strong pressure from within and outside. Intensive agricultural land use is unfavourable to the traditional concept of the countryside. A standardization of farming practice and an obsession with agricultural tidiness have both been much in evidence.

Moreover, pressure from non-agricultural 'development' is also acute, notably new housing, shopping centres and theme parks, while the rise in rural house prices is such that locals cannot afford them. The love of the countryside threatens to destroy it, as the desire to live 'in the countryside', one encouraged by romantic television programmes about rural life, is matched by the building of very large numbers of new homes. At the same time, although the key image for many remains that of England as a 'green and pleasant land', and of the Scottish, Welsh and Northern Irish equivalents, the focus of government concern, of consumerism and of most people has been on urban life. Legislation, such as the hunting ban under the Hunting Act of 2004 and the 'Right to Roam' under the Countryside and Rights of Way Act of 2000, both introduced by the Blair government (1997–2007), demonstrates the determination to push through urban norms on the countryside. Yet, it is in the cities that the changing nature of the British has been seen most clearly; and, ironically, many of those who live in rural areas now share the attributes of the urban life from which they often distance themselves.

6

CHANGING PEOPLE

More inhabitants and a new people. That appeared to be the prospectus, welcome or otherwise, during the period, and this prospectus was seen from the outset. More people were readily apparent as suburbia spread, notably, but not only, from London. Yet, a warning about the dangers of a new people arising from the cult of technological progress without a moral framework was provided by Aldous Huxley (1894–1963) in his novel *Brave New World* (1932):

> 'Stability', said the controller, 'Stability. No civilization without social stability. No social stability without individual stability. ... Hence all this.' With a wave of his hand he indicated ... the huge buildings of the Conditioning Centre. ... 'Fortunate boys ... No pains have been spared to make your lives emotionally easy – to preserve you, so far as that is possible, from having emotions at all.'

Population Growth
The period saw a major rise in the population of the United

Kingdom, from 46 million in 1931 to 50.2 million in 1945, 52.8 million in 1961, 55.9 million in 1971, 56.4 million in 1981, 57.4 million in 1991, 58.7 million in 2001 and 61.4 million in 2008. That of England and Wales increased from 40 million in 1931 to 49 million in 1991 (Scotland: 4.8 to 5.0 million; Northern Ireland 1.2 to 1.6 million). In 2008, there were 51,446,000 people in England, 5,169,000 in Scotland, 2,993,000 in Wales and 1,775,000 in Northern Ireland. At present, other than in apocalyptic scenarios linked to epidemic disease and environmental catastrophe, there is no sign that this increase will end, and, indeed, immigration has ensured that the rate of population increase has risen.

The overwhelming majority of the UK population lived, and lives, in England, and this is likely to become more marked. Immigrants focus on England in part because of the appeal of existing communities there, but also due to the extent to which nationalism elsewhere contributes to a less welcoming environment. The hostile treatment accorded to Romanian gypsies in Belfast in 2009 was especially notable, but, although less violent, the exclusivist nature of Scottish and Welsh nationalism, notably the emphasis on the Welsh language in the latter, is also significant.

England was, and is, the most densely populated of the major European countries, far more so than France, the country with which British people were most likely to compare their lot. The number of people per square kilometre was 244.2 in the UK in 2008 compared to 235.2 in Germany, 191.6 in Italy, 137 in China, 109.3 in France, and 31 in the US. This density has helped to define much of English history, both environmental and socio-political. Moreover, the density of England's population is more marked because of its concentration in the south east. This concentration feeds directly into the focus on house prices in English society. In part, this focus is a symptom of the stress and anxiety caused by crowdedness and by a sense of over-crowdedness.

Although the population has risen greatly, this rise was

below the general rate of increase in the world population, while, in addition, average rates of population growth in Britain have varied greatly during the period. Most notably, these rates were far lower in the inter-war period, when they fell to below replacement levels, than they had been in the nineteenth century. The number of children in an average family fell from three in 1910 to two in 1940. In addition, because childbearing was concentrated in the early years of marriage, the family-building period for most women fell in length, facilitating their employability or their role in voluntary activities. It became less common from the 1930s for women to have children after their mid-thirties.

The trend of fewer children, and of children being born earlier in marriage, began in middle-class groups but, in the inter-war period, spread to the working class. Repeated pregnancy became less common. There were significant economic consequences. The fall in the size of the average family cut expenditure on food and clothing, freeing funds for the consumer durables that were increasingly important, such as radios, but many (especially working-class) households did not experience such a fall.

Despite a post-war baby boom (birth peak) in 1947, and another in 1966, population growth rates continued to decline in the 1950s and 1960s, to almost a standstill in the 1970s and early 1980s, before rising. The population rose from 50 million in 1948 to 60 million by 2005. The higher birth rates in certain (but not all) immigrant groups in part reflected their adherence to different values, especially those of Islam; although, in practice, there was a range of Muslim views and these were implemented in terms of the particular family and communal practices of specific Muslim communities.

Birth control became more publicly discussed and available. The growing availability and acceptability of new or improved methods of contraception was important and included the growing use of the condom in the first half of the twentieth century, and of the pill, the coil and sterilization in the second half, as well as the legalization of abortion in 1967. Linking demographics and assumptions about gender, the pill became not only a symbol and means of the sexual revolution of the 1960s for women in particular, yet also for men, but also a fundamental aspect of the new, more planned, demographic regime, seen in particular in family planning clinics. From the 1960s, the ready availability of the contraceptive pill made it easier for women, both married and unmarried, to control their fertility. In 1961, the pill was made available on the NHS, and the NHS (Family Planning) Act passed in 1967 made no mention of marriage. This legislation was linked to the widespread breakdown in the relationship between sex and marriage, as well as to the rise of youth culture and the decline in the potency of the religious world view.

Key demographic, economic and cultural changes underlay the spread of effective contraceptive techniques, including lower levels of infant and child mortality; higher real incomes; the growing range of consumer goods and services, and the effect these had on spending patterns and expectations for ever higher standards of living; the increase in the proportion of married women in gainful employment; the growing willingness of the state to provide assistance for ill-health, unemployment and old age; and rises in the cost of educating and training children to meet the increasingly sophisticated demands of the workplace. Changing cultural values lessened the belief in childbearing as the major, if not sole, purpose of sexual intercourse, and instead, promoted a greater sense of individualism, especially for women, which, in turn, freed the individual from the traditional constraints of communal and family control.

Cultural changes were linked to shifts in religious practice. By the 1990s, only one in seven Britons was an active member of a Christian church, although more claimed to be believers. Both for most believers and for the less religious or the non-religious, faith became less important, not only to the fabric of life, but also to many of the turning points in individual lives, especially birth, marriage, dying and death. The failure in the 1990s of the 'Keep Sunday Special' campaign (heavily backed by the established Churches) to prevent shops from opening on the Sabbath confirmed the general trend. Churches used to play a major role in charitable functions and the provision of social welfare, but these have largely been replaced by the state, albeit with many gaps. Moreover, the lives of many politicians have ceased to be illuminated by religious values, although with Tony Blair (1953–) and Gordon Brown (1951–; Labour Prime Minister 2007–10) there was a shift back to earlier patterns of commitment. Margaret Thatcher also acknowledged her Methodist upbringing.

These shifts in religious practice took place alongside fundamental changes in personal and communal behaviour, with the 1960s, especially 1965–8, proving a turning point. An increasing percentage of the population, both male and female, had sex before marriage, and, on average, at a younger age. Cultural tropes and reference points, such as the significance of female virginity, changed dramatically, although, as with other changes, at differing rates.

From the 1930s to the early 1970s, age at marriage fell and marriage rates rose: the spinster ceased to be a characteristic feature of society, as did specific social arrangements for both spinsters and bachelors. From the 1970s, however, marriage rates fell, and there was an increase in the average age of marriage, because marriage in part has been replaced by a growth in co-habitation. Divorce was disapproved of in interwar society, and indeed Edward VIII's proposed marriage to a divorcee led to the Abdication Crisis of 1936: it was made clear to him by Baldwin, the Prime Minister, that he could not choose the personal life he wished, an approach that had the full backing of the Church of England and the editor of *The Times*, and the king, insistent on marrying the woman he loved, abdicated.

In contrast, divorce became much more common after the Second World War, especially from the 1960s, with the Divorce Reform Act of 1969 matching a powerful demand that reflected increasing expectations of marital harmony and higher standards for this harmony. Edward VIII's niece, Princess Margaret, had not been allowed to marry a divorcee in the 1950s, but she herself divorced in the 1980s.

Due, in large part, to divorce, the percentage of single-parent households headed by a woman rose: from 8.3 per cent of households with children in 1971 to 12.1 per cent in 1980. By 1990, the divorce rate had risen to 44 per cent of marriages contracted, and there was much talk of the breakdown of marriage.

Yet, in 1995, 71 per cent of families still consisted of couples living with their own children. Despite the increased frequency of step-parents, a frequency amply reflected in the plots of novels and television and radio dramas, such as *EastEnders* and *The Archers*, three-quarters of children grew up in families with both their natural parents. Furthermore, three-quarters of births outside marriage in 1995 were registered by both parents, a point that tended to be overlooked in the negative coverage of single parents.

In the 1990s, later births became more common and fashionable for a section of the population. This demographic was linked to significant changes in women's role in society and to economic factors. In 1975–2005, whereas the number of babies born to women aged twenty to twenty-four has more than halved, in 1995–2005 more women aged thirty to thirty-four have given birth than any other group.

A more fundamental shift, one common to the developed world, was rising life expectancy. It rose from 46 for men and 50 for women in the 1900s to 70 for men and 75 for women in 1979, to 77 for men and 81 for women by 2001, and in England to 77.7 for men and 81.9 for women by 2006–8. Whereas a sixty-year-old British man could anticipate another seventeen years of life in 1984, by 2006 the figure was twenty-one years: for women the figures were twenty-one years in 1984 and twenty-four years in 2006. By 2008, there were 1.3 million people aged eighty-five in the UK. As a result, the age pyramid altered. In County Durham, 45.5 per cent of the population in 1911 were under twenty, but only 32.3 per cent in 1971, whereas the percentage for those aged over seventy rose from 2 to 7.5. In 2009, the Office for National Statistics estimated that by 2033 nearly a quarter of the population would be over sixty-five and 18 per cent under sixteen.

Indeed, there was speculation that the likely impact of genetic knowledge and engineering was such that many (possibly a quarter of) babies born in 2009 will live till 100 and some might live till 150. This possibility has fundamental consequences for living arrangements and for individual family, community and state finances. Indeed, it is unclear how far society will be able to respond. The need, already, in terms of new facilities and changes in pension provision is readily apparent, but it is unclear that the political system will be able to provide the leadership and solutions necessary for over-coming the resulting strains.

It is all too easy to consider population shifts in aggregate terms, at the level of the nation, and, indeed, the basic character of change is similar across the country. This is especially true of the experience of ageing and the greatly increased use of contraceptives. Yet, there were also important social and geographical variations. Life expectancy was higher among the middle than the working class. Furthermore, in part due to age structure, birth rates were higher among communities based on immigration from New Commonwealth countries, such as India, Pakistan, Bangladesh and Jamaica, than among older-established groups. At the geographical level, population numbers in Scotland, Wales and north-east and north-west England did not grow markedly and, for much of the last twenty years, fell, but the situation was very different in south-east and south-west England.

Across Britain, the great mobility of the population affected demographic structures. The larger percentage of the popu-lation above sixty-five, greater disposable wealth on the part of much of the population, and enhanced mobility, combined after 1945 to ensure that a number of towns became especially associated with retirement to the seaside. This was true, for example, of Worthing, Hove, Eastbourne, Exmouth and Sidmouth on the south coast of England, and of Colwyn Bay in north Wales.

Furthermore, British membership in the European Economic Community – later European Union (EU) – from 1973 was followed in the 1980s by large numbers of British retirees emigrating elsewhere in Europe, especially to Spain. This movement was greater in scale than that in other European countries and reflected both opportunities and also a choice to leave a country that appeared crowded and troubled to many. The ability to move funds abroad that stemmed from the economic liberalism of the Thatcher government was important, as was the strength of sterling that resulted from North Sea oil and a monetarist fiscal policy with its control of the money supply. In part, moving abroad was an equivalent to the retirement of large numbers to the countryside or seaside. Each involved a departure from the cities that entailed a measure of cashing in on house values there as well as of 'white flight' from ethnically mixed urban neighbourhoods.

This trend of moving abroad accentuated the geographical spread of many families, creating problems for support within them. The spread was mirrored by rural youth depopulation in Wales and England. As a result of these and other trends, the old support network which the extended family provided ceased to exist. The family home is now less and less likely to contain grandparents, as well as parents and their children. Instead, with grandparents banished to care homes, the nuclear family unit became increasingly the norm in post-1945 Britain. The construction of new, out-of-town, housing estates reinforced this trend by making it more difficult for families to keep in regular contact. Instead, they began to spend less time together, and this affected all levels of society. As a result, the family as a means of transmitting behaviour patterns became less significant.

Immigration

Immigration played a major role in population changes, and by the 2000s was the dominant factor pushing growth. Until the 1950s, immigration was largely from elsewhere in Europe, although fresh restrictions on immigration in 1914 and 1919 had led to a decline in the 1920s and 1930s. Immigration was not then a major social or political issue, although there was a widespread low-level racism and anti-Semitism that could at times lead to violence, but which was more commonly a matter of social assumptions and institutional practices. Disapproval of inter-racial sexuality and marriage was an aspect of the social conservatism of the 1930s, a conservatism that was displayed across the political spectrum and by all social groups.

As with much else, the disruption of the Second World War altered the situation, providing large numbers of refugees, and also created new demands for labour within Britain; demands that in part reflected the fact that many men were occupied in military service well into the post-war period. Large numbers of Poles, mostly political refugees from communism, arrived after the war, or stayed on having reached Britain during the war, and the 1951 census recorded 162,376 people as Polish-born. Opposition to them was voiced at the TUC's annual congress in 1946, as well as by the Fascist Union Movement of Sir Oswald Mosley, who had backed Hitler in the 1930s and who continued to agitate, albeit with scant success, after the war. Immigration was also encouraged in order to cope with labour shortages: Estonians, Latvians, Lithuanians and Ukrainians arrived as European Volunteer Workers. Until Italian economic growth became more marked from the 1960s, the Italians were an important immigrant community, under-lining the need to remember the extent of white immigration after 1945.

The Irish were the largest group of immigrants. There was a major peak in Irish immigration during and after the Second World War, with labour actively recruited to help with wartime needs, while post-war reconstruction led to more immigration.

Even after Ireland left the Commonwealth in 1949, Irish
citizens enjoyed free access to the British labour market, as
well as the right to vote, a measure that greatly benefited the
Labour Party, and until 1971 the largest immigrant minority in
Britain came from the Republic of Ireland. That year, those
born in Eire (the Republic of Ireland, formerly the Irish Free
State) were 1.1 per cent of the British population. Whereas in
the nineteenth and early twentieth centuries, Irish immigrants
had focused on Lancashire and Scotland, from the 1940s they
switched to the Midlands and the south east, especially
London, Birmingham and Coventry, reflecting opportunities
in the labour market.

Immigration from the empire brought in Hong Kong
Chinese and Cypriots, and from the 1950s there was also large-
scale immigration from the New Commonwealth, principally
the West Indies, first, and South Asia, subsequently, although
many of the immigrants intended only a limited stay. A
temporary labour shortage in unattractive spheres of
employment, such as transport (especially the buses), foundry
work and nursing, led to an active sponsorship of immigration
that accorded with Commonwealth idealism. The over-
whelming majority of the West Indian immigrants who arrived
in the 1950s and early 1960s planned to save money in order to
buy land in the West Indies and return; but they gained only
low-paid jobs and never earned enough.

By the 1971 census, those born outside Britain amounted to
6.6 per cent of the total population, although, increasingly, this
statistic ceased to be a measure of the long-term impact on
society, because the children of immigrants, born in Britain,
had never known any other country. In the 1971 census,
707,110 people were recorded as New Commonwealth: they
were concentrated in London, the West Midlands and south
Yorkshire, including 7.1 per cent of the population of Bradford
and 6.7 per cent of Birmingham, and, within these areas, there
were further marked concentrations, for example in Balsall
Heath in Birmingham and Brixton and Tower Hamlets in

London. In contrast, relatively few New Commonwealth immigrants went to Scotland, North or central Wales, Northern Ireland, and rural or north-east England: the percentage for Newcastle was only 1.3. Economic opportunity played a role in these differences, but it was only partly responsible for them.

By then, concern about the scale of immigration, and growing racial tension, especially over jobs and public housing, had led to a redefinition of nationality. The British Nationality Act of 1948 had guaranteed freedom of entry from the Commonwealth and colonies, clearly differentiating immigration from both from that from elsewhere in the world, but this situation was changed by successive legislation of 1962, 1968, 1971, 1981 and 1988. For example, the Commonwealth Immigrants Act of 1968 deprived East African Asians with British passports of the automatic right of entry which they had been promised when Kenya won independence in 1963. This legislation became of particular importance when Idi Amin (c. 1925–2003), the dictator of Uganda, expelled the Asian population of the country in 1972.

The regulatory regime helped limit immigration, and in the 1970s and 1980s the UK was a net country of emigration, especially to North America and Australasia. Indeed, for 1980–5, there was an average annual net outflow of 50,000. Moreover, in the 1980s and early 1990s, primary immigration from the Indian subcontinent (Pakistan, India, Bangladesh and Sri Lanka) was limited, although admission for marriage and family reunion continued at about 25,000–30,000 each year. Nevertheless, by 1991 over 10 per cent of the population of six of London's boroughs – Hounslow, Ealing, Brent, Harrow, Redbridge and Newham – were of Indian background, while over 10 per cent of that of Tower Hamlets were Bangladeshi.

The situation totally changed in the 2000s, as the Labour government lost control of immigration and seemed unwilling to translate talk about action into action that was more than talk. Net immigration, the difference between those entering and leaving the UK, rose from 55,000 in 1996 to 237,000 in 2007, by when about a tenth of the population was foreign-born. In the 2000s, there were new strands of immigration from the Middle East, Somalia, the Balkans and Eastern Europe, especially Poland. By the end of 2006, a total of 580,000 people from the eight former Communist states that joined the EU had registered to work in the UK, 375,000 from Poland alone; although the true figure was seen as much greater. At the same time, earlier strands of immigration continued. In 2000, 50,000 people arrived from the Indian subcontinent, and 100,000 in 2006, in part due to a rise in the number of work permits and in part to a marked increase in the number of spouses and fiancé/es admitted. The total number of immigrants arriving from outside the EU with work permits rose from about 20,000 a year in the early 1990s to 145,000 in 2006.

The extent of additional illegal immigration adds a further complication, not least because it leads to uncertainty about total immigrant figures. Illegal immigration also linked with concerns about terrorism and this encouraged government interest in the 2000s in the idea of identity cards.

The religious balance changed greatly as a result of immigration. Whereas, in 1970, there were about 375,000 Hindus, Muslims and Sikhs combined in Britain, by 1993 the figure was about 1,620,000, with the rise in the number of Muslims particularly pronounced. Having been 250,000 strong in 1970 and 400,000 in 1975, the number of Muslims in the country doubled between 1980 and 1995, rising to 1.2 million.

The Muslims also became more active politically, not least as the notion of immigration leading to assimilation changed to the idea of multiculturalism. The alleged blasphemy of Salman Rushdie's (1947–) novel *The Satanic Verses* (1988) created a major controversy in 1989 because Islamic figures were outraged that Christianity, but not Islam, enjoyed protection under the blasphemy laws; not, though, that the Churches had much recourse to them. There were numerous demonstrations against the book in 1989, and in 1992 the controversy led to the first meeting of the (self-selected) Muslim Parliament of Great Britain.

Immigration pushed up the birth rate in Britain in the 2000s, because it added to the number of women of childbearing age. The average number of children born to each woman rose from 1.63 in 2001 to 1.96 in 2008, the highest fertility rate since 1973. In the year mid-2007 to mid-2008, a quarter of all babies had at least one foreign-born parent, and the fertility rate of mothers born outside the UK was 2.51 compared to 1.84 among UK-born women. As a consequence, the population rose 0.7 per cent in one year, to reach 61.4 million in mid-2008, a rate of increase that would lead, if extrapolated, to a figure of 76,676,688 by 2060, a figure that will lead to changes in most aspects of national life. The percentage of new births to mothers born outside the UK was particularly high in areas with concentrations of immigrants, such as Brent in London.

Health
While the ethnic composition of the British changed, their health was also transformed. New discoveries and their dissemination played a role, as did developments in the public provision of health and welfare, as well as more general improvements in housing and engineering, notably in the supply of clean piped mains water. A key discovery was that of penicillin. Bacterial infections of one kind or another were a very common cause of death in the first half of the century. Large numbers of children died then, the UK infant mortality rate being 58 per 1,000 in 1937, while the rate for Newcastle, where overcrowding remained very serious, rose to 91 per 1,000.

British scientists, notably Alexander Fleming (1881–1955), the discoverer of penicillin, the first antibiotic, in 1928, played a major role in the development of antibiotics in the early 1940s. After extensive use in the Second World War, penicillin was made available in 1946 as a prescription-only drug. It proved an effective weapon against post-operative infections, septicaemia, pneumonia, meningitis and endocarditis. Still serious in the 1930s, especially among the urban poor, tuberculosis was conquered from the mid-1950s thanks to the use of an American antibiotic, streptomycin, as well as to better diet, mass radiography, earlier diagnosis and the programme of mass BCG (Bacillus Calmette-Guérin) vaccinations of children. Antibiotics also helped with other bacterial infections, such as some venereal diseases and urinary infections.

The common childhood diseases that caused high mortality and high morbidity in children in the early part of the century, such as measles, whooping cough and diphtheria, had been declining since the First World War, but were further reduced by the post-1945 introduction of immunization programmes for the entire child population. The BCG injection scar on the upper left arm marked out a generational change and an aspect of a determined attempt to improve public health by securing the health and welfare of children. Despite controversy, the MMR vaccine, introduced in the UK in 1988, proved successful in tackling mumps, measles and rubella, although foolish refusals to take the vaccine increased the danger that these would reappear. From the 1970s, there was the introduction of limited population screening for the early detection and treatment of other diseases, such as breast and cervical cancer.

There was also a revolution in the treatment of mental illness, in which Britain played a major role. Knowledge, diagnosis and treatment changed, while the development, from the 1940s, of safe and effective drugs helped with major psychoses and depression, dramatically improving the care rate and improving the opportunities for community as opposed to institutional care. The range of surgical treatments also greatly increased, notably with the development of plastic surgery and of kidney transplants, as well as with a major increase in anaesthetic skills. Between the 1950s and the 1980s, the transplanting of human organs was transformed from an experimental, and often fatal, procedure into a routine, and usually highly successful operation, with the first heart transplants in Britain performed in 1980.

Yet, alongside general improvement there were important social and regional dimensions to health and mortality. The Depression of the 1930s had brought a high level of long-term unemployment and poverty to exacerbate the already difficult legacy of nineteenth-century economic change and social pressures. The number of registered unemployed rose from 1.46 million in 1929 to 2.95 million in 1932. The Welsh unemployment rate, which was higher than that in England, increased from 13.4 per cent in December 1925 to 27.2 per cent in July 1930, and to a peak of 37.5 per cent in 1932 (with Glamorgan and Monmouthshire having a rate of over 42 per cent); and, despite the recovery of the mid-1930s, was still 22.3 per cent in 1937. As the registered unemployed totally excluded the self-employed, agricultural labourers and most white-collar workers, the actual numbers of people without work was even higher.

Unemployment interacted with poverty to hit living standards. In Newcastle, an investigation into child health and nutrition in 1933 showed that about 36 per cent of working-class children were physically unfit and malnourished. Due to poverty, 33 per cent of the working-class families surveyed could not afford fresh milk.

Throughout the century, mortality rates were correlated with socio-economic indices. Moreover, socio-occupational differentials in mortality widened rather than narrowed. The upper and middle classes benefited more than the working class from a decline in death rates, and the welfare state created in the 1940s did not end this correlation. During the wartime Coalition government, there was planning for a post-war welfare state, notably the 1942 report *Social Insurance and Allied Services* drawn up by officials under the chairmanship of Sir William Beveridge (1879–1963). Bearing the imprint of his radical call for a 'comprehensive policy of social progress', this report advocated a compulsory national insurance scheme designed to provide state-supported security 'from the cradle to the grave', to cover ill-health, unemployment, retirement and family support. Much of this prospectus was based on existing principles, but Beveridge gave them a fresh lease of life and made it appear possible to use comprehensive social planning to overcome the effects of disease, unemployment and poverty. The 1946 National Insurance Act incorporated many of Beveridge's ideas, although he did not envisage the choice for long-term exclusion from the world of work that the ready availability of social welfare was shown to encourage during the boom years of the late 1990s and early 2000s.

In part, class contrasts in mortality rates arose because the social security system offered only minimal standards which were designed to prevent destitution rather than to provide comfort and security. The Black Report of 1980 showed that the working class had not benefited to the same extent from the National Health Service, vaccination programmes and improvements to the housing stock, as the upper and middle classes. Similarly, a British Medical Association report, *Growing Up in Britain* (1999), drew attention to major differences between the classes in infant mortality, accidental injury, chronic illness, height at birth and subsequently, breast-feeding, and diet. Heart attack rates varied greatly, with Glasgow proving a particular black spot.

These differences ensured significant geographical variations, variations that endured across the twentieth century. Thus, a comparison of data for England and Wales from the 1900s with figures from 2001, published in the *British Medical Journal* of 19 September 2009, indicated that, although inequalities in mortality had narrowed, the relationship between poverty and mortality remained strong across the whole of England and Wales, with a marked continuity in areas of mortality and deprivation. In the 1900s, the highest rates of deprivation and mortality were found in urban and industrial areas – notably inner London, South Wales, Liverpool, Manchester, Sheffield, Newcastle, Sunderland and Hull. Low rates were primarily rural, for example most of Northamptonshire. In 2001, the high rates were again concentrated in urban and industrial areas, although they had spread out, especially along the axis from Liverpool to Hull. Some rural areas, however, had become relatively worse off in mortality, as measured by the standardized mortality ratio; for example, much of rural Northumberland. More generally, there was insufficient expenditure by both government and the poor on preventative medicine, such as regular dental and optical check-ups.

The affluent were able to buy or rent better-quality housing, and to live at a lower housing density, than the poor, which lessened their exposure to infectious diseases and also brought psychological benefits. Lower-quality housing could be harder to keep warm and, in particular, dry. Although grants for the installation of basic amenities, such as lavatories, were available from 1959, much housing continued to pose problems for health, a problem exacerbated by the shortage of money for heating. Health was not the sole issue when housing was evaluated. For example, the sales of council houses under the 'Right to Buy' legislation of the Thatcher government's 1980 Housing Act were widespread but skewed. The better housing in the wealthier areas sold, while the public sector increasingly became 'sink housing', rented by those who suffered relative deprivation. In desperation, from the mid-1990s, local authorities increasingly demolished such housing, for example that in west Newcastle.

Health was even more of a problem for the large number of homeless, which rose, particularly in the 1980s. In part, this rise reflected the decline in the availability of low-cost housing, both public and private, for rent, but the closure of mental homes and the lack of care for ex-servicemen were also important. Each also reflected the serious limitations of the social welfare model of public provision.

Health, therefore, could not be separated from social welfare, and in particular the strengths and weaknesses of the welfare state, the system by which the government provides benefits and services, such as health care and pensions, for all members of society. Existing social welfare had proved unequal to the challenge of the Depression of the 1930s, leading, with the Unemployment Act of 1934, to a stronger conviction on the part of the intellectuals and university-educated public servants who were to become influential in the 1940s, that the central government must have an effective social policy.

The establishment of the National Health Service (NHS) in 1948 proved a far more prominent act by the post-war Labour government than the 1946 National Insurance Act. Inspired by egalitarian ideals, and in reaction to the variations and role of payment in inter-war health provision, the NHS was a system for state care. Its creation reflected the serious problems of the 1930s, when most local authorities did not have enough money for the municipal hospitals, while the voluntary hospitals also suffered from the impact of the Depression.

The solution was to integrate the voluntary and public (municipal) hospitals and to spread resources, and the NHS offered a new system through which central government expenditure could be directed and administered. The Second World War had shown that a regional system of health care and management could work, and the NHS provided this with new regional hospital boards under the Ministry of Health. The Minister of Health, Aneurin Bevan, a Welsh miner's son and committed socialist who loudly proclaimed his loathing for Conservatives, played the key role in creating the NHS. The creation of a national health service was Labour's election commitment in 1945, but Bevan, through his own personal pressure, managed to turn this into a commitment to a nation-alized health service, a service he later lauded in his book *In Place of Fear* (1951).

Health care was not only provided free at the point of delivery in hospitals. In addition, the General Practitioner (GP) Service was organized on the basis of a capitation fee paid by the government on behalf of every patient registered with a doctor. The new GP arrangements were an extension of the provisions under the 1911 National Insurance Act. Not all GPs joined the NHS, but the number who retained a private practice was small, and the combined impact of high taxation in the 1940s and the availability of free public treatment was important in limiting private health care, and thus ensuring that Britain took a distinctive health care trajectory, with state provision rather than mixed provision being a central feature.

However, the NHS was flawed from the outset by the classic problems of nationalized entities, including (frequently inconsistent) political intervention, the inflexible national policies that stemmed from centralized state control, funding difficulties in the face of competition for state expenditure, and poor management and labour relations. Moreover, the NHS was harmed by the measures taken to win the consent of interest groups, particularly doctors and dentists, although the British Social Attitudes Survey consistently showed the NHS to be the most popular service of the welfare state.

From the beginning, the NHS suffered from rising expectations of treatment, the greater cost of care that stemmed from an ageing population, and the growing expense of medical treatment. The subsidized availability of drugs under the NHS, with most prescriptions provided free, was both socially progressive and highly expensive, even though the NHS was able to act as a quasi-monopolistic purchaser, and thus to bargain over prices (and wages). The NHS also rapidly encountered problems in dealing with demand for spectacles and dentures, with massive waiting lists reflecting pent-up demand. There was serious political controversy within the Labour government in 1951 over the introduction of charges, with resignations from the government by left-wingers, including Bevan, who saw himself as the government's socialist conscience.

From the 1970s, moreover, there was declining confidence in the ability of the health system to solve problems, at once the product of a general sense of malaise in Britain, of a decline of faith in modernist solutions, and of specific concerns about the NHS. Whereas the jolly 'Doctor' films, beginning with *Doctor in the House* (1954), had presented a benign image of the NHS (albeit one in which doctors and surgeons treated patients like slabs of meat), Britain was seen as a strike-wracked and run-down NHS hospital in Lindsay Anderson's depressing satirical film *Britannia Hospital* (1982).

More generally, histories written prior to the mid-1970s tended to adopt an optimistic note about the expansion of publicly provided social welfare, although, in practice, many of the social problems of the 1930s had eased rather because of post-war economic expansion which greatly reduced unemployment. Moreover, economic growth helped state provision by providing the wealth for higher levels of taxation, which was why, when the economy ceased to grow in the 1970s, many on the right of politics began to argue that Britain could no longer afford a welfare state grounded on universalism, as opposed to means-testing. The percentage of the GDP taken by tax rose from 30 per cent in 1937 to 32 per cent in 1960, but then, in a period largely under Labour government, to 43 per cent by 1980.

The sustainability of this seemed highly unlikely to commentators. In addition, the desirability of targeting resources at the really needy, in order to reduce the escalating welfare bill, of moving from universal provision to 'residualism', also proved a thorny subject for Labour, with some politicians moving in this direction during the Blair and Brown governments (1997–2010).

Government spending on health care rose above the rate of inflation under both the Conservative and Labour Parties, and there was less direct private contribution to individual health care than in France and Germany, let alone the US. Concern about creeping privatization in the NHS led Blair to make electoral capital in 1997 with his pledge to 'Save the NHS' (which was not in fact in danger). Expenditure on the NHS rose under Blair and Brown, and Cameron felt it necessary to promise that it would be safe under him. The NHS was, and is, Western Europe's largest employer.

Such expenditure affected the government funds available for other activities. In particular, spending on health (and other aspects of social welfare) reduced the state's capacity to spend on economic investment, transport infrastructure and military expenditure. To American critics, the last was a key aspect of a more general facet of European politics and society. Ironically, expenditure on health care in Britain in 2007 was only 8.4 per cent of GDP, compared to 16 per cent for the US, and there were 8.2 MRI (magnetic resonance imaging) scanners per million people in Britain compared to 25.9 in the US: it was social welfare that took more in Britain. Yet, despite less spending in Britain, health outcomes were better than in the US.

Improved health care played a role in longer life expectancy and in major changes in the causes of death. Whereas infections and parasitic diseases were a major cause of death for the entire population in the first half of the century, today infections and parasitic diseases generally only kill people who are suffering from associated disorders and who are at the extremes of life. Respiratory diseases have also declined in importance.

Instead, late-onset diseases, especially heart disease and cancers, are now far more important, and help encourage the government role in discouraging smoking and drinking to excess. Cancers were responsible for 25.6 per cent of all deaths in England and Wales in 2001, followed by ischaemic heart diseases (19.9 per cent) and strokes (11 per cent). Death rates from heart disease are among the highest in the world. In September 2009, the European Heart Network reported that, of sixteen European countries, Britain had the sixth highest death rate for coronary heart disease among men under sixty-five and the fourth highest for women under sixty-five. Lifestyle is a major issue, with much of the population clinically overweight or obese, which partly helps explain the high rates of heart disease. Climate may also play a role, notably in higher rates in Scotland, although diet is also cited as a factor there.

Moreover, the British people are literally changing shape, becoming broader and taller and having more fat. Between 1951 and 1999, the average female bust size increased by 2 inches (5 centimetres), while women grew taller by about half an inch (12 millimetres) and heavier by 6.6 lbs (3 kilograms) each decade. Average shoe sizes rose from 4 to 5½ (37 to 38½), and waist sizes from 25½ to 28 inches (65 to 72 centimetres). There were similar changes for men. The cult of exercise had little impact on these trends. Another change linking social trends with health was that of the marked rise in sexually transmitted diseases. Between 1998 and 2007, chlamydia increased by 150 per cent, herpes by 51 per cent and gonorrhoea by 42 per cent.

Class and Economy

Average changes were played out through major social and regional variations, a situation readily seen in the 1930s. An instructive contrast from 1936 was that between the unemployed Jarrow shipworkers who drew attention to their plight with a march on London, and the new Carreras cigarette factory opened at Mornington Crescent in London and employing 2,600 workers. This regional contrast ensured that it continued to be unhelpful to think of a common working- or middle-class experience, and this situation obviously inhibited the development of class consciousness. The gender dimension was also significant.

Social differences had a regional component throughout the period, with ownership of electrical goods, as well as of cars and telephones, and electricity consumption, higher in the south east than in poorer areas, such as South Wales. Whether defined in terms of income or occupation, the middle class were proportionately far more important in London and the south east than in any other region.

The Second World War, however, encouraged an inclusive idea of nationhood resting on shared experience and common purpose. An emphasis on the Home Front made social distinctions seem unacceptable, and the rationing of food, clothes, petrol and much else rested on a theory of equality. Although the extent to which, during the war, the classes mingled, for example in work, should not be exaggerated, such mingling was stressed as a desirable goal and was more extensive than before the war.

The war was followed by a degree of collectivism under the Labour governments of 1945 to 1951. The welfare state built up under Labour was seen as an aspect of the continued process of state control over society and economy, while nationalization of much of the economy consolidated the trend towards national control, planning, products, conditions, pricing and wage settlements. These collectivist aspirations were to be contested, however, not only by political opponents, but also, notably from the 1960s, by the rise of an individualist culture and one in which class categories were affected, indeed undermined, by a new and more vocal interest in youth, gender, and race (see p. 271–3, 276–8).

Nevertheless, class remained an important dynamic, although not the anticipated rise of the working class but, instead, a major expansion of the middle class. In 1900, 75 per cent of the labour force were manual workers; by 1974, 47 per cent and, by 1991, only 36 per cent. In contrast, in 1971, male employment in administrative, professional and other service occupations was below 25 per cent in only three counties in England and Wales: Montgomery, Radnorshire and Carmarthen, all agricultural counties in Wales. The trend in employment reflected the extent to which heavy industries were hit hard by economic change. The expansion of the late 1940s, which led, for example, to the massive and modern Port Talbot steelworks, opened in 1951, was succeeded by closures and massive lay-offs. In Wales, the Ebbw Vale Steelworks closed in 1975–6, the Shotton steelworks following in the 1980s. Moreover, London ceased to be a city in which manufacturing was a central element of the economy.

This de-industrialization was a dramatic change on the situation in the 1850s when Britain was the 'workshop of the world'. As with many other trends covered in this book, this was not one unique to Britain. Instead, there were problems general to heavy industry, coal-based manufacturing and the European economies. Yet Britain fared worse than the other economies of Western Europe, and it was not only heavy industry that was hard hit in Britain. The reasons for industrial problems were much debated among economists but included very poor labour relations, notably in the 1970s, frequently indifferent management, incoherent government policy and a fiscal environment that was not focused on industrial production.

A good example was provided by shipbuilding, in which Britain led the world until 1955 when it was supplanted by Japan. In the late 1940s and early and mid-1950s, British shipyards benefited from rising world demand, but by the 1960s they were losing orders to the lower charges of foreign yards. In addition, the latter were able to promise earlier and more reliable delivery dates, a result of the lack in Britain of modern yards able to offer flow-line production and, therefore, higher productivity. This absence reflected problematic labour relations and a lack of investment, born of short-term attitudes and limited planning for the longer term.

As the market became more competitive from the 1960s, the decline of British competitiveness in this sphere hit hard. Business was lost and shipyards were closed, so that, whereas the UK had delivered 12.4 per cent of the ships that entered service in the world in 1962, by 1971 the percentage was down to 5.1; although, in terms of tonnage, there had been an increase. The Suez Crisis of 1956 exposed a particular problem in British shipbuilding capacity, as it led to a shift towards supertankers, designed to take oil from the Middle East round Africa rather than to go through the Suez Canal, a challenge that British yards, with their limited facilities on narrow rivers such as the Clyde and the Tyne, could not meet.

Britain's merchant marine also declined, with, again, a major implication for the nation's once close relationship with the sea. In 1900, the UK owned about half of the merchant shipping afloat, and in 1914 39.3 per cent. Thereafter, there was a serious decline, to 29.9 per cent in 1930, 26.1 per cent in 1939, and, after the wartime destruction of other merchant navies, a rise to 32.4 per cent in 1948. By 1960, the share was down to 16.3 per cent. This was due not only to the growth in the shipping of other countries, but also to serious problems in the British industry, especially labour disputes, anachronistic working practices, poor management and under-investment: labour problems hit profits, ensuring limited investment, which in turn affected British shipbuilding.

Although Britain's merchant fleet was not to reach its post-war peak until 1975, in 1967 it lost its position as the world's leading shipper to Liberia, which operated as a flag of convenience for the US, helping to provide American-owned shipping with lower taxation and cheaper crews. Merchant shipbuilding was in terminal crisis by the 1970s. As with the car industry, the Labour government of 1964–70 went for larger groupings, rather than the reform of working practices. In 1977, Labour nationalized the industry, which by 1978 was launching only 5.2 per cent of world output. Trading losses and a lack of support from the Conservative government and the European Union compounded the problem, and by 1992 the relevant percentage of world output was 1.2, while most British shipyards had closed.

More generally, the manufacturing base declined, and notably as a source of employment, as the nature of much of the work in it became more skilled, restricting opportunities for the less skilled, and the service sector grew. Average incomes for those in work rose appreciably, ensuring that, whether they thought of themselves as working class – as in the case of John Prescott, Labour's deputy leader from 1994 to 2007 – or not, much of the working population could afford a lifestyle associated with middle-class occupations. Commentators discerned embourgeoisement among Luton car workers from the 1960s. The rise in home ownership, the decline of trade union membership, and the creation of 'New Labour' in the 1990s, with its conscious breach from the trade unions, were all aspects of this change.

The rise in the service sector was linked to a growth in consumerism that reflected the increase in prosperity, but also owed something to a major extension of personal borrowing that was partly a product of technological development, not least in the shape of credit cards and, later, internet purchases. Thanks to the state provision of free or subsidized health care, education, council housing, pensions and unemployment pay, rising real incomes fed through into consumption, although, for many, rising incomes led to expenditure on forms of private welfare, such as private and occupational pensions, school fees, private medicine and, increasingly, private housing. Indeed, the last became a key aspect of expenditure.

Government action was important. Purchase tax on consumer durables was cut from two-thirds to half in 1953, as the Conservatives, who had gained power in 1951, replaced Labour austerity with consumer demand. As a result of a surge in consumption, the number of households owning a washing-machine rose from 25 per cent in 1958 to 50 per cent in 1964 and 88 per cent in 1991, so that going to the laundrette became a minority activity. For cars, ownership by 25 and 50 per cent of households was reached in 1956 and 1965, and for fridges in 1962 and 1968. Thus, for many, the 1960s meant the affluent society in the shape of washing-machines, cars and fridges, rather than pop music and drugs.

The transition to the service economy was true even of traditional centres of heavy industry. In 1901, 15 per cent of the inhabitants of Newcastle were employed in shipbuilding and engineering, but by the late 1970s the largest employers were the City Council, the Department of Health and Social Security, the Area Health Authority, and the university. More generally, social structures and practices were remoulded across Britain with the decline of industry, and traditional assumptions of, and about, class were altered. Both middle- and working-class assumptions about behaviour – their own and that of others, and how it placed people socially and exemplified different values – were challenged. In John Osborne's biting play *Look Back in Anger* (1956), what made the central character, the anti-hero Jimmy Porter, so angry were the limits to social mobility in class-ridden Britain. Despite his university education, Jimmy would never be able to escape his working-class background and, as a result, he chose to run a stall, rather than accept a form of employment which his educational qualifications would allow him to undertake.

Class, however, lost its power to unleash such scathing anger, for to move from the 1950s to the 1960s was to move to the world of *Alfie*, a film character of 1966 (played by Michael Caine) for whom women, clothes and cars were graspable commodities that proved that one could get on in the world without the privileges of birth and education. His determination to enjoy life to the full, and his ability to do so, gave him no time to be angry.

As class-based criteria became less prominent in public discussion and government policy supported home ownership, the core description of the majority of the British by the 1990s was of a capitalist, consumerist, individualist, mobile, predominantly secular and urban, property-owning democrat. Moreover, compared with 1851, or indeed 1931, national broadcasting, state education and employment, nationwide companies, unions, products and pastimes had all brought a measure of convergence in behaviour and attitude. This convergence was seen in the decline of dialect and of distinctive regional differences in practice, for example in cookery. House types and furnishing were more uniform than in most other countries of comparable size.

Yet, there were variations within this society. The decline of the aristocracy robbed the upper class of symbols of differences, and the wealthy professionals who benefited from the expansion of the City of London were able to present themselves as middle class, although some gloried in a 'barrow boy' East End image. Yet, there were still major differences in opportunity within society, and there was also what was increasingly termed in the 1990s the 'underclass'. This was not a new problem, and there were parallels with Victorian ideas of the unsocialized residuum, but there was a striking contrast between general affluence and, on the other hand, the homeless sleeping rough, notably in cardboard settlements, as on London's South Bank, or the poverty and despair of run-down industrial areas.

Social classification was unsettled, with Thatcher claiming in 1987 that there was 'no such thing as Society', while in 1990 John Major talked about a 'classless society'. A lack of clarity both affected political assumptions and created problems for politicians. It was unclear whether the basic distinction was of a broad propertied stratum and a disadvantaged underclass, or whether it was more appropriate to highlight contrasts among the propertied. Differences in disposable wealth were linked to variations in consumption patterns, such as car ownership and tourism. The creation and expression of social distinction through contrasting consumption patterns links this chapter to the discussion in Chapter 8. They also serve as a reminder of the extent to which real social contrasts existed alongside the creation in the 1940s of a war state and a welfare society both based on the idea of national unity.

Education

Education represented a key way in which the nation changed. In part there was a bringing to fruition of earlier plans for changing the educational system in order hopefully to forward the prospect for a new society. The latter theme, indeed, was a significant one throughout the period. Thus, the close of the First World War had seen not only the introduction of universal male suffrage, votes for women, and a government subsidy for council house building, but also a major reform of the education system. The 1918 'Fisher' Education Act raised the school leaving age from twelve to fourteen and planned a further rise to fifteen. It was assumed that at fourteen most people would enter the workforce, but attend 'continuation schools' once weekly until sixteen. Government subsidies to local education authorities were increased.

This, however, was not a comprehensive change, and in that it reflected the extent to which state-directed change in a democracy, with its habit of ensuring powerful safeguards for other interests, did not equate to the totalitarian changes seen for example in the Soviet Union. The Fisher Education Act did not include the numerous Church or independent schools, let alone the universities. Moreover, the Act did not change the curriculum, and that reflected the conservatism of much of British public culture and ideology and, in particular, a reluctance to discard past methods in favour of new possibilities. Thus, the new Act offered little scope for science, technology and modern languages.

Furthermore, the implementation of the Act was partial, again a characteristic of much government (and not only in Britain), with implementation generally not matching up with legislative decision or administrative dictat. Local authorities, which enjoyed considerable independence, frequently acted slowly, employers did not wish to pay for workers to go to continuation schools, the 'Geddes Axe' of 1922 ended these schools, and the increase of the leaving age to fifteen was postponed indefinitely. An attempt to reach this limit was made under the second Labour government (1929–31), but was blocked in the Conservative-dominated House of Lords. In 1936, the age was raised to fifteen with effect from 1 September 1939, but with the outbreak of the Second World War this was further postponed.

As with much else, the Second World War led to plans for post-war social renewal that reflected both concern about pre-war conditions, wartime aspirations for a better society and the belief that state provision was best. The crucial measure for education was the 'Butler' Education Act of 1944, drawn up by the liberal Conservative R.A. (Richard Austen) Butler (1902–82), who was Minister of Education and whose legislation brought proposals to fruition during the war, unlike the Beveridge Report. With its statement that pupils should receive an education relevant to their 'age, abilities and aptitudes', the

Act of 1944 had a clear social agenda. The minimum school leaving age was raised to fifteen from 1947, and fees in state-supported secondary schools were abolished. Legislation in 1947 extended the provisions to Scotland and Northern Ireland. The abolition of fee-paying in grammar schools would, it was hoped, encourage the entry of children from poorer families as entry into schools was to be on the basis of the eleven-plus examination. The Education Act obliged every local education authority to prepare a development plan for educational provision and the Ministry of Education imposed new minimum standards in matters such as school accommodation and size. This division was typical of the trend in relations between central and local government from the mid-nineteenth century: one in which the autonomy of the latter was gravely, and increasingly, limited. This trend gathered pace from the 1940s, in part due to the war, but was also due to the assumptions of the post-war Labour government.

The Act did not prescribe the types of secondary school. That came in subsequent guidance to local authorities and reflected the recommendations of the Norwood Report of 1943, which claimed that there were three kinds of minds: abstract, mechanical and concrete. This led to a tripartite structure of secondary schools: the grammar, secondary modern and secondary technical. In the event, successful pupils at the eleven-plus went to the grammar schools; the next tranche to secondary technical schools, very few of which were built; and the 75 per cent who failed, to secondary modern schools, which drew heavily on working-class pupils.

To some critics, this system was unfair and socially discriminating, and criticism increased from about 1950: already in 1945–7 Ellen Wilkinson, the Labour Minister of Education, had fought strongly for the comprehensive principle, with individual schools incorporating all pupils in their catchment area. Although popularly acclaimed in 1944, the Butler Education Act was academically reviled by 1956. Moreover, there was rising social disquiet because, although most grammar school pupils continued to come from the middle class, the grammar school system did not satisfy enough of them. In part, this reflected the inability of the grammar schools to expand to cope with the post-war baby boom, and, on a longer time scale, the problems posed by wide variation in grammar school provision across England and Wales.

The comprehensive model was tested in the late 1940s and the first purpose-built comprehensive school, Kidbrooke, in south-east London, opened in 1954. Two years later, Anthony Crosland, an able and determined theorist of the left, published, in his *Future of Socialism*, a call for egalitarianism through comprehensive education. He vowed to close every grammar school, and, when he became the Minister of State for Education in Harold Wilson's Labour government, he set comprehensivization in process with Circular 10/65 of 12 July 1965. This obliged local education authorities to draw up plans for replacing the tripartite system. In education, Labour's re-election in 1966 was crucial, for by the time the Conservatives returned to power in 1970 much of the old system had been destroyed. Margaret Thatcher (1925–), as Secretary of State for Education, replaced the Crosland Circular, but a large number of comprehensive school approvals came during her period as Secretary of State and the number of pupils in comprehensives rose through the 1970s, so that the system became the norm.

The school leaving age was raised to sixteen in 1972, but many pupils continued to leave school without the necessary literacy and numeracy to make them readily employable. Moreover, despite their deficiencies, grammar schools may have achieved greater social mobility than comprehensives, an issue that contributed to the ideological battleground over education. There were also serious problems with education from the economic point of view. Technical skills among school-leavers remained deficient, in part because of the perceived superiority of academic over vocational education. The situation in Germany, Japan and China was very different, and this difference can be linked to their greater economic growth. The bulk of the British workforce certainly did not measure up to their Continental, East Asian and American counterparts in many respects, and this contrast owed something to educational factors. It has been argued both that too much emphasis was placed on equality and social opportunity and too little on raising educational standards, and also, from a different direction, that there was too great an emphasis on education, rather than training in skills. These views were aired extensively from the 1980s, but it was unclear how best to remedy the problem, and the granting of university status to the polytechnics as a result of the Education Act of 1992 made the situation more problematic at the level of higher education.

Both political parties sought to address the problem at the school level. Distrustful of local government, the Conservatives attempted, with the 'Baker' Education Act of 1988, to raise standards by creating a national curriculum. Established practices in teacher training, school government, and educational supervision were all replaced, but it proved difficult to use the educational system to address more widespread social issues affecting educational aspiration and performance. These included widespread poverty, poor housing and low expectations.

All remained serious issues affecting the health and education of much of the population. Tony Blair came to power in 1997 emphasizing his commitment to 'education, education, education', but was also unable to do much to improve the situation. In practice, the national straitjacket of control was measured in terms of more exams and a greater role for national standards, the results of which were presented in school league tables, but education failed to deliver the 'outcomes' anticipated by the government.

Conclusions
This failure contributed to the sense of national malaise, not least to a mismatch between claims and reality that hit the

Labour government hard. It could press buttons, as when ASBOs (anti-social behaviour orders) were introduced to try to control bad behaviour, but could not seem to affect public attitudes or conduct. Thus, the Conservative opposition referred in the late 2000s to a 'broken society', one of people excluded from the benefits of economic activity, let alone growth.

Indeed, in 2009, when, at a time of high unemployment, an unprecedented 477,000 people enrolled in university, there was no adult working in 16.9 per cent of working-age households, a percentage that reflected a lack of ability, opportunity and drive, as well as the social benefits system, notably the 'welfare trap' discouraging the unemployed from seeking work. This high percentage contributed to a reality and sense of poverty, and notably the psychological poverty seen in families in which more than one generation had no or little experience of work. This situation, and the anxieties it gave rise to, contributed to opinion polls that indicated that, although the British lived longer, many were dissatisfied with the nature of British society and fearful of the future. Polls also indicate that many are fearful, for example on 'sink' housing estates where ASBOs have failed in practical terms to curb or control anti-social behaviour, especially among young people.

Meanwhile, the unprecedented rate of large-scale immigration constituted an experiment with the very nature of the people. In 1997–2007, the total net inflow of foreign citizens was 3 million strong, about 5 per cent of the population, a figure that excluded illegal immigrants, who possibly comprised another 600,000 people. The resulting pressure on housing and infrastructure is relatively apparent, and there is also the central question of the consequences of clashing values in an increasingly heterogeneous society.

7
EMPIRE TO EUROPE

The transition from world's leading empire to a member of the European Union was one of the most significant of the period, and one that captured the decline in Britain's role and reputation in the world. This decline continues to attract attention elsewhere, and not least because the former empire comprises much of the world. It was not apparent at first, and indeed Britain played a key role in the Second World War, but by 1965 the empire was largely gone, and the context of British power was transformed as a consequence.

The Empire of the 1930s
The empire was still a reality in the 1930s, even though there was Arab violence in Palestine in 1936–9, as well as resistance in Waziristan on the 'North-West Frontier' of India (now the border between Pakistan and Afghanistan), and pressure for independence from the non-violent Indian National Congress. These were serious problems, but containable ones, not least due to the military resources provided by the empire,

especially the Indian Army, the largest volunteer army in history. Instead, British military resources were put under mounting pressure from outside the empire, from the need to consider German rearmament, Japanese aggrandizement and Italian ambitions, and from the constraints created by domestic financial problems.

Alongside tensions within the empire, disparate elements also interacted to create a sense of imperial partnership, camaraderie, even nationalism. New air routes linked the empire to Britain, while Imperial Trade Preference, introduced in 1932 as part of the new protectionist regime, helped ensure that trade within the empire held up better than that with other countries. Imperial protectionism benefited from the lack of energy in the long-established Free Trade arguments at a time of heightened international protectionism during the Depression, although an over-reliance on easy and guaranteed imperial markets helped dull the competitive edge of British business, a predicament underlined subsequently when such trade became less important to the economy. Commitment to the empire in the 1930s was demonstrated, in different forms, by the major and expensive new naval base for the defence of the Far East built at Singapore, and by the majestic buildings designed for the official quarter in New Delhi.

Empire was also important in British consciousness. The demand for empire was seen in inter-war films such as *The Drum* (1938) and *The Four Feathers* (1939). Based on A.E.W. Mason's (1865–1948) novel of 1902, the latter was a presentation of imperial endeavour in Sudan as a definition of manliness and heroism. Now, instead, there is a pervasive anti-imperial liberalism that excludes earlier narratives of national glory, presenting them as anachronistic. Yet, on Empire Day in the 1930s, schools staged pageants and displays, souvenirs were issued, and large parades were held in Hyde Park. The *Daily Express* launched an 'Empire Crusade' and legislation sought to give substance to imperial interests. The Government of India Act of 1935 moved India towards self-government, but was designed to ensure British retention of the substance of power.

The strength of the empire in the 1930s puts into perspective the later sense that its collapse was inevitable, and the same point can be made for the imperial hub, Britain. In comparison with the weaknesses and collapse of democracy over much of Continental Europe in the 1930s, the success of the National Government was a triumph, and one that was important to national survival in the Second World War. In opposition to the Communists and to Sir Oswald Mosley's British Union of Fascists (established in 1932), which he presented as un-British, Stanley Baldwin, the dominant figure in the National Government from 1931 to 1937 and Prime Minister from 1935 to 1937, stressed national identity, continuity, distinctiveness and solid common sense. Baldwin did so not in order to embrace political reaction, but rather to use images to lessen tensions arising from economic change, particularly rivalry between capital and labour. He was photographed with pigs and five-bar gates, helping to underline an identification with an image of rural values.

More valuably, alongside the serious hardships of the 1930s, with 2.2 million people still unemployed in 1938, there was also much prosperity. GNP (Gross National Product) in 1934 returned to its 1929 figure, the economy recovered more than the economies of France and the US, about 2.6 million jobs were created in 1933–8, real wages rose, and prices fell. This improvement helped explain the National Government's over-whelming victory in the general election of 1935, its ability to act as a force for stability, and Britain's success in holding political extremism at bay. Thanks in part to the absence of any system of proportional representation, the British Union of Fascists did not win council seats in elections. In addition, Mosley failed to contest the general election in 1935; his earlier New Party had been unsuccessful in 1931.

The success in overcoming extremism was underpinned by the optimistic emphasis on social cohesion and patriotism offered by films and news reels. Lord Rothermere's influential *Daily Mail* backed Mosley in 1934, but dropped him as he resorted to violence and increasingly strident anti-Semitism. Conservatism was not just a matter of politics. D.C. Thomson and Mills & Boon, two of the most successful publishers of popular fiction, actively disseminated conservative social and moral standards: sexual energy was restrained, while radicalism, social strain and moral questioning were ignored.

Approach to War

This was the idea of nation and empire that played the key role in resisting Hitler's Germany in 1940–1 after the conquest of France in May–June 1940 left Germany dominant in Western Europe. In the 1930s, Britain had not been prepared for sustained and extensive Continental warfare. Its society was patriotic and, at times, jingoistic, but it was not militaristic. Unlike in much of the Continent, there were few men in military uniforms on the streets, no peacetime conscription and only a relatively small standing army. Moreover, both the Treasury and most domestic opinion were against an arms build-up and rearmament was not pressed hard until 1938.

The Labour opposition was also for long unsure about how best to respond to Hitler. Due to a strong pacifist component, Labour was divided over rearmament, and in the 1935 election Labour politicians denounced warmongering. Yet, when it became clear that Hitler was not going to stop expanding beyond Germany's 1919 treaty frontiers, the Labour leadership pressed for a firmer British response and for rearmament, as did a number of Conservatives not in office, most prominently Winston Churchill.

German rearmament, publicly announced in 1935, made the situation in Europe more menacing. German expansionism indeed placed the spotlight on Anglo-French preparedness. In 1938, in the Munich Crisis, Hitler successfully intimidated Britain and France over the future of Czechoslovakia, leading to the Munich Agreement, which proved the centrepiece of the

British attempt to secure a negotiated settlement to satisfy German ambitions, but at the cost of major territorial losses by Czechoslovakia that lessened its ability to resist Germany.

The British service chiefs urged caution on the government, which anyway did not want to fight. Conscious of numerous global commitments, they warned about the dangers of becoming entangled in major military action on the Continent. There was particular concern about the likely impact of German bombing of civilian targets. The major impact on public morale of German raids on London in the First World War seemed a menacing augury. Anglo-French fears of war with Germany may have been excessive in 1938, given the weaknesses of the Nazi regime, including a lack of enthusiasm among German military leaders, but this is unclear, and, anyway, there was a well-founded fear of causing a second 'Great War'. Furthermore, the military was poorly configured for war with Germany. As the Deputy Chief of the Imperial General Staff noted in May 1939,

> ... under the plan approved in April 1938, the Field Force was to be organized primarily with a view to reinforcing the Middle East. The crisis in September 1938 ... focused sharply the fact that, even when the programme was complete, our forces would be inadequate for a major Continental war.

Delay in fighting Germany at least permitted investment in improved military effectiveness, as well as strengthening the moral case that Britain had tried every avenue to avoid war. In response to the threat from German bombers, attention was switched from building up a bomber force to fighter defence, with the development of the Hawker Hurricane and the Supermarine Spitfire. These aeroplanes, which were the product of a key capability in British industry, reflected the transition of fighters from wooden-based biplanes to all-metal cantilever-wing monoplanes with high-performance engines

capable of far greater speeds, range and armament. Alongside
early-warning radar, a major achievement of applied industry,
they were to be key to resisting successfully the air assault that
Germany launched in 1940.

In opposing the Munich Agreement, Churchill told the
Commons on 5 October 1938 that 'maintenance of peace
depends upon the accumulation of deterrents against the
aggressor, coupled with a sincere effort to redress grievances'.
The build-up of British forces did not provide a deterrent to
further German action, but it was to help strengthen Britain's
defences. However, although Britain was allied to France in
seeking to deter Hitler, the Soviet Union was willing to coop-
erate with Germany in 1939, while the US was not interested in
action. As the US was the world's leading industrial power, this
gravely weakened the possible response to Fascist aggression.
Indeed, the lack of Anglo-American cooperation in the 1930s
was a major feature in international relations, and one that
affected Britain's options.

The occupation of the remainder of Czechoslovakia in
March 1939 starkly demonstrated Hitler's failure to stick to the
Munich Agreement and led the government, since 1937 under
Neville Chamberlain, to join France in guaranteeing Poland
and Romania against attack. As a result, the German invasion
of Poland, in turn, led Britain and France to declare war on
3 September 1939. Parliament and public opinion now saw
conflict with an untrustworthy Nazi Germany as inevitable.
Churchill, who had been a harsh critic of the appeasement of
Germany, especially the Munich Agreement, told the House of
Commons that day:

This is not a question of fighting for Danzig [Gdansk] or
fighting for Poland. We are fighting to save the whole world
from the pestilence of Nazi tyranny and in defence of all that
is most sacred to man. This is no war for domination or
imperial aggrandizement or material gain; no war to shut
any country out of its sunlight and means of progress. It is a

war, viewed in its inherent quality, to establish on impregnable rocks, the rights of the individual, and it is a war to establish and revive the stature of man.

The Second World War, 1939–45

Once war had broken out, however, the Anglo-French forces were unable to provide any assistance to Poland, not least by attacking German forces on the French frontier. The British forces sent to France in 1939 were small, short of equipment, particularly tanks, transport, artillery, small arms and ammunition, and poorly trained for conflict with the Germans. Churchill, who had become First Lord of the Admiralty with the outbreak of war, advocated the dispatch of a fleet to the Baltic specially prepared to resist air attack, but this rash idea was thwarted by his naval advisers.

Despite the rapid fall of Poland in 1939 and Hitler's subsequent call for negotiations, Britain and France were determined to fight on in order to prevent German hegemony. They were correctly distrustful of Hitler, wrongly sceptical about Germany's ability to sustain a long war, and confident that, as in the First World War, the Allied forces in France would be able to resist attack. In practice, military activity on the Western Front in what was the particularly bitter winter of 1939–40 was very limited, leading to its description as the 'Phoney War'. The Anglo-French forces failed to respond to German success in Poland with altered training regimes. Instead, training was conventional, and there was little preparation for mobile tank warfare, although more than was subsequently alleged. The British Expeditionary Force, and the Allies generally, were not lacking equipment compared to the Germans, nor was the equipment really inferior; instead, it was a matter of operational vision, and command and control in the mobile battle that were deficient. Conscription, introduced in Britain in 1939, produced a large army, but, once the Germans attacked, neither the troops nor the officers proved able to respond adequately to the pace and character of the German attack.

Chamberlain's hope that a limited conflict, including the naval blockade of Germany, would lead Hitler to negotiate, or would result in his overthrow, rapidly proved abortive. Germany conquered Denmark, Norway, the Netherlands, Belgium and France in early 1940. In Norway, the hastily thrown together British force suffered from inadequate training and equipment and a lack of air cover and appropriate artillery. The Germans proved better able to seize and maintain the initiative.

In the France campaign, the Allies were also outfought. The British were tied to French strategy and this bears much of the blame for failure, but the British also suffered from particular deficiencies, including poor training and command. The British were driven from the Continent, although much of the Army was successfully evacuated from the beaches near Dunkirk on 27 May to 4 June: the Navy evacuated most of the troops, but private boats also took off an important number, and this provided an important image of national resolve and unity.

Britain, nevertheless, appeared to have lost the war. Defeat in Norway had helped discredit the leadership of Chamberlain, who had already been affected by disquiet over the energy and style of his war leadership. The need to bring Labour into the ministry and the unwillingness of the Labour leadership to serve under Chamberlain contributed to the change of government, and Churchill's reputation as a resolute opponent of Hitler helped ensure he became Prime Minister. A National Government under Churchill was formed on 10 May 1940 with a Cabinet including Conservative, Labour and Liberal members. Clement Attlee (1883–1967), the Labour leader, became Churchill's deputy. However, in the aftermath of the fall of France, a defeat far greater than anything suffered in the First World War, several leading politicians felt it necessary to consider a negotiated peace. These included the Foreign Secretary, Halifax (1881–1959), who had come close to succeeding Chamberlain. Moreover, David Lloyd George thought he might be able to succeed Churchill and settle with Hitler.

Churchill, however, refused to trust Hitler and was determined to fight on with the backing of Labour and many backbench Conservative MPs. He successfully outmanoeuvred his rivals in the government, but the military situation was still parlous. Late 1940 and early 1941 was the nadir of Britain's twentieth century. Isolated, apart from the crucial support of the empire, and effectively bankrupt, it suffered further defeats, notably with the fall of Greece to Germany in April 1941.

Yet Operation Sealion, the planned German invasion of southern England, had been called off, after the German air force failed, in the Battle of Britain in July–September 1940, to gain air superiority over southern England, the English Channel and the invasion beaches. The strength of the British Navy made German air superiority crucial. In the event, British fighting quality, command decisions, growing numbers of fighter aeroplanes and radar, led to the outfighting of the Germans. Initial German attacks on the RAF (Royal Air Force) and its airfields, in what was an air superiority campaign, designed to force the British to commit their fighters and then to destroy them, inflicted heavy losses on the British, especially on pilot numbers. By early September, Fighter Command, under remorseless pressure from larger forces, seemed close to defeat.

However, fighting over Britain, the RAF benefited from the support provided by the ground control organization and could more often recover any pilots who survived being shot down. Furthermore, RAF fighting quality, which had been underestimated by the German planners, was seen in the heavy losses inflicted on the Germans, and the Germans did not appreciate the extent to which the RAF was under pressure. Yet, although success in the Battle of Britain was crucial, it was a victory only in that it denied Germany triumph. There was still no sign that Britain was strong enough to challenge German control of the Continent, a situation that encouraged the traditional British recourse to a strategy based on maritime control and on diversionary attacks in secondary theatres, which was to mean in 1940–1 the Mediterranean and East Africa.

German pressure on Britain increased, however, in the winter of 1940/41. The 'Blitz' – the bombing of Britain that began in September 1940 and lasted until May 1941, with later less intensive but still serious revivals – was very damaging, and made it clear how far Britain had been pushed back on to the defensive. The German decision to bomb London and other cities was designed to put the *Luftwaffe* (German air force) centre stage by bombing Britain into submission. Cities such as Coventry, London and Southampton were devastated, although fatalities were fewer than had been feared before the war, when large numbers of cardboard coffins had been prepared and there was widespread preparation for airborne gas attacks that were never mounted. Nor was industrial production badly hit by air attack.

German indiscriminate bombing, intended to destroy civilian morale, failed in its purpose, and, indeed, the experience of 1940 helped fashion a renewed patriotism, not least because it proved easier to support the war when there seemed no alternative and when Britain was unencumbered by allies whose policies led to criticism. German air attacks served to demonstrate the morality of the struggle against Hitler, as well as encouraging the sense that everyone, irrespective of their background, was under attack and 'taking it'. This had a considerable effect, both at the time and for post-war Britain. As Churchill told the Commons on 21 November 1940, 'The War Damage (Compensation) Bill … will give effect to the feeling that there must be equality of risk and equality of treatment in respect of the damage done by fire of the enemy.'

Unsurprisingly, there is some evidence that spirits were lower than has been popularly thought. In Southampton, there was low morale and the mayor and civic leaders slept outside the town to avoid bombing, while ordinary citizens could seek the same only by sleeping on the common in summer. After a government report, the mayor resigned in disgrace. Yet, this response was unusual. On the whole, morale remained high, and fortitude in the face of the attack became a key aspect of national identity. In particular, there was no panic in heavily bombed London, and the docks continued working.

Attempts to shelter from the bombing led some Londoners to seek refuge in the Underground system. Although initially banned from doing so, as the system was still running, citizens crowded into Tube tunnels, providing images for artists such as Henry Moore (1898–1986).

The devastation in London and in other heavily bombed cities, such as Exeter, Liverpool and Plymouth, was one of the most important long-term consequences of the bombing. About 115,000 houses in London were destroyed, while 288,000 required major repairs. The damage to the built environment was accentuated by post-war reconstruction, much of which was of poor quality; although allowance has to be made for the cost of reconstruction, the massive need for new housing, and the extent of other burdens on the national finances.

Britain was also under pressure by sea. U-boat (submarine) attacks on British trade routes, especially the crucial supply route from North America, threatened the economy and food supplies. In the 'Dig for Victory' campaign people were urged to grow their own food. The fall of France had increased British vulnerability, as German submarines could now be based on the west coast of France, as had not been the case in the First World War.

The Germans also challenged Britain's position in north Africa. Italy under its Fascist dictator, Benito Mussolini (1883–1945), had entered the war as an ally of Germany in June 1940, and Mussolini launched attacks on British positions in East Africa and Egypt. These were swiftly checked and the Italian armies in their neighbouring colonies of Ethiopia and Libya were heavily defeated in December 1940 to early 1941. However, the Germans sent a force that in April 1941 drove the British back into Egypt. The Germans also defeated the

British in Greece. The tempo of the German advance, especially its rapid use of airborne troops and armour, brought a decisive advantage, as did the effective use of ground support artillery. Churchill, who had backed the expedition to Greece in order to show that Britain was supporting all opposition to the Axis, swiftly recognized this as an error. Defeat in mainland Greece was followed by the successful German invasion of Crete.

The empire played a key role in the war in Africa and the Middle East. Australian and New Zealand units took a major part, while Canadian forces were significant to the strategic reserve in Britain. Moreover, the degree to which most of the non-white empire was loyal was an important indication of imperial solidarity. Indian and African forces proved crucial in the defeat of the Italians in east and north Africa, as well as in the conquest in 1941 of Iraq, which was seen as a potential German ally. If nineteenth-century imperialism lacked a clear moral basis, the empire demonstrated one in 1940–1 by giving Britain the ability to fight on. This role, however, has been underplayed in subsequent attempts to provide a sense of common history that could include immigrants from the Commonwealth.

There were also signs of American support for Britain, valuable signs in light of the strength of isolationism there: indeed, the US had earlier followed policies towards German expansion that were as bad as those of the appeasers. In September 1940, as an important gesture to Britain, the US provided fifty surplus destroyers (seven of them to the Canadian navy) in return for ninety-nine-year leases on bases in Antigua, the Bahamas, Bermuda, British Guiana (now Guyana), Jamaica, Newfoundland, St Lucia and Trinidad. In practice, the deal was of limited value to Britain, as the ships took time to prepare, but, aside from the psychological value at a time when Britain was vulnerable, no other power was in a position to provide such help.

Moreover, thanks to the passage by Congress of the Lend-Lease Act in March 1941, the President, Franklin Delano

Roosevelt (1882–1945), was granted a total of $7 billion for military *matériel* that he could sell, lend or trade to any state vital to American security. This opened the way for the shipping of American military supplies to Britain. That July, furthermore, American forces replaced the British in Iceland, keeping it out of German hands. The Americans also took a role in protecting convoys in the western Atlantic from submarine attack.

Despite American support for Britain, Hitler mistakenly hoped that the British people would realize their plight, over-throw Churchill, and make peace. In the event, in the face of British obduracy, Hitler was reduced to trying to link his policies by believing that the defeat of the Soviet Union on which he focused in 1941 would make Britain ready to settle and to accept German dominance of Europe.

In the meantime, the British were unable to mount a serious challenge to the German position in Europe, and were obliged to continue a reliance on a peripheral strategy, hoping that blockade, air attack and sponsoring resistance in occupied Europe would weaken the Germans. This approach made the best of the current situation, but it did not promise much, and, ultimately, Churchill depended on something turning up, notably in the form of American intervention. It did, but it is interesting to consider what would have happened had the war not expanded in that fashion.

The total change in the situation in 1941 owed little to Britain. Hitler's attack on the Soviet Union, Operation Barbarossa, launched on 22 June, and his declaration of war on the US, following his ally Japan's attack on its base at Pearl Harbor (and on British and Dutch colonies) on 7 December 1941, were what led to the total defeat of Germany and Japan in 1945. Ultimately, this widening of the war was to be decisive in Allied victory, but, in late 1941 and 1942, German and Japanese advances were still very serious. The Germans made major gains at the expense of the Soviet Union. The British rapidly lost Hong Kong, Malaya and Burma to the Japanese, and the surrender of Singapore on 15 February 1942, with

62,000 troops, was a major blow. The British had been outfought by a smaller Japanese army in the Malaya campaign, and the surrender shattered British prestige in Asia: it was later described by Churchill as the 'greatest disaster in British military history', and the defeat badly strained relations between Britain and Australia, already troubled by competing priorities over the use of imperial forces.

A general problem of excessive commitments hit the British hard. The Germans under Rommel pushed into Egypt, leading to criticism of the British Army and of Churchill's war leadership. The fall of Tobruk and its large garrison on 20 June led to a parliamentary vote of confidence on 2 July 1942, which Churchill won by 476 to 25 votes, but there was considerable uneasiness about the management of the war alongside the enormous public respect for Churchill.

Moreover, German submarine attacks continued to inflict heavy losses in the Atlantic. By then, Britain's role in the war was very much as part of an (unstable) alliance, with the Soviet Union the major opponent of Germany, in terms of German forces engaged, and the US that of Japan. Relations with the Soviet Union were characterized by mutual suspicion, with Churchill rightly concerned about Soviet intentions in Eastern Europe. There were also tensions over strategy and goals in the Anglo-American relationship, not least Churchill's opposition to Roosevelt's anti-imperialism and to his hostility to Imperial Trade Preference. Nevertheless, the relationship was pivotal to the successful prosecution of the war.

Hitler's declaration of war on the US let Roosevelt off the geopolitical hook, since he agreed with Churchill that Hitler was a greater menace than the Japanese, although not all of American opinion shared this view. The declaration led to the 'Germany-First' strategy, which was to see the bulk of American land and air assets allocated to preparing for the invasion of Europe. Roosevelt supported this emphasis because of his concern that Britain might otherwise collapse in the face of German pressure.

After American entry into the war, the British continued to play the leading role on certain fronts: against Germany in Egypt and against Japan in Burma (and, later, providing much of the manpower for the war with Germany in Italy and France); while also being crucial to the air and sea wars against Germany. The sea war, which focused on anti-submarine operations in the Atlantic, was scarcely a peripheral struggle, as it was central to the eventual ability to build up British and American forces in Britain in preparation for an invasion of German-held France. In addition, the British conquest of Iraq, Lebanon and Syria in May–July 1941, the Anglo-Soviet occupation of Persia (Iran) from August 1941, and the British conquest of Madagascar in May–November 1942, all ensured that the worlds of German and Japanese expansion would be kept well apart, and that the Allied world would not be fractured. The Allies were able to pursue a global strategy but their opponents could not.

The Germans and Japanese advances were eventually held in 1942, including by the British in Egypt and on the India–Burma border respectively; and serious defeats were inflicted. The Americans beat the Japanese at Midway in the Pacific, the British defeated the Germans at El Alamein in Egypt, and the Soviets forced a German army to surrender at Stalingrad in early 1943.

Germany and Japan were driven back in 1943, with the Germans defeated at Kursk by Soviet forces and cleared from north Africa by Anglo-American forces which pressed on to invade Italy. The Battle of the Atlantic against German submarines was won in early 1943. The wartime peak of tonnage sunk by the Germans was reached in November 1942, but in 1943 success was won by the Allies with improved resources, tactics and strategy, including more effective anti-submarine air tactics and the extension of air cover over the Atlantic thanks to the use of long-range planes and the establishment of a base on the Azores. Moreover, the failure of the U-boat offensive was clarified by the massive scale of

American shipbuilding which made it possible to cope with losses.

France was invaded with the D-Day landings on 6 June 1944. The British, Canadian and American forces benefited from absolute air and sea superiority and from a successful deception exercise, which ensured that the landings in Normandy were a surprise to the Germans. It proved difficult to break out of Normandy but, greatly helped by air power, the Allies finally succeeded in doing so at the close of July. This victory was followed by the speedy liberation of France and Belgium, before the Germans successfully stopped the Allied advance in late 1944, notably by defeating a British airborne force at Arnhem.

Meanwhile, the Soviets advanced across Eastern Europe, and the Americans 'island hopped' towards Japan. In 1945, Germany was invaded from west and east, Anglo-American forces crossing the Rhine in March and reaching the Elbe in April. Hitler committed suicide on 30 April as the Soviets fought their way through Berlin, and Germany was forced to surrender unconditionally on 7 May. If the Soviets played the key role on land against the Germans from June 1941, the British, too, played an important part, particularly at sea and in the air. Japan was driven to surrender on 14 August 1945 by the American use of atomic bombs, but the Japanese had already been outfought on land: by the British in Burma as well as by the Americans in the Philippines and by the Soviets in Manchuria.

The empire continued to play a major role until the war's end. By 1942, 500 Canadian warships were in commission. Canadian troops played a major part in European operations in 1944–5, and Canada at the close of the conflict had the world's third largest navy and the fourth largest air force. It also provided Britain with crucial financial support, and on more generous terms than the US.

The war had underlined Britain's vulnerability. The preservation of national independence had traditionally required a strong fleet, but insistent German aeroplane attacks from 1940, and, with the coming of the V-1, missiles revealed that command of the sea could no longer protect Britain from bombardment, even if it could still thwart or inhibit invasion. Although the Germans did not develop a long-distance heavy bomber force, their bombers could attack Britain from bases in north-western Europe, while the V-2 rockets, which could travel at up to 3,000 mph (4,828 kph), could be fired from a considerable distance. The Germans also bombarded Dover with long-range guns from the other side of the Channel. The defensive perimeter of the country was thus extended.

Over 60,000 civilians were killed in air and missile attack, nearly half of them in London. The strain was heavy. Swansea was bombed forty-four times in 1940–3, with 1,238 people killed or wounded, over 7,000 made homeless, and the town centre destroyed. In 1942, three of the twelve houses in the Exeter street in which I live were destroyed, as was much of the city centre.

In response to the air attacks, there were large-scale evacuations of children. Indeed, these evacuations were the biggest state-directed movement of civilians in British history. At the start of the war, 690,000 children were evacuated from London alone. There were problems with homesickness and with parents missing children, while evacuation revealed the gap between the life experiences of inner-city children and those of rural Britain.

Wartime disruption hit family life and affected social behaviour. Notably, there was more freedom for women because far more were employed while there was a general absence of partners, as well as more flexible attitudes to sexual behaviour. Despite the wartime problems, the black market encouraged by shortages and rationing, and a surprisingly troubling level of labour disputes and strikes, especially among the miners, there was a high degree of acceptance of the need for sacrifice, and morale and popular resolve were strong.

The midwife of change, war boosted the role of the state and the machinery of government. It was necessary to produce formidable amounts of equipment, to raise, train, clothe and equip large numbers of men, to fill their place in the workforce, and to increase the scale and productivity of the economy. The experience of state intervention in the First World War ensured that it was more effective in the Second. The Emergency Powers (Defence) Act, rapidly passed on 22 May 1940, gave the government power to order anyone to perform any action, the power being exercised through defence regulations. Censorship was imposed and the general election due for 1940 postponed. The Churchill government greatly expanded the hitherto limited mobilization of national resources, which was necessary because the war savaged the economy. Free trade and hitherto largely unregulated industrial production were both brought under direction; and consumption and the manufacture of consumer goods were successfully cut in order to free labour and other resources for wartime goals. Indeed, despite war damage, production of war *matériel* rose, that of aircraft from 7,940 in 1939 to 26,461 in 1944.

Conscription was introduced more rapidly than in the First World War: of men in 1939 and of women in 1942. The size of the armed forces rose to 4.7 million men and 437,000 women by 1945. At its peak, 1.79 million people served in the Home Guard and many joined other voluntary organizations such as the Royal Observer Corps. Many young women served in the Land Army.

Moreover, government regulation became ubiquitous and the number of non-industrial civil servants rose from 400,000 in 1939 to 722,000 in 1944. Food rationing began in January 1940, and the Ministry of Food encouraged consumption patterns and recipes that would make the best use of scarce foodstuffs; whale meat was one recommended dish. Clothes rationing followed in 1941, and indeed the combination of the Depression followed by the war created a generation focused on thrift. All areas of life were regulated. For example, the hospital sector was reorganized under the Emergency Medical Service.

New ministries were created in 1939 for economic warfare, food, home security, information, shipping and supply. Later additions included aircraft production (1940), fuel and power (1942) and production (1942). These creations were aspects of an impressive and generally effective administrative machinery. There were still serious problems. National wage negotiating machinery was established in the coal industry, and a National Coal Board was created to supervise production, but these measures did not prevent a serious miners' strike in early 1944. Indeed, 55.7 per cent of the days lost to strikes in the war occurred in the coal industry. Government expenditure and taxation rose markedly.

What the post-war world would bring was unclear. Imperial power was still a major theme. In April 1944, the Admiralty discussed plans for a big heavy cruiser; discussion of new battleships and carriers followed in May. In 1945, authority was reimposed in areas that had been conquered by Japan, such as Hong Kong and Malaya. Britain still had the largest empire in the world, and there were even ideas of extending British power, both north from India and into the former Italian empire, notably Somalia and Libya. In 1946 Admiral Willis (1889–1976), Commander-in-Chief Mediterranean, could write about his optimism for a long-term, albeit smaller-scale, British presence in Egypt.

The Cold War and the End of Empire
Post-war politics, however, were to lead to very different priorities. Britain had lost about 25 per cent of its national wealth during the war, as well as key export markets, for example in Eastern Europe, and merchant shipping, and its dependence upon wartime loans (mainly from the US) made it the world's greatest debtor nation in 1945. This was not the best basis for the formidable challenge that was to be posed by confrontation with the Soviet Union during the Cold War that followed the Second World War and lasted until the fall of the Soviet Union in 1991. Already, in mid-1944, planners for the

Chiefs of Staff were suggesting a post-war reform of Germany and Japan so that they could play a role against the Soviet Union. By early 1945, differences with the Soviets over the fate of Eastern Europe, especially Poland, were readily apparent, while British troops were opposing the Communists in Greece. In March 1946, Churchill, then in opposition to the Labour government, claimed that an Iron Curtain was descending from the Baltic to the Adriatic, dividing Europe between free and unfree.

In response, an American alliance appeared essential, not least because the other Western European states were weak. In 1947, the British acknowledged that they could no longer provide the military and economic aid deemed necessary to keep Greece and Turkey out of Communist hands. Instead, the British successfully sought American intervention, in Europe and South-East Asia. This policy was criticized from the left of the Labour Party, especially in the 'keep left' campaign of May 1947 when what was seen as a dependence on the US was castigated.

Confrontation with the Soviet Union did not drown out two other themes: first, a period of fundamental change in the empire and, secondly, faltering steps with regard to European cooperation. The Second World War was far more damaging than the First for the empire. Churchill considered the annexation of Libya, as well as acquiring the Kra peninsula from Thailand; but such views were now anachronistic, not least because they were inimical to the new world order of independent, capitalist democracies which the US wished to see. Instead, much of the empire was given independence in 1947–8. The granting of independence to the Indian subcontinent, which became the separate states of India, Pakistan, Ceylon (Sri Lanka) and Burma, in 1947–8, was followed by the ending of the Palestine mandate in 1948, a key step in the troubled origins of Israel.

These steps, however, were not intended to mark the end of empire, but, rather, Indian independence was viewed as providing the means for continued informal control in south Asia, while, elsewhere, a major effort was made to keep both the idea and practice of empire alive. Indeed, the government sent troops to maintain the British position in the economically crucial colony of Malaya, in the face of a Communist insurrection: it took 300,000 men to defeat a Communist force that never exceeded 6,000. The government also hoped to use imperial economic and military resources to make Britain a less unequal partner in the Anglo-American alliance, while major efforts were made to improve relations with Australia, Canada, New Zealand and South Africa.

Nevertheless, India had been the most populous and important part of the empire and the area that most engaged the imaginative attention of the British. Once India had been granted independence, it was difficult to summon up much popular interest in the retention of the remainder of the empire. Yet Britain did not join what was initially called the Common Market – European Economic Community (EEC) – the basis of the modern European Union, because it was seen as a means to reintegrate the economies of Continental Europe, which Britain had never seen as economically crucial to its interests.

Instead, British politicians saw the US and the empire as more vital economic and political links. This view was strengthened by the economic, political and military weakness of the Western European states, and by the willingness of the US to avoid isolation, unlike after the First World War. The North Atlantic Treaty Organization (NATO), created in 1949 and of which Britain was a crucial founder member, replaced the idea of a Western European 'Third Force'. Britain became a major NATO military base, with American planes joining the RAF in eastern England, providing the key force with which the Soviet Union was to be bombed in the event of war.

There was a deeper reason, however, for distance from Europe. In Western Europe, old elites and many earlier political parties, especially those on the right, had been discredited by the events of the 1930s and 1940s, and political structures, notably the powerful state, had been found inadequate. This created a situation of political and governmental fluidity, and led to a sense that change was necessary. The creation of the EEC under the Treaty of Rome of 1957 was part of a process in which the political structures and party politics of France, Germany and Italy were transformed between 1945 and 1958.

In contrast, Britain was separate from this process. It also lacked the direct experience of territorial invasion and devastation that affected France and Germany. In political and institutional terms, therefore, the creation of the EEC was both cause and effect of a divergence between Britain and the leading western European states. The difference was seen further when the British inspired a European Free Trade Association (EFTA) of countries not in the EEC, established by the Stockholm Convention of 1960. It initially included Britain, Denmark, Norway, Portugal, Sweden and Switzerland. EFTA was restricted to commercial matters, and lacked the idealistic and federalist flavour of the EEC.

The Cold War gathered pace from 1947, as Britain and the US responded to the consolidation of Soviet power in Eastern Europe. Clement Attlee, the Labour Prime Minister, also decided by 1947 to develop a British nuclear bomb, a policy regarded as necessary for Britain's security and influence: the bomb was ready by 1952. The Cold War certainly entailed heavy costs. Under American pressure, Britain embarked in 1950 on a costly rearmament programme that undid the economic gains made since 1948 and that strengthened the military commitment that was to be such a heavy post-war economic burden. The British were to devote a higher percentage of national resources to defence than economic rivals such as Germany, which handicapped the British economy. Furthermore, high defence spending was to influence economic policy.

The crisis in public finances in 1951 also reflected Labour's efforts to fund a major expansion in social welfare. This provided another instance of the tensions between welfarism, military expenditure and financial/taxation considerations already seen with the Liberal government of the late 1900s and early 1910s during the naval race with Germany, and seen again in the late 2000s. Also, in 1950 Britain sent the third largest contingent to fight in the American-led United Nations forces engaged in the Korean War (1950–3), against Communist North Korea and its Chinese ally: although, in July 1953, at 14,198, the contingent was far smaller than the South Korean (509,911) and American (302,483) ones.

The policy of the Attlee government was supported by the vast majority of the Labour Party and trade union movement. Communist and Soviet sympathizers within both were isolated and the Communist Party was kept at a distance. This situation helped prevent the development of a radical left and was linked to the alliance between labour and capital that was to be important in the post-war mixed economy.

Britain still saw itself as a major imperial power. When Churchill regained office in 1951, he had no intention of dismantling the empire. Although global commitments were reduced in some areas, elsewhere they were maintained and even expanded. In 1956, however, under Churchill's Conservative successor, Anthony Eden (1897–1977), the weakness of the imperial response and the limited domestic popularity of empire were exposed in the Suez Crisis. Britain and France attacked Egypt, an intervention publicly justified at the time as a way of safeguarding the Suez Canal, which had been nationalized by the aggressive Egyptian leader Gamal Abdel Nasser (1918–70), who was regarded as a threat to British and French imperial interests.

The invasion was poorly planned, but was a major display of British military power, and it was abandoned not because of failure on the ground but in large part because of American opposition. Concerned about the impact of the invasion on attitudes in the Third World, the Americans, who were ambivalent about many aspects of British policy, refused to extend any credits to support sterling, blocked British access to the International Monetary Fund until Britain withdrew its troops from Suez, and were unwilling to provide oil to compensate for interrupted supplies from the Middle East. American opposition, which underlined the vulnerability of the British economy, was crucial in weakening British resolve and led to a humiliating withdrawal that provided a clear indication of Britain's loss of world power. Failure in the Suez Crisis can be seen as the end of Britain's ability to act wholly independently; from then on, there was an implicit reliance on American acceptance.

Decolonization and greater Dominion autonomy also ensured that Britain could bring less to the strategic table. Indian independence in 1947 was particularly important, as Indian troops had been crucial to Britain's expeditionary capacity in Asia, Africa and the Middle East. The loss of these troops removed an important mainstay of the military dimension of the empire so that, whereas in 1941 Indian forces had played a major role in the successful invasion of Iraq, overthrowing its pro-German government, a decade later, when Britain was in dispute with the nationalist government in Iran over its seizure of Britain's oil interests, Plan Y, the plan for a military intervention by the seizure of Abadan, was not pursued, in large part because, without Indian troops, and with British forces committed in Germany and Korea, it no longer seemed militarily viable. Political pressures also played a role as both the US and Arab states warned Britain against invasion.

There were no Indian troops to help in the Suez Crisis, nor to participate in the Vietnam War, had that been a goal. Thanks in part to the fact that Britain could no longer deploy imperial military resources, intervention in the two Gulf Wars (1991, 2003) was very much as a junior partner of the US, and with Britain as much a symbolic partner as a crucial supplier of support. By then, the idea that Britain might have fought in part by deploying Indian troops was no more than a distant memory. It was not only a lack of imperial assistance that was at issue. In addition, the British had been far more successful when they attacked Egypt in 1882 than in 1956, a contrast reflecting a major shift in Western attitudes towards force projection and in the ability to coerce a compliant response.

Government attitudes to empire changed significantly after the Suez decade. As Conservative Prime Minister in 1957–63, Harold Macmillan set out to restore relations with the US, rather than to preserve, let alone try to strengthen, the empire. There was a wave of decolonization, and much of the empire was dismantled in a rush, especially in Africa, but also in the West Indies and Malaysia, as well as other colonies, including Cyprus and Jamaica. Churchill would have been less willing to abandon the empire at this rate. Decolonization was hastened by a strong upsurge in demands for independence which the government did not know how to confront. Although criticized by some right-wing Conservatives, decolonization was not a central issue in British politics. There was fighting in the last stages of empire, notably resistance to nationalists in Malaya (which gained independence in 1957), Kenya (gained in 1963) and Aden (gained in 1967); but nothing on the scale that the French faced in their attempt to retain Indo-China (1946–54) and Algeria (1954–62), nor that the Portuguese confronted in their African pretensions.

It is unclear how far a major nationalist rising in, or foreign invasion of, a British colony would have led to a substantial response that might have proved bitterly divisive within Britain. Certainly, decolonization did not prove as divisive for the Conservatives as relations with Europe did from the late 1980s. In part, this was because, despite the anomaly of the Falklands War in 1982, the empire was seen as being transformed into the Commonwealth, rather than lost. Thus, the logic of Britain's imperial mission, allegedly bringing civilization to backward areas of the globe, allowed the presentation of independence as the inevitable terminus of empire.

This end to empire was also relatively painless because interest in much of it was limited from the 1950s. This was not the case with some traditional Conservative groups, such as the military, but was the case with much of the party's middle-class support. The balance between the generations was also important, with the young not experiencing the sense of discontinuity felt by their elders. This difference constitutes an instructive contrast between the historical memory and imagination of the generations.

As empire receded fast, Britain appeared a diminished power, although it had an enhanced military capability as a result of becoming the third state in the world to develop the atom bomb (1952), followed by being the third with the hydrogen bomb (1957). From 1960, American nuclear submarines equipped with Polaris intercontinental missiles began to operate from the Holy Loch in Scotland, and in 1962 Macmillan persuaded President Kennedy to provide Britain with the submarine-launched Polaris missile system, which offered Britain a global naval capability, although American agreement was dependent on the British force being primarily allocated for NATO duties.

Indeed, if imperial diehards, such as the Suez Group, represented one critique of government policy and the foreign policy consensus, another was provided by the Campaign for Nuclear Disarmament (CND), launched in 1958. That year, 9,000 people marched in protest from London to the Atomic Weapons Research Establishment at Aldermaston. In 1960, the philosopher Bertrand Russell (1872–1970) organized a campaign of non-violent civil disobedience. Its impact, however, was limited.

Support for joining the EEC became more widespread in British political circles as it became clear that the organization would be a success, especially in terms of the level of economic growth enjoyed by the member states. Rapid growth in the economies of Germany, France and Italy, and, outside the EEC, Japan, helped make Britain appear unsuccessful. The relative decline of the British economy was particularly pronounced in manufacturing, although in some sectors, such as pharmaceuticals, Britain remained a market leader.

The loss of British influence in Washington was also an issue, as America was keen for Britain to join the EEC, and indeed continues to press Britain to support European integration. However, in 1963, the French President, Charles de Gaulle (1890–1970), vetoed the British application, declaring at a press conference, 'England is insular ... the nature and structure and economic context of England differ profoundly from those of the other states of the Continent'. De Gaulle also argued that Britain was too close to America.

Though there was a degree of opposition to entry in the Conservative Party, the Labour Party was more ambivalent, in part because of fear that Continental workers would accept lower levels of social protection and welfare, and thus price their British counterparts out of work; a process that was to be more clearly the case with east and south Asian competition. Hugh Gaitskell (1906–63), Labour's leader, declared in 1962, significantly in a television interview, that entry into the EEC 'means the end of Britain as an independent nation; we become no more than Texas or California in the United States of Europe. It means the end of a thousand years of history.' From the perspective of 2010, this proved a perceptive forecast.

There was a rethink when Labour came to power in 1964 under a new leader, Harold Wilson (1916–95). He had initially hoped to maintain Britain's role as a major independent power, and grandiloquently sought to act as a leading figure on the international stage, not least by revitalizing the Commonwealth. In support of India against China, which had successfully attacked the former in 1962, Wilson declared 'Britain's frontiers are on the Himalayas'. However, the attempt to act as a major independent player failed. This goal had to be abandoned in part because Britain lacked the necessary diplomatic strength, for example to mediate over Vietnam, but also in the face of the country's severe financial problems, which led to a serious sterling crisis in July 1966 and a major devaluation of sterling in 1967. This blow made Britain look weak and Wilson seem ridiculous.

As a result of a new sense of overreach, the government decided in January 1968 to abandon Britain's military position 'east of Suez'. British forces were withdrawn from Aden in 1967, and from the Persian Gulf and (largely) Singapore in 1971. Unlike Australia and New Zealand, Britain did not come to the assistance of the US in Vietnam. Meanwhile, decolonization continued, and by 1971 there was little left of the empire, apart from such far-flung outposts as the Falkland Islands, Gibraltar, Hong Kong and some small islands in the south Atlantic and West Indies, including Ascension, Tristan da Cunha and St Helena. Instead, Britain's international commitments and defence priorities were increasingly focused on Western Europe from 1966–7, with the focus on NATO tasks a military equivalent to a drive to join the EEC.

At sea, a focus on the NATO area was a consequence of the drawing back from imperial commitments east of Suez and of the build-up of the Soviet navy from the 1950s, and much of the British fleet was allocated to the Naval Force Atlantic, a NATO command established in 1967. Multilateralism within NATO, which became the consensus for Britain's defence in the 1960s, greatly diminished the independent role of British strategy, and this was taken further in 1966 with the cancellation of the planned CVA-01 fleet carrier, which would have been the first large carrier to be built in Britain since the Second World War. The Minister of Defence (Navy) resigned over the decision to end an independent British intervention capability. It was envisaged that, after the existing aircraft carriers, with their distant strike capability, came to an end of their service, naval air power would amount essentially to helicopters designed to act against Soviet submarines in the Atlantic. An ability to support amphibious operations no longer seemed necessary, which amounted to a major shift in military tasking.

Indeed, British forces were already in Western Europe, in the former occupation zone within West Germany, as the British Army of the Rhine, so that, in the event of a conflict, there would be no equivalent to the need to move troops to the

Continent seen in 1914 and 1939 when troops had been moved to France. British defence priorities were focused on Western Europe and the North Atlantic, the British being obliged to maintain 55,000 troops in Germany in order to man 40 miles (65 kilometres) of the West German border. If numbers were reduced, for example to help in the situation in Northern Ireland, it was necessary to seek NATO permission and to promise to restore the agreed strength. The Army as a whole was equipped and trained primarily for this task, with the strategic, operational and tactical emphasis on resisting heavily armed and more numerous Soviet forces. No longer an imperial force, the British military had moved far from its role during Queen Victoria's reign.

Joining the Common Market

Under Wilson, after the serious sterling crisis of July 1966, there was a new bid in May 1967 to join the EEC, but it was rejected anew by De Gaulle in May and again that November. Britain's options seemed no longer to be those of independence and alliance from a position of strength, but, instead, to be those of joining the American or European system. Not keen on close cooperation with the US, Edward Heath, Conservative Prime Minister in 1970–4, pushed hard for entry into the EEC, seeing this as crucial to his vision for the modernization of Britain, and as a way to play a convincing role on the world stage. De Gaulle's resignation in 1969 cleared the path, not least as Georges Pompidou (1911–74), his successor, wanted Britain in the EEC in order to balance West Germany, and in 1972 Britain signed the Treaty of Accession, which took effect the following year.

The negotiations were relatively easy for two reasons. First, Heath was prepared to surrender much in order to obtain membership. In particular, he accepted the EEC's Common Agricultural Policy, although it had little to offer Britain. Cheap food from the Commonwealth, especially New Zealand lamb, was to be excluded, in order to create, and then maintain, a market for more expensive, subsidized Continental products. Secondly, there was only limited opposition within the Conservative Party, still less the government. Membership was criticized most strongly on the left wing of the Labour Party, whose dominance forced Wilson to declare that he opposed entry on the terms which Heath had negotiated, although Labour supporters of EEC membership led by Roy Jenkins (1920–2003), were willing to vote with the government, thus providing crucial parliamentary support. Heath pushed membership hard on its economic merits, arguing that it opened up markets, but he said little about possible political consequences, ignoring warnings about the potential impact on national independence.

When Wilson returned to power in 1974, EEC membership was re-examined, in large part in an effort to quieten critics on the Labour left, although there were prominent Labour opponents of membership who were not on the left, notably Peter Shore (1924–2001). This was not the first occasion on which foreign policy was subordinated to domestic considerations. The government entered into a largely cosmetic renegotiation of Britain's terms of entry, and then launched a constitutional novelty: a referendum campaign in which the principle of collective Cabinet responsibility would not apply. This was seen as the best way to surmount party divisions and keep the government together.

In the referendum on Britain's continued membership of the EEC, held on 5 June 1975, 67.2 per cent of those who voted favoured membership, the only areas showing a majority against being the Shetlands and the Western Isles of Scotland. The available evidence suggests that public opinion was very volatile on the EEC, implying a lack of interest and/or understanding, and that voters tended to follow the advice of the party leaderships, all of which supported continued membership. Although opposition came from across the political spectrum, it was stigmatized as extreme.

The referendum result was decisive. Britain stayed in and the

EEC was not to become a divisive political issue again until it emerged in the late 1980s as the focus for tensions within the Thatcher government. In the mid-2000s, no comparable referendum was allowed by Blair or Brown on the Lisbon Treaty, a key measure in the development of the European Union, the successor to the EEC, although referenda were conducted elsewhere, including in France, the Netherlands and Ireland. Such an approach encouraged a Euroscepticism that reflected widespread concern, largely in England, about a loss of sovereignty, British identity and national interests.

Northern Ireland

In the late 1970s, other issues took centre stage. The economy and trade union relations were more pressing as domestic issues, and there was a sense that the country was ungovernable. This sense was particularly acute in Northern Ireland. It was scarcely surprising in the 1960s, a decade in which there were numerous demands for change, that the situation there should be scrutinized critically. However, the background was not totally bleak. An IRA campaign launched in 1954 had had little success and was formally suspended in 1962. Captain Terence O'Neill (1914–90), who became Prime Minister of Northern Ireland the following year, sought greater harmony between Catholics and Protestants, and hoped that economic growth would help to ease sectarian tensions. In 1968, he launched a programme for the removal of discrimination against Catholics in housing, local government and voting arrangements.

Nevertheless, despite encouragement and some pressure from the Labour government in London, the pace of change proved insufficient to diffuse a sense of discrimination, and the continued Unionist ascendancy, backed up by the police, led to tension. A civil rights movement, modelled on that in the US, developed, complaining about the position of Catholics. A harsh and insensitive police response led to fighting in October 1968, beginning in Derry (Londonderry) on 5 October, when an attempt to prevent a banned protest demonstration led to violence. The summer of 1969 witnessed a breakdown in law and order, with open communal violence.

The Labour government was determined not to use troops to maintain order, and, in July, the Cabinet agreed to the use of CS gas by the police in an attempt to avoid such a deployment. However, in the face of rioting in Derry and Belfast, the Cabinet, the following month, reluctantly agreed to accept the use of troops to restore peace. They were intended as a short-term measure, to be withdrawn as soon as peace was restored, and to protect Catholics as much as Protestants, but, instead, their very presence became an issue and a cause of further violence.

The Labour government did not wish to impose direct rule from London, and succeeded, in the short term, in restoring order, but no long-term solutions were provided, and order remained fragile. The attempt to impose a curfew on the Falls Road in Belfast in July 1970 was rejected by its Catholic community, while the authorization in August 1970 of the internment (imprisonment without trial) of suspected terrorists increased tension in 1971, which witnessed the first killing of a British soldier by the Provisional IRA.

The following year, there were widespread shootings and bombings, including 'Bloody Sunday' in Londonderry and 'Bloody Friday' in Belfast. The first, in which fourteen civilians were shot dead on 20 January 1972, marked the moment when the Nationalist community in Northern Ireland came to regard British troops as an occupying force.

The Provisional IRA, founded in 1970 as a violent alter-native to the older official IRA, and the (Protestant) Ulster Volunteer Force and Ulster Freedom Fighters, pushed terrorism up the political agenda, as both communities became engulfed in paramilitary-led violence. The British government reacted with a determined attempt to reimpose control, increasing the number of troops from 6,000 in 1969 to 20,000 in 1972. In Operation Motorman, the Provisional IRA's 'no-go' areas in Londonderry and Belfast were reopened for military and police patrols, which led the Provisional IRA to abandon attempts to stage a revolutionary war, an important moment in the history of the UK, and, instead, to turn to terrorism.

The continued intractability of the situation resulted in the imposition of direct rule from London: the Unionist regional government and the Stormont Assembly were suspended in March 1972, but the Heath government assumed that this would be a temporary measure, and there was no attempt to integrate Northern Ireland into the United Kingdom. Instead, Heath wished to establish the conditions under which Northern Ireland could become self-governing again, but on a different basis than before: this time there would be a genuine cross-community government in Northern Ireland. The government sought, with the Sunningdale Agreement of 1973, and the creation of a non-sectarian power-sharing Executive, which took office in 1974, to negotiate a settlement, but these measures did not command sufficient cross-community support. In an echo of the role of the National Union of Mineworkers in bringing down the Heath government, the Ulster Workers strike of May 1974 and the collapse of the power-sharing Executive led to the resumption of direct rule that spring. At a distance, the Sunningdale Agreement prefigured the eventual Good Friday Agreement, but the time was 'wrong' in 1973, whereas in the 1990s it was clear to the Provisional IRA that they could not win.

In 1974, Northern Ireland seemed completely ungovernable. Instead, the Army had to maintain a semblance of order sufficient to demonstrate to the terrorists that they could not win, and also to encourage intransigent Catholic and Protestant politicians eventually to talk with each other, a very long-term task. Provisional IRA terrorism made it difficult for the Army to fraternize with the population, and ambushes ensured that garrisons had to be supplied and reinforced by helicopters. Furthermore, the Provisional IRA found shelter in the

Republic of Ireland and it proved impossible to control the border. The Army acquired considerable experience in anti-terrorist policing, but the difficulty of ending terrorism in the absence of widespread civilian support became readily apparent. Policy would probably have been different had there been a conscript army. Conscripts might have been unwilling to serve in Northern Ireland, and the deployment and tactics employed might have placed a greater emphasis on avoiding casualties.

Foreign Policy from the 1970s

Meanwhile, and also unexpectedly, the international body that seemed most powerful and effective in Britain was not the EEC, but the International Monetary Fund (IMF), which was designed to stabilize the international economy by helping states with a liquidity or balance of payments crisis. In the face of a serious economic and fiscal crisis, the Callaghan government (James Callaghan; 1912–2005) sought a loan in 1976, and had to accept public expenditure cuts. Moreover, the constitutional issue that was most prominent in the late 1970s was relations within Britain, specifically Scottish and Welsh devolution, not relations within the EEC.

Imperial fragments continued to gain independence in the 1970s, for example the Ellice Islands (as Tuvalu) in 1978 and the Gilbert Islands (as Kiribati) in 1979. However, the empire's replacement, the Commonwealth, amounted to little in the international system or even in British foreign policy. It had been seen as a way to retain imperial cohesion and strength, and thus to strengthen Britain, as well as to serve as the basis for an international community spanning the divides between First and Third Worlds, white and black. In 1949, the prefix 'British' was discarded from the title of the Commonwealth, and it was decided that republics might remain members, a measure that allowed India to stay in. Commonwealth unity was fostered by a Secretariat, established in 1965, and by Heads of Government meetings.

However, the idea of cooperation succumbed to the reality of different interests and concerns. Relations with white-ruled South Africa, Britain's immigration policies and the consequences of Britain's concentration on Europe all led to differences between Britain and Commonwealth partners, but the absence of common interests and views was of greater significance.

Margaret Thatcher, Conservative Prime Minister from 1979 to 1990, and a politician of conviction and vigour, sought to centre Britain's international position on alliance with the US, not membership of the EEC, still less the Commonwealth. She was helped by her close relations with Ronald Reagan (1911–2004), Republican President of the US from 1981 to 1989. Both were firmly opposed to communism, and Cold War tensions revived with the Soviet occupation of Afghanistan in late 1979. Reagan, in turn, was willing to let Thatcher take a role that was disproportionate to the respective strength of the two countries. Although she did not always take his lead, the relationship was special to Thatcher, for it gave her great influence on a world scale.

Moreover, American logistical support greatly aided the British in the Falklands War of 1982. This conflict, the last fought by the British alone, was begun when the Argentinians successfully invaded the British-owned Falkland Islands in the South Atlantic. The islands had a British settler population and had been under British control since 1833, but they were claimed, as the Malvinas, by the Argentinians, then under the rule of a new military junta which was convinced that Britain would not fight, a conviction owing much to the withdrawal of Naval coverage in the South Atlantic. Rejecting mediation attempts that would have left the Argentinians in control, the British sent a task force that reconquered the Falklands. Running down the Navy, the Thatcher government had not been prepared for the conflict, the focus of its defence planning having been on the Cold War.

Nevertheless, the government benefited in the crisis from an upsurge in domestic popularity. Despite Nationalist graffiti in

Northern Ireland praising the Argentinians, British Catholics did not play a hostile role comparable to that of some Muslims when British forces were committed in Iraq from 2003. Furthermore, the opposition Labour Party leader, Michael Foot (1913–2010), badly misjudged the Conservative response. Thinking that this was another instance of Conservative appeasement, a re-run of 1936–8, Foot pressed for action against Argentina, a right-wing dictatorship (he was far more tolerant of the left-wing variety), only to find Thatcher provide it.

As a result, it was Labour that was split (although only a minority of the Labour Party opposed the war), with, in contrast, very few Conservatives critical of the leadership. The failure before the conflict to provide deterrent signs to Argentina was not brought home to the government at this stage, and critical later enquiries were to lack political weight.

Internationally, the dictatorial nature of the Argentinian junta, and the fact that the Falklanders did not want to be ruled from Buenos Aires ensured that Britain benefited from a more supportive response than that shown during the Suez Crisis. American policy, however, proved a particular difficulty, as the Reagan government supported conservative dictatorial Latin American regimes and did not wish to see a war between two allies. Indeed, the American response was a reminder of the conditional nature of alliances, and of the need, in reply, to rely on resolution and to benefit from divisions among the policy-makers of allied states. Initially, the British found President François Mitterrand (1916–96) of France more ready to offer support, not least information on the Exocet missiles France had sold to Argentina. The claim by Mitterrand's psychoanalyst that Thatcher threatened the use of nuclear weaponry against Argentina unless France provided such information is implausible.

The successful resolution of the conflict strengthened Thatcher's reputation for resolve, and led to the fall of the military junta in Argentina. Moreover, despite CND protests and a women's encampment outside the base in Greenham

Common, American cruise missiles were deployed in order to provide added strength against the Soviet Union; while, in 1986, American bombers attacked Libya from British bases.

The close relationship with the US proved divisive within Britain, because the Labour Party's move to the left in the early 1980s led to a rejection of key aspects of foreign and defence policy, including the country's status as a nuclear power, a status that rested on the intercontinental ballistic missiles carried by Britain's nuclear-powered submarines. The relationship also affected Britain's position within the EEC, as although she did support the American invasion of Grenada in 1983, Thatcher instinctively preferred to side with the US. Indeed, differing attitudes towards the US were part of a wider contrast between Britain and its European partners.

Thatcher was especially critical of what she saw as a preference for economic controls and centralist planning in the EEC. In 1988, she declared, in a key speech at the College of Europe in Bruges, 'We have not successfully rolled back the frontiers of the state in Britain, only to see them reimposed at a European level, with a European super-state exercising a new dominance from Brussels.' In this and other respects, Thatcher's government was more influenced than its Continental counterparts by the emergence of neo-liberal free market economics in the 1980s.

Moreover, contributing to this contrast, she, and the British public, were at least partly shielded from the implications of economic decline by the extraction of large quantities of oil from under the North Sea from the mid-1970s. By 1986, oil production constituted 5 per cent of British GDP. Seeing off the miners' strike of 1984–5, and thus defeating the hopes nurtured by the far left for a collapse of capitalism, Thatcher favoured the extension of free trade within the EEC, but was highly critical of the federal pretensions and policies of EEC institutions; and, with the battle over the British rebate in the mid-1980s she fought hard to reduce Britain's disproportionately high financial contribution to the EEC.

Yet, by signing the Single European Act in 1986, Thatcher gave new powers to the European Parliament and abolished the veto rights of a single state in some key areas of decision-making. Exemplifying the degree to which British politicians did not understand the momentum towards federalism integral to the EEC, Thatcher did not appreciate what she was doing. She no more realized what would flow from the Single European Act, as the momentum for the creation of a single European market gathered pace, than she understood the consequences of her failure to retain support among Conservative backbenchers. Indeed, as a politician, Thatcher was gravely weakened by her inability to appreciate the potential strength of those she despised. Her own attitude towards the EEC was more bluntly put by Nicholas Ridley (1919–93), a minister close to her who was forced to resign from the Cabinet in 1990 after calling the European Community 'a German racket designed to take over the whole of Europe'. For many (but not all) of those whose experiences had been moulded during the Second World War, the situation seemed particularly troubling.

Thatcher's alienation from the EEC, by then the European Community (EC), became more serious as the EC developed in a more ambitious direction. The Delors Report of 1989 on economic and monetary union proposed a move towards a single European currency. Thatcher found herself pushed towards closer links by her leading ministers, and eventually took Britain into the Exchange Rate Mechanism (ERM) of the European Monetary System (EMS) in October 1990, but also made it clear that she would never accept a single currency. However, her reluctance over European integration had frac-tured Cabinet loyalty, and this provided the lightning rod for dissatisfaction with her leadership within the Cabinet and parliamentary party.

Thatcher's successor as Conservative Prime Minister, John Major (1943–; Prime Minister 1990–7), initially spoke about his desire to place Britain 'at the heart of Europe', but, nevertheless, resisted the concentration of decision-making within the EC at the level of supranational institutions. In the Maastricht Agreement of December 1991, Major obtained an opt-out clause from Stage Three of economic and monetary union, the single currency and from the Social Chapter, which was held likely to increase social welfare and employee costs and to threaten the competitiveness and autonomy of British industry. Major also ensured that the word 'federal' was excluded from the Agreement.

Major's reputation, nevertheless, was wrecked by Europe. He had supported entry into the ERM at an overvalued exchange rate because he believed that this would squeeze inflation out of the British economy, but, in the midst of grave economic circumstances, the government found itself obliged to respond to the financial policies of Germany, the strongest economy in the ERM. Crucially, the Bundesbank did little to help Britain. Its different fiscal priorities forced Britain first to raise interest rates to a damagingly high level and then, in 1992, to leave the ERM in a humiliating fashion on 'Black Wednesday', 16 September 1992.

The reputation of the Major government for economic competence was destroyed. Paradoxically, however, this product of fiscal weakness helped maintain a degree of national autonomy, notably with a free-floating exchange rate and with the Bank of England setting interest rates. This autonomy was furthered at the close of the decade when Britain stayed out of the Euro despite the wishes of Tony Blair, who became Labour Prime Minister in 1997.

After the exit from the ERM, Europe continued to be a divisive issue within the Conservative Party and government. It became more so, because the general election of 1992 had left the government with a parliamentary majority that was so small that it was very vulnerable to dissent; and there was dissent aplenty over Maastricht.

Conservative disunity and failure over Europe – an inability to shape the EEC, or to limit its consequences and its impact on

British politics – contrasted with a more assertive stance elsewhere abroad. The end of the Cold War in 1989 brought to an end one era of competition between the great powers, and Britain was on the winning side. Britain also took a prominent role in the American-led coalition that in 1991 drove Iraq from Kuwait, which it had conquered the previous year. This war was both successful and did not have divisive consequences at home. The Americans very much took the leading role, but the British made a contribution, at sea, in the air and on land. The war did not lead to any occupation of Iraq, and the ease of exit from the conflict contrasts markedly with the Gulf War of 2003.

Tony Blair sought anew to square the circle of differing international interests and identities for Britain. Like Heath, he was convinced that closer European integration was central to his strategy for modernization, and, under Blair, there was an erosion of national sovereignty and a reckless transfer of powers to European institutions; an erosion that was in the logic of the 1986 Single European Act. Yet, despite Blair's wish to join the European currency, the Euro, he felt obliged to be cautious, because of the more sceptical nature of public opinion, the caution of his powerful Chancellor of the Exchequer, Gordon Brown, and the different circumstances of the British economy.

Political contrasts emerged more clearly in 2003 when Blair supported the US in the invasion of Iraq, a step France and Germany publicly opposed. This invasion followed British military commitment against Islamist fundamentalists in Afghanistan after the 11 September 2001 attacks on New York and Washington, and represented a return to an 'east of Suez' commitment that contrasted markedly with the trend of British policy from the late 1960s.

Yet, the basis of this commitment was no longer that of supporting an imperial presence. Instead, the British government saw itself as playing the role of key member of the Western alliance, and, in particular, vital ally of the US. Blair captured the national mood in 2001 when he declared, on the evening of 11 September, that 'we in Britain would stand shoulder to shoulder with our friends in the United States against the evil of mass terrorism'. Against Iraq in 2003, Britain played a secondary role, but an important one because of the potential for overstretch created by the relatively small size of the American force. The 2003 Defence White Paper argued that 'priority must be given to meeting a wider range of expeditionary tasks, at greater range from the United Kingdom and with an ever-increasing strategic, operational and tactical tempo'.

Yet, the ability of Britain to sustain this ambitious policy was far less clear. Moreover, with the US becoming less powerful in the world, at least in relative terms, the prudence of this expeditionary warfare seemed uncertain. Indeed, the ability of British policymakers to adapt to a multipolar world in which China is more powerful is at issue. Furthermore, the political context of British military activity in the 2000s was very different to that of the 1950s. A combination of the individualist and anti-Establishment culture of the 1960s, the end of national service, opposition to the Vietnam War and the impact of the Campaign for Nuclear Disarmament had greatly strengthened anti-war feeling.

Much of this focused on the First World War. The 'lost generation' and the futility of this war were myths so deeply imbedded in popular consciousness that, for some, they became irrefutable facts, as well as folk memory passed down through families, and any scholarly attempt to disabuse believers was treated with hostility.

In many respects, this response, already seen in the 1930s, continues to mould the more general perception of war held by a society that is singularly lacking in bellicosity. This is linked to the need to adopt a moralistic attitude to foreign military commitments in order to win support for them, a marked characteristic of the politics of the 1990s and 2000s.

If these circumstances provide an important element of contemporary strategic culture, it is far from apparent how the situation may change in the future. The implications of terrorism, growing European Union direction, not least after the Lisbon Treaty came into force in 2009, and resource crises on military activity are all unclear; a situation which underlines the need, when looking at the past, present and future, to avoid both the pitfalls of clear-cut accounts of change, and determinism. For example, the aftermath of the military commitment to Afghanistan, which itself became increasingly problematic in military and political terms in 2009, is uncertain.

Economic Changes

Political and strategic changes in Britain's international position were accompanied by major shifts in other respects, both economic and cultural. In particular, the empire's role as an economic partner and support ceased. In 1935–9, the empire took 49 per cent of British exports, and, until the 1967 devaluation of sterling, the currencies of most Commonwealth countries, bar Canada, were fixed in value relative to sterling, and they conducted their international trade in sterling. Moreover, many of these states held large sterling balances, which helped support the currency, just as today foreign holdings of dollars support that currency. The role of sterling, however, declined alongside Britain's economic and military position.

This process was notable in the former empire. The US replaced Britain as the biggest source of foreign investment in Canada in the 1920s, and as Canada's biggest export market after the Second World War. Australia came increasingly to look to east Asia for economic partners. Moreover, Britain's economic place in Asia was substantially reduced in the second half of the century. This was the case both in former colonies, such as India and Malaya, where the role of British companies declined, and in other countries, notably China and Iran, where Britain's role had been important.

Yet, despite the loss of empire, the British economy still differed from that of Continental Europe. The special financial status and influence of the City of London was distinctive. Even in relative decline, notably compared to its position in the 1920s, the City proved effective at developing trading in new financial instruments such as Eurobonds, futures and derivatives. Partly as a result, the City became more prominent in the British economy and also more closely linked into a world network of financial centres, the other key points in which were New York, Tokyo and Hong Kong. London benefited from its time zones which enabled it to do business while New York, Tokyo and Hong Kong were open.

At the same time, the City's financial place within Europe was challenged by Frankfurt, although, as part of this challenge, German and Swiss banks established themselves in London, in part by purchasing British merchant banks. Indeed, the effectiveness of the City, despite the relative decline of the British economy and the loss of sterling's role as a stable international reserve currency, owed much to the liberal attitude of the Thatcher government to the growing role of overseas banks in the City.

Substantial fortunes were made, helping fuel the property market in London, while a speculative building boom changed the face of the City. The functionalism of large, open trading floors prevailed in skyscrapers such as the NatWest Tower and 30 St Mary Axe (the 'erotic gherkin').

There were, therefore, significant changes in Britain's economic relationship with the rest of the world. These affected the world of goods, which was important to the sense of identity. As imports of manufactured goods became greater, especially after the Second World War, so British products became less distinctive and characteristic. In addition, within Britain, they became less effective as signifiers of style and quality.

American Influence
The impact of American cinema was particularly prominent. British culture, history and society were interpreted and

presented for American, and thus, also British, audiences by American actors, directors and writers, or by their British counterparts responding to the American market. Thus, Dorothy L. Sayers' (1893–1957) Lord Peter Wimsey, a fictional epitome of the best of the British aristocracy, was played by an American, Robert Montgomery, in *Busman's Honeymoon* (1940). George Orwell referred to the pressure of Americanization and the dissolution of values in the war years when, in his essay 'Decline of the English Murder' (1946), he contrasted a recent case with the years 1850–1925, which he characterized as the age of 'the old domestic poisoning dramas, product of a stable society where the all-prevailing hypocrisy did at least ensure that crimes as serious as murder should have strong emotions behind them'.

American links, a positive image of the US, and a habit of looking at Britain through the American prism were all greatly accentuated by the Second World War, and were maintained in the Cold War. President Truman's (1884–1972) Democratic administration (1945–53) was far from identical with the Attlee Labour governments (1945–51), with their nationalizations and creation of a welfare state, but it was possible to stress a common language and values, certainly in comparison with the Communist Soviet Union. Moreover, the American emphasis on the free market appealed to more groups in British society, not least to commercial interests, than the more statist and bureaucratic Continental European societies did.

In practice, cooperation with the US did not separate Britain from the Continent. Other European states were also founder members of NATO, American economic assistance under the Marshall Plan was important in the recovery of Western Europe, and the Americans played a role in thwarting Communist activity in France and Italy. Cultural Anglo-Americanism was matched by closer links between America and Western Europe as a whole. Their cultures weakened or discredited by defeat, collaboration or exhaustion, much of Western European society was reshaped in response to

American influences and consumerism, which were associated with prosperity, fashion and glamour. Britain's economy and society were wide open to the stimuli coming from the most developed and powerful global economy.

At the same time, the impact of empire declined. Britain's cultural, social and political influence in former imperial possessions ebbed rapidly. The percentage of the Australian and Canadian populations that could claim British descent fell appreciably from 1945, as they welcomed immigration from other countries, for example Greeks and East Asians into Australia. America came to play a more prominent role in British culture, with American soap operas being shown frequently on television. In some respects, the US served as a surrogate for empire, for both Britain and the Dominions, providing crucial military, political, economic and cultural links, and offering an important model. Encouraged by the role of American programmes on British television, and American or American-derived products in British consumer society, the American presence in the British economy, and the more diffuse, but still important, mystique of America as a land of wealth and excitement, grew. America thus became very important to British culture in the widest sense of the term, and helped to alter the latter.

The suburban culture and society that was prominent in Britain in the 1950s was particularly accessible to American influences. This trend was seen in popular music, for example the songs of Perry Como (1912–2001) and Elvis Presley (1935–77), the cult of the car, the use of 'white goods', especially washing-machines, and electricity (rather than coal), the rise of television, and a suburbia of modern detached houses. Through popular music and the increasingly ubiquitous television, American influence grew rapidly in the 1950s. It became the currency of the affluence that replaced the austerity of the 1940s. American soap operas and comedy programmes set standards for consumer society, notably in female clothes and hair and household accessories. While the US was a model

of individualism and, albeit to a lesser extent, for democratization, the consumerism was particularly apparent, and not
least with iconic television shows, from *I Love Lucy* in the
1950s to *Dallas* in the 1980s. These series took forward the role
of film in the inter-war years in proposing a model of fashionable and comfortable living that was open to 'ordinary
people', as opposed to the idea that such living should be
derived from the habits and hobbies of an ancestral social elite,
which had been the British pattern in the nineteenth century.
American 'soap operas' were generally set in spacious housing,
mostly in suburbia, and they provided a pattern of life for
suburban, car-owning Britons.

Competing Identities

There were also important Continental intellectual and
cultural influences, in part stemming from the large number of
refugees who fled the traumas of its politics, notably Jews who
entered Britain in the 1930s. If this process entailed an
openness to Continental influences, it did not, however, imply
a sympathy for political developments there. Immigrant
professors and architects can be more widely influential than
might be apparent at first glance, but, nevertheless, their
influence is generally indirect.

There have also been more direct links between Britain and
the Continent, of which one of the most important has been
tourism. To an unprecedented extent, much of the British population, male and female, young and old, became aware that there
is an 'other': other places, other peoples, and other ways of
organizing life. The impact of such experience was lessened by
many of the aspects of package holidays (in which travel, accommodation and, often, meals were sold as a unit by a British travel
agent), specifically going abroad to 'cocoons', environments in
which the foreign is tamed or lessened, and in which there are
aspects of Britishness, not least other British tourists.

In the first half of the twentieth century, although the 1938
Holidays With Pay Act provided a legislative support for

leisure, tourism was limited due to war and the relatively high cost of foreign travel. Moreover, fashion and habit helped to restrict the lure of abroad. Thus, the working class was apt to go to the seaside resorts developed in the Victorian period, such as Blackpool, Skegness and Southend, while, with the social divisions characteristic of Britain (and other countries), much of the middle class went to more 'select' coastal resorts such as Sidmouth and Torquay on the 'English Riviera'. The more affluent were familiar with the Alps or the French Riviera.

In contrast, far greater numbers travelled for pleasure from the late 1950s, a consequence of greater disposable wealth among the working class, especially skilled artisans, the development of the package holiday, the use of jet aircraft, in which Britain played a key innovative role, and the spread of car ownership. As a consequence, although a large number never went abroad, in part because of poverty, far more inhabitants of Britain than ever before visited the Continent. Furthermore, unprecedented numbers made a regular habit of doing so, and some went several times a year. If many visited 'little Britain' in resorts such as Benidorm in Spain, which was purpose-built from the 1960s to cater to the mass-tourism market, others did not. Exotic holidays on low-cost airlines or cruise ships subsequently became more common.

Moreover, a growing percentage of the population chose to live abroad, especially in retirement, or had second homes there. This became particularly the case in France and Spain in the 1980s and 1990s, and was a consequence of the liberalization of financial controls under Thatcher. It became easier to transfer funds abroad and to own foreign bank accounts.

Such links were an important aspect of a reconceptualization of relations with the Continent in which the latter became more familiar. This familiarity was related to a shift in the notion of patriotism. Patriotic sentiment was less frequently expressed from the 1960s, and attitudes towards abroad became less adversarial. The extent to which major football teams, for example Arsenal and Chelsea, had foreign players and managers was particularly notable in the 2000s.

Thus, notions of identity and habits of expressing identity were both in flux in the closing decades of the century and in the 2000s. It would be mistaken to pretend that they had ever been constant, but the last half-century was one of particular fluidity. The loss of empire, the lasting alliance with the US, and membership of the European Union, were all far more than simply political issues.

In the 1990s and 2000s, issues of identity focused on Europe. Britain was, and is, a European country, affected by similar social, and other, trends as the other countries. That, however, did not mean that British participation in the movement that successively spawned the EEC, EC and EU should be seen as inevitable. Europe could, and can, have different, indeed very different, forms and meanings, and it is difficult to argue that they were, and are, inevitably reduced to the EU, and in its current form. The Swiss and Norwegians are Europeans but not members of the EU.

Moreover, although some opponents of the movement for European unification might have been self-confessed 'Little Englanders', others could legitimately claim that they were in no way 'anti-European', but simply wanted to see 'Europe' developing along different lines, which was Thatcher's position. In addition, she prided herself on the role that Western firmness had played in the freeing of Eastern Europe from Soviet hegemony and Communism. Nevertheless, the identification of Europe with the EEC and, even more, the EC and the EU, had a major impact in British discussion, such that Thatcher's views led to her being presented as 'anti-European'.

More generally, openness to the outside world became more intense in the twentieth century, and did so as part of the process of accelerating change that characterized the age. That, however, should not lead us to assume that shifts in national identity have largely been a response simply to this changing relationship. It is also important to note changes within

Britain, both between, and within, areas and social groups, so that the impact of the outside world rested in part on its inter-relationship with developments within Britain.

Thus, in the 1950s, the availability of American role models, such as James Dean (1931–55) and Elvis Presley, was important in the definition of youth identity, while youth culture was transformed when rock 'n' roll arrived with the playing of Bill Haley and the Comets on the soundtrack of the film *Blackboard Jungle*, which was released in Britain in 1956. The growing cult of youth helped explain the importance of these models. Indeed, in the 1960s this cult focused on The Beatles, who listened to imported American records but were not American.

Thanks to film, television and travel, the immediacy of foreign exemplars became more urgent, but this was more than a matter simply of opportunity. In addition, there was an important loss of confidence within Britain that encouraged the search for foreign models. This was not new – Germany had been an important source of models in the late nineteenth century, one, for example, advocated by Prince Albert – but the search became more insistent. The process was facilitated by the presentation of the US as an ideal in both film and tele-vision. This was the most important source of change in terms of Britain's relations with the outside world, in large part because this presentation of the US as an ideal drove expecta-tions and habits within Britain. Britain was an ally of the US, not simply in political and military, but also in wider social and cultural terms, unlike say, American allies such as Saudi Arabia.

The sway of American culture was such that the shift from the period of British great power status to that of American hegemony, a shift accomplished in the 1940s, and with the consequences readily apparent in the 1950s, was managed without conflict. The process of decline was largely hidden from British eyes, and most of the public adapted to the conse-quences, a situation eased not only by the American alliance but also, from the 1970s, by the availability of North Sea oil, which enabled Britain to continue without addressing fundamental structural problems. The loss of great power status proved far harder for British politicians than for the public, but the major role of the state in the domestic economy and in social welfare was such that the politicians also had a difficult domestic agenda to address.

Multiculturalism

Neither the US nor power politics were the sole issues in Britain's engagement with the wider world. For example, the nation's diet changed greatly. There is now greater consumption, via restaurants and supermarkets, of products and dishes from around the world, notably Chinese, Indian and Thai cuisine, which reflects the extent to which the British have become less parochial and readier to adopt an open attitude – although these cuisines had to be adapted to British tastes. Indeed, British travellers in India and China swiftly realized that the restaurants in Britain were different, not only in providing more meat but also in offering tastes and dishes that were believed to be appropriate for the British palate.

Increased foreign travel and intermarriage are further aspects of a relatively unxenophobic and continually changing society, most of which was anyway far less prejudiced and racist than critics frequently suggested. Indeed, a tolerant multiculturalism characterizes much of British life, and is one definition of its society. Multiculturalism itself is a ping-pong issue, swinging back and forth between tolerance and diversity on the one hand and pressure for integration and full participation in Britishness on the other. Nevertheless, to contrast Britain with countries from which it receives many immigrants, Britain is more tolerant than Muslim societies, while the attitude towards homosexuality is far harsher in many countries, including Jamaica and Nigeria. The open-ended nature of British society, the sense that change and continuity are a joint dynamic, has been under challenge from differing definitions of this dynamic;

but there was, and is, an overall willingness to accept this formulation of nation and country as tolerant.

However, by 2009, the population exceeded 61 million, and the trend remains strongly upward. Concerns about the limits to multiculturalism and diversity, and about the success of integration, have become more pronounced, and have been exploited by the extremist British National Party, which became more prominent in 2009, doing well in the European elections that year.

These concerns are driven not so much by the rise in population, acute as that is as an issue in the discussion of immigration, as by the willingness of a small number of Islamists to take part in murderous plots, such as the 2005 Tube bombings in London, that reflected a total alienation from British society; and by polls suggesting that many more rejected much of British society. Moreover, this alienation was not necessarily a matter of recent migrants, but, rather, a symptom of a failure on the part of their children to accept Britishness. This issue was given fictional form in Sebastian Faulks' (1953–) novel *A Week in December* (2009), a state-of-Britain novel set in 2007, in which, while an Asian entrepreneur who has made money producing chutney for the British market and who argues that terrorism cannot be justified by the Koran, prepares to collect an OBE, his teenage son learns bomb-making through the local mosque.

The consequences of the strong links between some immigrant communities and the Pakistani homeland underlined the question about whether the consequences of multiple identities could be as benign as they were in most other cases. This situation has had political consequences, not least because of debate over whether a multicultural society can work. In particular, it is unclear how far, if such a society lacks a strong common culture, it is compatible with democracy, which depends on the minority accepting broadly the wishes and lifestyle of the majority. Particular problems arise with education and health care, notably (but not only) of women.

Declining Distinctiveness and the National Interest

Multiculturalism also represented an aspect of an engagement with the outer world in which Britain seemed less confident and distinctive, and understandably so in a world increasingly characterized in terms of globalization. In many respects, Britain became more similar to the societies of Western Europe, although this is also true of societies such as those of Australia and Canada, and this similarity led to comparisons between countries, for example of the relationship of state education to multiculturalism in France and Britain: in France there is a greater expectation of conformity with state norms. The similarity of societies was a consequence of broadly parallel social trends, including secularization, the emancipation of women and the move from the land. Sexual permissiveness, rising divorce rates, growing geographical mobility, the decline of traditional social distinctions and the rise of youth culture were all shared characteristics. Deference, aristocracies and social stratification all declined.

The result was a lessening of a sense of national distinctiveness, and this lessening played a role in relations with both the US and 'Europe', the two key poles of Britain's engagement with the outer world. It became harder to articulate a robust patriotism to serve as a cultural basis for a clear-cut presentation of the national interest. This issue very much affected the politicians who followed Margaret Thatcher. She had many faults, but was clearly able to articulate such a sense of interest. If it was largely in terms of traditional assumptions and a conventional vocabulary, this was understandable; Thatcher was able to link the 1980s to the formative experiences of her youth and those of many of her listeners, notably the Second World War, its aftermath, and the last stages of Britain as a great power and an empire. The Falklands War of 1982, moreover, provided her with an opportunity to deploy a strong and uncomplicated patriotism.

At the same time, her government proved far less successful in taking forward this patriotism for the next generation. To criticize successive governments for the consequences of a broader pattern of cultural development is misplaced, but politicians can be faulted for failing to understand the changes that have occurred and for assuming that nationalism is an automatic response. The results became clear after 1990 in the difficulty in articulating a coherent and commanding sense of national interest during the Major, Blair and Brown governments. Instead, there was very much an ad hoc quality to the discussion of policy over a wide range of issues, including foreign policy, military planning, immigration, human rights and other aspects of Britain's relationship with the wider world. This situation is ongoing and affects for example plans for a Strategic Defence Review after the 2010 election, to follow the review of 1998, because it is clear that there is no consensus on the nature of Britain's national interests.

A lack of consensus could of course be found on earlier occasions, for example over appeasement in 1938, but it is striking that differences in policy in that case drew more on a widely held set of beliefs and assumptions about Britain, its interests and its role in the world, than is the case today. The range of factors responsible for this change links this chapter with the others in this book, because they include Scottish nationalism and large-scale Muslim immigration, but, however important and easy to attach blame, such separatist strands are not solely at issue. Instead, it is the fundamental cultural shift in the bulk of the population that is a key element, one addressed in the next chapter. A society that puts such a stress on individualism, in the sense of self-fulfilment, finds it hard to define priorities and policies in a competitive and difficult world.

8

TO THE PRESENT

The narrative of ministries scarcely captures the fundamentals of political change in this period, nor its implications for society. Instead, the key point in this chapter is to link culture and politics, and to argue that the account of ministries, elections and government policies takes on much of its significance only alongside an understanding of broader themes in Britain's development, notably the moods of public culture. The latter owe something to government action, particularly with the liberal legislation of the 1960s, and also to the activities of public bodies, especially the BBC, but it is wrong to see culture and society as simple products of such governmental and institutional action and direction. This is notably the case if a global perspective is taken, as that reveals a general trend. Indeed, it was a widespread shift in norms, beliefs and practices that constituted 'the Sixties' and their consequences. This shift can be linked to consumerism and democratization as key aspects of the general trend in values in Britain over the last half-century.

It is important to focus on the 1960s as they were a key period of cultural discontinuity, a period very much seen in those terms, both at the time and subsequently. The 1960s certainly destroyed a cultural continuity and sense of continuity that had lasted very obviously from the Victorian period, and, in doing so, reflected the impact of social and ideological trends, including the rise of new artistic forms and of a new agenda moulded by shifts in the understanding of gender, youth, class, place and race.

Society Before the 1960s

Despite a feeling of uncertainty and dissolution after the First World War, as well as the new artistic and cultural forms of the 1920s, this transformation had scarcely been readily predictable in the 1930s. Then, the dominant collectivism (by modern British, though not 1930s Soviet, standards) of society and politics also had a strong moral dimension. This dimension rested on the long-established notion of Britain as a Christian state, one sharpened by concern about the unruliness of the public. This was not simply a political culture of conservatism for the left drew on a strong Nonconformist tradition that entailed a cultural puritanism directed against drink, gambling and self-indulgence and focused, instead, on exemplary self-improvement.

Public morals and popular culture had for long been policed, but this policing was accentuated in the mid-twentieth century, because fears of subversion and the disruptive consequences of individualism influenced attitudes to practices that were not in the accepted social mainstream, such as drug-taking. Moreover, the pronounced stress on the collective culture and effort, whether in the shape of the National Government (1931–9), the war effort (1939–45) or post-war socialist planning by the Labour governments of 1945 to 1951, led to an intolerance towards those who did not accept norms. Not filling in forms or not having a fixed address was a defiance of bureaucracy, but there was also a moral policing that criminalized habits judged unacceptable, for example drug-taking. Abortion, homosexuality, prostitution and suicide were all long-standing criminal offences, and actively treated as such by the police and courts; and consenting adults had therefore no privacy. Policing had a clear and well-advertised moral component, and politicians and newspapers actively pressed for the enforcement of these laws.

The press drew on the treatment of these activities as criminal in order to underline their discussion of them as unnatural; and this created a context within which politicians discussed legislation, a context that was not simply, or even largely, that of Christian morality. As a result of legislation such as the Offences Against the Person Act of 1861 and the Infant Life Preservation Act of 1929, abortion was a crime that led to prosecution, and early campaigners for publicly available contraception were also prosecuted. In light of the subsequent rush of legislative change, it is notable that Parliament for long resisted it. Thus, in 1960, the House of Commons rejected the recommendation of the 1957 Wolfenden Commission for the liberalization of the laws on homosexuality.

Restrictive divorce laws affected marriage, child care and sexuality, providing a staple of gossip, community assumptions and plots for writers and dramatists; while censorship played a major role in what could be read, seen and listened to. Literary merit was no defence against charges of pornography, as Penguin Books was to discover when it published an edition of D.H. Lawrence's novel *Lady Chatterley's Lover* in 1960, although the failure of the resulting prosecution proved a key moment in the breaching of the established moral code.

Censorship of the theatre and stage by the Lord Chamberlain's department, which was not abolished until 1968, served to maintain moral conventions on topics such as sexuality, abortion and birth control. Moreover, the leisure activities of the many were regulated by law, whether drinking, gambling or watching television. There were legal hours for drinking in pubs, and, in the case of gambling, no off-course cash betting, a measure, of course, that did not affect those with the leisure and means to afford to go racing. Such restrictions made criminals out of the large numbers who broke them, while also exposing social distinctions. In practice, the laws were broken, notably with backstreet bookies and with 'lock-ins' in pubs allowing drinking after hours.

Force and violence played a role in the legal and social systems. Corporal punishment (beating with the cane, slipper or, in Scotland, tawse) remained common in schools. Young men were brought under the sway of the state through conscription, which was continued after the Second World War, in part in order to provide the manpower to defend empire, notably in response to the Communist insurrection in Malaya, but also in order to compensate for the loss of the Indian Army, and was not phased out until 1957–63. Although capital punishment – hanging – was imposed only for murder, the ability of the legal system to deliver such a verdict contributed to the sense of a powerful state with clear moral codes that it was determined to enforce. Attempts to end capital punishment, attempts that drew on liberal criticism, were unsuccessful. The House of Lords rejected abolition in 1956, although there were relatively few executions in the last years of capital punishment. These executions, nevertheless, attracted great public attention, not least because of some important miscarriages of justice.

Culture Before the 1960s
A similar emphasis was seen in much of the cultural activity of the period, although this conservatism is underplayed if the stress instead is on Modernism, the movement which aimed to make a break with the past and to find new forms and means of expression. Fashionable circles, notably the inter-war Bloomsbury Group associated with the writer Virginia Woolf (1882–1941), had little time for popular writers of the period, or for commercial mass culture, but, despite later fascination

on the part of critics, Modernism had only limited popular appeal, certainly compared with many of the 'middle-' and 'low-'brow writers of the period, and had little airing on the radio. The rising disposable income of the inter-war period, especially of the 1920s, the ready availability of inexpensive books, and increased leisure, helped the popular writers of the period, such as Hugh Walpole (1884–1941) and J.B. Priestley, as well as the sales of the works of earlier writers, notably Arnold Bennett, John Galsworthy, Rudyard Kipling, G.K. Chesterton and Hilaire Belloc.

A self-conscious Yorkshireman, Priestley had an interest in English character and valued ordinary people, but his distance from cosmopolitanism and his socialism did not make him a provincial drudge. Instead, he took forward the realist tradition associated with Dickens, a tradition that was despised by the Modernists.

Another Yorkshire writer, the feminist Winifred Holtby (1898–1935), also offered a strong sense of place in her last novel *South Riding* (1936), a depiction of a Yorkshire community with a headmistress-heroine. This tradition of writing based on a strong sense of place continued in much of the popular novel writing of the later twentieth century, for example the works of Catherine Cookson (1906–99), which were mostly set in her native Tyneside. A sense of place was also seen in television dramas, for example 'soaps' such as *Till Death Us Do Part*, *Coronation Street* and *EastEnders*, and also detective stories set in particular locations.

An inter-war musical equivalent to the success of traditional rather than Modernist forms can be sought in the popularity of the pastoral work of Ralph Vaughan Williams and Percy Grainger (1882–1961); which, however, was criticized by the composer and critic Constant Lambert (1905–51) as the 'cow-pat school' of British music. Similarly, the music of Edward Elgar remained popular in concert programmes, gramophone record sales and BBC broadcasts. Elgar, Vaughan Williams and Sir William Walton (1902–83) were very different composers, yet each was seen by audiences as quintessentially 'English'. They took certain elements of tradition, bonded them with foreign or modern influences, and produced something entirely fresh, yet seemingly eternal, the invention of tradition in action. Vaughan Williams' *The Lark Ascending* regularly tops Classic FM's poll for popular classics. BBC broadcasts and concert programmes, for example those of the Proms (Promenade concerts in the Albert Hall), were also conservative in their treatment of foreign music.

Moreover, many of the painters of the period produced portraits or landscapes that paid scant tribute to fashionable themes. In the inter-war years, the Royal Academy Schools were characterized by a conservatism greatly at odds with Modernism, while James Bolivar Manson (1879–1945), the Tate Gallery's Director in the 1930s and a painter of flowers, was opposed to Cubism, Expressionism and Surrealism. Works by painters such as Picasso could be bought in London galleries, but their wider impact was limited. In the Second World War the War Artists Advisory Committee, which sought to use painting to maintain public morale, had little interest in abstract and non-objective art, and, instead, sought to preserve a bucolic sense of national identity. It was only in 1945 that the trustees of the Tate Gallery in London agreed to the opening of a small room devoted to abstract art.

Despite works by architects such as the Georgian-born and Continental-trained Berthold Lubetkin (1901–90), Modernism also had little impact in architecture in the inter-war years. Instead, pre-war styles, both revised classicism and Arts and Crafts, remained very strong, as in the Liberty department store in London.

Much of the culture of the period was not designed to challenge established practice and social order. Although the independent-minded and free-living character of Harriet Vane in Dorothy L. Sayers' detective novels was striking, not least for having sex before marriage, most popular female novelists, such as Agatha Christie (1890–1976), Ivy Compton-Burnett

(1884–1969) and Daphne Du Maurier (1907–89), focused on stable sexual and class identities. This was part of a conservative disposition that was very pronounced in the 1930s. Moreover, Du Maurier's novels, such as *Jamaica Inn* (1936) and *Rebecca* (1938), had a particularly strong sense of place, a characteristic of much of the culture of the age and one that reflected both the interest in nature and location, and also the existence of regional voices.

The 1930s also saw a rise in a 'Condition of Britain' culture – attempts to present the life of the poor and to do so in a way that emphasized hardship, although they also reflected and reinforced the social research of the time. These attempts, which drew on radical political commitments and a determination to vindicate the arts by showing life as it is, included George Orwell's bleak description of working-class life in northern mining communities, *The Road to Wigan Pier* (1937), as well as Walter Greenwood's (1903–74) depiction of the harshness of unemployment in *Love on the Dole* (1933). As with much else, there were Scottish and Welsh equivalents to this literature, which influenced the attitudes that were to rise to the fore after the Second World War.

The Second World War and its aftermath in the austere, regulated late 1940s, provided the occasion, if not the cause, for a shift to a new seriousness, notably with the bleak world depicted by George Orwell in his futuristic novel *Nineteen Eighty-Four* (1949) and the harsh tones of the music of Benjamin Britten (1913–76) and Michael Tippett (1905–98), as in Britten's opera *Peter Grimes* (1945). Architecture was now dominated by Modernism. The progressive style of the 1930s became an orthodoxy that was used for the widespread post-war rebuilding necessary after German air attacks, for urban development and for the new construction made possible by the investment in hospitals, schools and New Towns.

A centrepiece was the first major post-war public building, the Royal Festival Hall (1951), which was the lasting legacy of the Festival of Britain of that year. Intended to mark a century since the Great Exhibition, this festival was held on the bomb-damaged south bank of the Thames. It brought together an incoherent melange of themes, including new technology, a better Britain and aspects of traditional culture. The Festival, which was visited by close to 8.5 million people, reflected confidence, or at least interest, in new solutions and a Labour vision of progress, but, in fact, most people were less confident than at the time of the Great Exhibition.

Whatever the success of the Royal Festival Hall, the ugliness of much subsequent Modernist building led to depressing, if not inhuman vistas. Unfortunately, the Modernist movement in architecture was visibly important in the transformation of British cities from the 1960s, not least in the building of new city centres and tower blocks, although less so in small-scale domestic architecture.

Like the First World War, the Second hit religious belief and observance. There was a fall in denominational membership, especially of the Church of England. The 1950s, however, were not a period of obvious crisis. Church attendance ebbed, for both the Church of England and the Methodists, but not greatly; while the Catholic Church and the Church of Scotland remained strong. Elizabeth II's (1926–) coronation in 1953 was very much an Anglican ceremonial, and there were many signs of vitality. These included the building of a new Coventry Cathedral, the construction of churches in New Towns and other newly built neighbourhoods (which was a major drain on Church revenues), and the popularity of Billy Graham's (1918–) evangelical missions and of the theological writings of C.S. Lewis (1898–1963), such as *The Screwtape Letters* (1942) and his spiritual autobiography, *Surprised by Joy* (1955). Graham is an American, and his impact displayed the multi-faceted nature of trans-Atlantic relations. Significantly, he also operated outside the context of the established Churches.

The successful staples of the 1950s, on the West End stage and in the lending libraries and the standard bookshops, largely echoed those of the 1930s. Audiences flocked to see plays by Noël Coward (1899–1973), both old, such as *Private Lives* (1930), and new, for example *Look After Lulu* (1950), as well as plays by Terence Rattigan (1911–77) (*The Winslow Boy*, 1946) and William Douglas Home (1912–92) (*The Chiltern Hundreds*, 1947). The audiences were also very large for the short stories Agatha Christie adapted for the stage, notably *The Mousetrap* (1952). Hercule Poirot, like P.G. Wodehouses's Jeeves and Wooster, still appeared in novels that offered nostalgia but without appearing helplessly anachronistic, which in many respects they were. Christie herself acknowledged this in her novel *At Bertram's Hotel* (1965), as the pre-war opulence and level of service could be maintained only by the criminal underpinning of the hotel.

Yet, there were also changes. The late 1950s were to be the stage for the 'Angry Young Men', a group of writers who felt very much at odds with their Britain as a result of their sense that the post-war reforms of the Labour government, followed by 1950s affluence, had produced a vulgar materialist society that was disagreeable in itself and frustrating to them as individuals. They were impatient alike with traditionalism and the new, commercial values of ITV, the independent television channel, and they struck at what they presented as the 'phoniness' of social mores. These works, by John Wain (1925–94), Kingsley Amis (1922–95), John Braine (1922–86), John Osborne (1929–94) and Alan Sillitoe (1928–), however, were less a cause of long-term cultural change than were the pressures stemming from the greater post-war impact of American culture (much deplored by Priestley) and the foundation in 1955 of ITV.

The 1960s

Although prefigured in the 1950s, the causes and symptoms of long-term cultural change (as well as of short-term fashions) came thick and fast from the 1960s. The post-war baby boom and increasing affluence both had a major impact. Youth culture in particular became much stronger and also had a far more powerful influence on the overall cultural life of the country. Whereas, in the late 1950s, British singers had essentially imitated American models, The Beatles were home-grown and were exported successfully to the US, which was rare for British popular culture. In the winter of 1960–1, in a period with rising sales of records, they established themselves as the band for Liverpool teenagers. Yet, to become national, The Beatles had to be repackaged to conform to what was seen as appropriate at that level. In 1961, the band abandoned their leather jackets for smart suits, and their manager, Brian Epstein (1934–67), gained them a recording contract with the music giant EMI. It was newly responsive to the commercial possibilities of pop, cutting-edge popular music aimed at the young, and understood that it was no longer appropriate to expect performers to behave as they had been told to do in the 1950s.

The Beatles' debut single, 'Love Me Do', was released in October 1962, and they set the sound for change. The popular music gave Britain a 'feel' that was very different to the 'feel' it had had as the world's leading empire. So, more generally, did the 'Swinging Sixties' and the London of Carnaby Street and the mini-skirt. On 25 June 1967, 500 million people, the biggest live television audience of the era, saw The Beatles perform 'All You Need is Love' on the BBC's *Our World* programme, an attempt to show what the newly developed satellite-linked TV could do to create one world.

The popularity of The Beatles and other exponents and signs of the new, in turn, sapped respect for older patterns of behaviour. Conformity to the rules of the past was out, and the relationship between the social hierarchy and the 'Swinging Sixties' was uncertain; and one negotiated by this hierarchy accommodating new patterns of behaviour.

The Beatles came from the north of England, but soon left for the capital. Just as, in film, working-class dramas set in the north had a vogue, but were subsequently absorbed by a more metropolitan focus, so the same was true of popular music. Indeed, British youth culture was soon reconfigured towards fashionable middle-class interests. Thus, the hippies and drugs that became prominent in the late 1960s reflected the affluence, ethos and Americanism of middle-class south-eastern youth, such as Mick Jagger (1943–), rather than their northern working-class counterparts. The Beatles took to the new culture, especially to drugs and Asian mysticism, providing it with a 'sound'. The Beatles changed their style and sound, from their debut album *Please Please Me* to the 1964 album *A Hard Day's Night*, and then to the 1967 *Sgt. Pepper's Lonely Hearts Club Band*. The role of students in the pop culture of the 1960s was particularly important, and the majority of them came from a middle-class background. Many of these students had the money to spend on drugs, attending pop concerts and playing at radicalism in large part because of the affluence of their parents.

In the 1960s, massive open-air concerts focused the potent combination of youth culture and pop music, but this music, and its commercialism was, subsequently, to be challenged by punk, a style that set out to shock and to transform popular culture. Yet, to reach a wider audience, punk, in turn, had to be taken up by record companies and television.

There were also potent shifts in society as a whole from the 1960s, with a stress on the individual, and on his or her ability to construct their particular world. It would, however, be misleading to ignore earlier pressures for change in the 1950s. Indeed, images of sex played a much greater role in life in the late 1950s, not least in newspapers, novels and films, than they had done a decade earlier. Nevertheless, the outcome of the 1960 *Lady Chatterley* trial, with Penguin Books acquitted of the charge of obscenity, indicated that the new decade would be one of change, and this rapidly followed from 1963, gathering pace thereafter. This was a period in which fashions, such as the mini-skirt and popular music, both stressed novelty. Songs and films, such as the film *Tom Jones* (1963), featured sexual independence.

Hedonism focused on free will, self-fulfilment and

consumerism, and the last was the motor of economic consumption and growth. The net effect was a more multi-faceted public construction of individual identities. This stress did not lend itself to a classification of identity, interest and activity in terms of traditional social categories, especially class.

The nature of social developments can be gauged by considering changing assumptions. The mores expressed by detective writers reflected their eye for social values. In Patricia Wentworth's (1878–1961) *The Listening Eye* (1957), Ethel Burkett writes to her aunt about her sister

> ... who had taken the unjustifiable step of leaving an excellent husband whom she complained of finding dull. 'As if anyone in their senses expects their husband to be exciting' wrote Mrs Burkett. 'And she doesn't say where she is, or what she is doing, so all we can hope and trust is that she is *alone*, and that she hasn't done anything which Andrew would find impossible to forgive. Because what is she going to live on?'

Thus, Ethel's sister is demanding change and willing to seek it herself, notably by breaking family constraints; while Ethel still offers a traditional view of husbands sitting in judgment.

Whatever the developments of the 1950s, the 1960s did represent change, not least in legislative action, although this was scarcely a situation unique to Britain. The death penalty was abolished and racial discrimination declared illegal in 1965, while abortion was legalized in 1967 by the Abortion Act. Homosexual acts between consenting adults were legalized in 1967 by the Sexual Offences Act; although the Act was in part designed to control homosexuality, while the legislation was not extended to Scotland until 1981. The Divorce Reform Act of 1969 and the Equal Pay Act of 1970 sought to improve the position of women, although the latter Act excluded the large number of female part-time workers, a group that also received scant support from the trade unions. As more generally throughout the Continent and in North America, social paternalism, patriarchal authority, respect for age and the nuclear family, and the stigma of illegitimacy, all declined in importance.

Religion

Although Churches played a role in reform, notably in opposing capital punishment and (in some cases) supporting the decriminalization of homosexual behaviour, the permissive legislation of the 1960s flew in the face of Church teachings, and left the Churches and particularly the Established Churches confused and apparently lacking in 'relevance'. This was especially serious for an age that placed more of an emphasis on present-mindedness than on continuity with historical roots and teachings. Belief in orthodox Christian theology, especially in the nature of Jesus, and in the after-life, the Last Judgment and the existence of hell, lessened, while Christian social behaviour in the shape of activities such as membership in Church clubs and attendance at Sunday school declined. Absolute and relative numbers of believers fell rapidly, particularly for the Church of England, the Church of Scotland, the Methodists and the Scottish 'Wee Frees'. Already in 1951, Rowntree and the Lavers' *English Life and Leisure* had noted a decline in attendance among Nonconformist congregations.

The Church of England appeared divided and unsure of itself (see also p. 268). The issue of relevance was raised in 1963 in *Honest to God*, a widely read book by John Robinson (1919–83), Anglican Bishop of Woolwich, that sought to address the inability of the Church to cater for many, especially in run-down urban areas, by pressing the need for a determination to respond that would include a new liturgy. Cranmer's prayer book English, based on the Book of Common Prayer of 1549, was criticized as antiquated, and was replaced by a series of new liturgies. These themes echoed down the following decades. Weekly attendances by Anglican congregations fell below a million in 2007, and, with congregations ageing and churches crumbling, Stephen Cottrell (1958–), the Bishop of Reading, complained in 2009 that the Church of England did not reach out to the bulk of the population. It was symptomatic of the role of consumerism that his analogy was to shopping: 'we have become known as just the Marks and Spencer option when in our heart of hearts we know that Jesus would just as likely be in the queue at Asda or Aldi'.

The Established Churches also had to confront challenges from within the world of religion. Aside from serious internal rivalries, they were affected by other Christian Churches, by traditional non-Christian faiths, and by new cults. The tensions within the Church of England reflected long-standing differences, but were also indicative of a rapidly changing public culture, as well as of profound divisions. Liberal Anglican theologians challenged conventional views and caused great controversy, notably David Jenkins (1925–), Bishop of Durham from 1984 to 1994, who held unorthodox (but widely representative) views on the Virgin Birth and the bodily resurrection of Jesus. York Minster, where he was consecrated, was struck by lightning in 1984, which was seen by some evangelical critics as divine judgment. The vote by the General Synod in 1992 to accept the ordination of women priests led over 440 clergy to leave the Church of England, mostly for the Roman Catholic Church. In 2009, Pope Benedict XVI (1927–) permitted Anglicans to join an ordinariate that would bring them into full communion with Roman Catholics while retaining elements of their Anglican identity. By then, the issues of homosexuality and of women bishops had proved highly divisive.

Individualism in society and culture and the rise of the 'private sphere' was also seen in religion, notably in the extent to which individuals chose (and changed) their churches, rather than being bound by that of their forebears. The rise of 'fundamentalist' evangelical Christianity, inspired from

America, notably with Billy Graham's crusade in the 1950s, focused on a direct relationship between God and worshipper, without any necessary intervention by clerics and without much, if any, role for the sacraments. Certain aspects of this Christianity, especially its charismatic quality, appealed to some Anglicans, creating tensions within the Church of England.

The Christian tradition also became more diverse, in part as a consequence of the participatory character of worship introduced by immigrants from the West Indies. In addition, non-Trinitarian religions, that do not regard Jesus as the Son of God, such as the Christadelphians and Jehovah's Witnesses, grew in popularity in the 1980s and 1990s. The long-established Mormons had 90,000 members in Britain in 1970 and 150,000 in 1992.

Moreover, from the 1960s both 'new age' religions and Buddhism appealed to large numbers who would otherwise have been active Christians. They proved better able than the Churches to capture the enthusiasm of the many who wished to believe amid a material world where faith had become just another commodity. Faddishness also played a part, as with The Beatles' pursuit of Indian mysticism. In 2006, the Home Office approved a pagan oath for use in the courts. The 2001 census recorded 31,000 pagans, but estimates suggest that the real figure is over 120,000. The popularity of cults was also a reflection of the atomization of a society that now placed a premium on individualism and on personal responses. Such a society was peculiarly unsuited to the coherence and historical basis of doctrine, liturgy, practice and organization that was characteristic of the Churches.

This point begs the question of whether the earlier decline of religious practice and belief had not itself permitted the development of just such a society, rather than the society causing a decline. In part, it is necessary to stress the diversity of the 1960s and subsequent decades, and to note our limited knowledge and understanding of popular religion and what is termed folk belief. It is unclear, for example, how best to understand the lasting popularity of astrology, which was a staple in the popular press. More generally, Christianity did not collapse; it declined, and there were still many committed Christians, as well as a large number who claimed to be Christian but did not go to church or chapel, and also of conforming non-believers. Nevertheless, belonging without believing and believing without belonging became more significant in Christian attitudes and practice.

Gender

Women's liberation arose as a second wave of feminism, although, as with other movements lacking a centralizing structure, this was highly diverse. Conventional assumptions were widely attacked, including nuclear families, the authoritarian role of men within households, and sexual subservience. Demands for the recognition of an independent sexuality focused on heterosexual activity, with an assertion of women's rights to enjoy sex, to have it before marriage without incurring criticism, and to control contraception, and, thus, their own fertility.

There was also pressure for more radical options. Lesbianism was affirmed, and connections opened with the gay men's movements. Legislation played a significant role, as with other social changes of the period. Indeed, for change to become reform it had to pass through legislation. The Sex Discrimination Act of 1976 had considerable impact on the treatment and employment of women. The police were encouraged to take a firmer line against wife-beating and child abuse; and major efforts were made to alter public assumptions about rape. Thus, the idea that clothes or conduct of a certain type in part excused rape was totally rejected, although the percentage of rape allegations successfully prosecuted remains very low. Aside from demands for legal changes, feminism led to calls for changes in lifestyles and for social arrangements that put women's needs and expectations in a more central position.

Jobs and lifestyle became more important as aspirations for women, complementing, rather than replacing, home and family. The number of married women entering the job market escalated from the 1960s, and more women returned to work after having children; a marked change to the social assumptions of the first half of the century. The expansion of white blouse occupations brought increased opportunities for women to choose their own lifestyle. Positive discrimination in favour of hiring and promoting women, however, worked most to the benefit of middle-class women, fortifying social differences and, thus, serving as a reminder of the continued role of class as an issue. The expansion of higher education, from the implementation of the Robbins Report in the early 1960s, contributed greatly to the growth in opportunities. By 1990, 14 per cent of women were educated past the age of eighteen, compared with only 1 per cent in 1959.

Gender was an issue for men as well as women. The loss of empire and the end of conscription affected notions of masculinity. Although these ideas remained important in some spheres, notably the military, among black youths, and as far as boys' attitudes towards certain subjects in schools were concerned, less emphasis was placed overall on what had been seen as masculine values, and some of these values and practices were questioned, indeed mocked, not least in the satirical programmes that became increasingly common on television from the early 1960s, notably *Beyond the Fringe*. The decline of manual work and the growing importance of women workers also contributed to the same sense of changing, indeed, in some contexts, imperilled, masculinity. Different attitudes to homosexuality contributed powerfully to this sense, as did the marginality of men in many families, especially with the growing significance of single mothers. The role of women in the workforce was also important as women became primary wage-earners in many individual households. Moreover, more men had to answer to female managers and to adjust to women as equals in the workplace.

As well as gender, ethnicity was an increasingly important ·theme from the 1960s. The Race Relations Act of 1965 was an attempt to include immigrants within the nation without any demand that they assimilate, the latter possibly a mistake. The Act made it illegal to discriminate in public places, and established the Race Relations Board to tackle complaints. Housing and employment, both major spheres of serious discrimination, were excluded until the second Race Relations Act of 1968, and a third Act followed in 1976. Legislation was made contentious by Enoch Powell's 1968 speech warning of the baleful consequences of mass immigration; Powell (1912–98), a Conservative MP, was sacked from the Shadow Cabinet for this speech. Race relations also came to play a role in school curricula and citizenship ceremonies.

Race relations legislation failed to convince many immigrants (understood as New Commonwealth immigrants and their descendants) that they were not the victims of a racialist system, but it marked a major advance on the earlier situation when no such legal protection existed. Nevertheless, race relations continued to be high-profile and contentious, with particular concern about policing by immigrants arguing that they suffered unfair treatment, and about crime by both immigrants and 'whites', each alleging undue criminality on the part of the other group. At the same time, it would be mistaken to consider immigrants as a bloc and race relations as a simple issue of their relationship with the native 'white' community. For example, there were also serious tensions between Asians and West Indians, while the caste-like attitude of some Asian communities, not least towards marriage, was highly exclusionist.

Society in Flux
Society was in a situation of greater flux than in the 1950s, let alone the 1930s, and the alignments and classification of the nineteenth century were no longer relevant. This situation was matched in the cultural world, which was one of bewildering

complexity and of artistic hierarchies under repeated challenge. Yet, alongside the rhythm of cultural change, there was a continuing fissure between elite and popular cultural forms, and a wide disjuncture between 'high-' and 'low-'brow works. The overwhelming characteristic of popular 'low-'brow works was a reluctance to experiment with form and style. A pattern of contrast that was essentially set earlier in the century, with the impact of Modernism, ensured that there were very differing understandings and experiences of culture and the arts. These differences reflected the wider cultural politics of a society containing highly varied levels of income, education and expectation.

Yet choice existed: in social behaviour, personal mores and artistic taste. The role of choice was true more generally in the reaction against deference and hierarchy, which affected all organizations and careers. The royal family faced public criticism, not least on the grounds of cost and relevance. George VI (1895–1952; r. 1936–52) had won respect by his resolution during the Second World War, notably staying in London during the Blitz. Moreover, the coronation of Elizabeth II in 1953 proved a key moment of national pride, identity and occasion for the society of the 1950s, and, as queen from 1952, she helped maintain the nation's sense of continuity. The royal family's support for good causes, notably voluntary organizations, contributed to a strong sense that the monarchy had an important purpose.

However, there was mounting criticism from the 1960s and, in particular, the 1990s. The death of Princess Diana, the ex-wife of Charles, Prince of Wales, in 1997 led to a large-scale public outpouring of grief that contrasted with earlier habits and yet also focused a sense that the royal family (as opposed to the estranged 'People's Princess') was out of date. In addition, when the queen's sister, Princess Margaret, died in 2002, there was a display of critical comments that contrasted notably with the deference shown to the royal family in 1930, the year of her birth.

The abandonment of deference was wide-ranging. Thus, a willingness to question the police became more pronounced from the 1960s, and the police, like other public and private bodies, had to devote more time to establishing a complaints procedure and to addressing criticism.

More generally, the strength of consumers within a market economy that, after the end of post-war austerity and rationing, had been expanded by growth and large-scale privatizations, promoted democratization, as, however guided by advertising, consumers made their own purchasing decisions. In addition, taxpayers were encouraged under Margaret Thatcher in the 1980s to see public expenditure as questionable and open to challenge: taxes were 'our' money, spent by the state. Under John Major, Conservative Prime Minister from 1990 to 1997, the Citizens' Charter (and all its variants: Patients, Schools, Further Education, etc.) promoted a culture of complaint and redress, admittedly most heavily used by the middle class. This process was taken forward by the Human Rights Act of 1998 which undermined traditional structures of deference and authority by enshrining rights over regulations.

The consequences of the extension of rights proved very varied, as did their political context. Most obviously, individuals were given legal rights at work in 1963, and individual rights were pushed actively by the Thatcher government as it sought to establish a new practice of employment and a culture of work focused not on the traditional collective bargaining, which affirmed the role of trade unions, but on legal regulation – regulation therefore established by Parliament and regulated by the courts. As a consequence, the culture of redress led to defensiveness on the part of institutions and individuals, and thus, ironically, expanded the size of the bureaucracy.

Accountability was pushed by consumer groups, notably the Consumers' Association, from mid-century with comparative testing magazines, for example *Which?* and *Consumer Reports*, encouraging the centrality of informed consumer choice. Moreover, the endless satisfaction survey/market research/focus groups of the 1990s and 2000s promoted a sense of democratized (public) services, an idea pushed by Tony Blair who greatly favoured policy by market research. Accountability, transparency, consultation and openness became 'buzz' words and oft-cited ideas, with the very concept of the 'buzz' word reflecting the vogue for the fashionable.

These tendencies, however, accompanied the contrary collectivism stemming from universal public provision in crucial fields such as education and health, again underlining the tensions at play in society. Thus, alongside democratization came the anti-democratic rise in the power of quangos: government-appointed bodies that, despite their frequent talk of consultation, lacked accountability and instead often existed to advance and enforce centrally fixed standards.

Politics, 1945–64

Collectivism stemmed in part not from socialism but from a strengthening of the earlier commitment to government-directed reform. In the 1930s, there was a widespread sense that government had to act in response to the Depression, and there was a wave of what was later termed 'middle opinion', which began to champion the ideas that would later underpin the post-war consensus. For example, in 1931 the pressure group Political and Economic Planning was formed to promote planning and a more interventionist style of economic management. However, there was far less intervention in the economy than critics thought appropriate.

From 1945, the policies of successive Labour governments further strengthened this identification of reform with government action. Labour thinkers in the 1930s elaborated ideas of corporatist socialism that were implemented by the 1945–51 Attlee governments, with intellectual approaches given particular credence. The academics who had entered government service during the war provided a new definition of expertise; although it often lacked a pragmatic feel or a grasp of economic realities. Planning reflected a strong current of collectivism; self-help had gone, as well as the laissez-faire state. 'Welfare' in part represented the triumph of human agencies in society over spiritual responses to life, while the memory of widespread unemployment in the 1930s encouraged government action.

Until the advance in the late 1970s of the neo-liberal free market economics that were to be associated with Thatcher, state intervention in the economy was conventionally seen in terms of reform. Although particularly associated with Labour, it was also supported by Conservative governments, as with the establishment of the Central Electricity Board (1926), the British Broadcasting Corporation (1926), the London Passenger Transport Board (1933) and the British Overseas Airways Corporation (1939). Furthermore, under the Conservatives, there was also considerable regulation in other sections of the economy, for example the rail system. Moreover, in 1938, it was agreed that coal royalties would be nationalized from 1942.

This situation did not represent some lack of confidence in capitalism by Conservative governments, but, rather, a pragmatic willingness to consider a range of options for the organization of sections of the economy, and a belief, looking back to late-nineteenth-century attitudes, that public ownership could be a positive step. Competition was not seen as a goal in itself. Instead, public ownership was viewed as a potentially effective form of management, as with the creation from 1933 of the National Grid by the Central Electricity Board. These policies were developed by the Labour governments of 1945–51.

Egalitarianism represented another current of reform thought, indeed a secular ideology, although, within the Labour Party, there was a tension between gradualist, Fabian approaches and those which called for a true socialist overturning of the old order. A belief that people are equal, and should be treated equally, had been associated from the outset with Labour, and it lay behind the creation of the National Health Service, which was both an assertion of the importance of equality within the community and a device to achieve it. Whereas the National Insurance Scheme of 1911 had been intended to help transfer income over the lifetime of an individual in order to provide for health care, the NHS offered state provision paid for by taxation. Moreover, family allowances were introduced in 1945, and paid from the outset to mothers, not fathers.

The creation of the NHS was a good example of Labour's success in adapting socialist ideology to the British political and government system. Labour's overwhelming electoral victory in 1945 reflected considerable support for its policies from both middle- and working-class voters, and support for collectivist assumptions, but other factors also played a role, notably the degree to which Labour's role in the wartime Coalition proved that they could run things. Moreover, there was a rejection of the 1930s' Depression and, in part, of the image of pre-war society as class-oriented, and these attitudes led to opposition to the Conservatives.

On the whole, state provision and control were pushed most strongly by Labour governments, which nationalized coal in 1947, the railways and electricity in 1948, gas in 1949, and iron and steel in 1951, and wished to nationalize much more, including wholesaling, while Conservative administrations adopted a more ambivalent position. Notably, when the Conservatives, still under Churchill, returned to power after the election of 25 October 1951, with 321 seats to Labour's 295, they did not return to the policies of the 1930s. Instead, there was much with which Churchill would have been familiar as a reforming Liberal imperialist in the 1900s. Accepting the consequences of 1945, the adaptable Conservatives continued the welfare state and, indeed, much of Labour policy. Only the recently nationalized iron and steel, and road haulage were denationalized, both in 1953; the railways, gas, coal and electricity remained in the public sector. There was no equivalent to the Thatcherite privatizations of the 1980s.

Allowing for the importance of debates and divisions within

the political parties, the Conservatives did not wish to lose support by being associated anew with the policies of the 1930s, and, in particular, successfully worked to keep the centrist Liberals weak. Prosperity was to be ensured, Churchill pressing in 1951 a policy of 'houses, red meat, and not getting scuppered'. A continuity of economic policy between the Labour Chancellor of the Exchequer, Hugh Gaitskell, and his Conservative replacement from 1951, R.A. Butler, including a fixed exchange rate for sterling, Keynesian demand management and a commitment to 'full' employment, led to the phrase 'Butskellism' being coined by the *Economist* in 1954. The Conservative government decided that it was not sensible to legislate against trade union rights, such as closed shop agreements and the legal immunities the unions had gained in 1906, and, from the later standards of Thatcherism, the unions were appeased. Indeed, Churchill urged his naturally emollient Minister of Labour, Walter Monckton (1891–1965), to give in on pay awards in order to avoid strikes. Moreover, in the early 1960s, the Macmillan ministry sought to develop economic planning.

There was also continuity in foreign and imperial policy after 1951: the Churchill government was equally, if not more, supportive of the Atlantic (Anglo-American) Alliance, NATO and the Commonwealth. The consensus of the 1950s was not a new departure, but, in many senses, a reworking of the consensus policies and attitudes of the 1920s and of the war years. It drew on the prolonged boom in the Western economy between 1945 and 1973, which helped underwrite policies of full employment and which kept unemployment relatively low.

In practice, however, consensus was not universal. Although continuing the welfare state, the Conservatives did not make it more generous, as Labour, now in the luxury of opposition, advocated. There was also a Conservative determination to resist higher taxes. Thus, very different policy goals between the major parties ensured that elections mattered. Aside from these differences, there were also contrasting responses to circumstances. The Conservatives saw Labour as overly socialist and as unreliable against Soviet Communism, while, in opposition from 1951, Labour sought to replenish its ideological identity and to distinguish itself from the government. Yet, it did so without going far to the left. Indeed, the limited extent of political radicalism was readily apparent in 1945–65. Nazi activities had discredited the extreme right, and, although Oswald Mosley continued his Fascist electioneering, he had less prominence than before the war; while the policies and eventual failure of the Soviet Union struck successive blows at the credibility of the far left. The registered membership of the Communist Party fell from 56,000 in 1942 to 25,000 in 1958.

The Liberals pursued a centrist policy in the late 1940s and early 1950s and they sought to offer a radical, but non-socialist, opposition to the Conservative government, but they lacked parliamentary weight and won only six seats in each of the elections of 1951, 1955 and 1959.

The Conservatives held office until 1964, with Churchill as Prime Minister until 1955, Sir Anthony Eden in 1955–7, Harold Macmillan in 1957–63, and then Sir Alec Douglas-Home. We tend to judge the past from the present, and notably so when using the same terms. Thus, most readers will associate Conservative governments with those of Margaret Thatcher and John Major in 1979–97, but that is not the background from which to look at their predecessors in 1951–64. There are significant comparisons between the two periods, not least a determination to support the American alliance, but there was no attempt in 1951–64 to change dramatically, or even significantly, the welfare state or labour relations. Instead, there was a 'one nation' Tory paternalism that was later to be anathema to Thatcher, a paternalism, moreover, that matched the cultural conservatism of the 1950s.

The Tories handsomely won re-election in 1955 and 1959; which underlines the political change that the 1960s represented. On 26 May 1955, the Conservatives, under the newly appointed Eden, won 49.7 per cent of the vote and 345 seats, compared to Labour's 46.4 per cent and 277 seats. In the 1950s, most seats were won by the two major parties. The Liberals won only six seats, while the Scottish and Welsh nationalist movements did not gather strength until the 1960s.

In 1959, the Conservative hoardings proclaimed 'Life's better with the Conservatives, Don't let Labour ruin it', and there is little doubt that a sense of affluence helped greatly in their electoral victory, as, more broadly, did the growth in the middle class and the expansion of owner-occupation of housing. 'Most of our people have never had it so good', a phrase Macmillan had employed in a speech in July 1957, was much used during the next election campaign. On 8 October 1959, the Conservatives won 365 seats, their best post-war figure until Thatcher's second victory in 1983.

This was the first time during the age of mass democracy in Britain that a party had won three successive general elections; the last time that there had been three successive victories was in the 1830s. At 49.3 per cent, the Conservative percentage of the vote was slightly down on 1955, but Labour's fall, to 43.9 per cent, was far greater: Labour won 258 seats. The modest revival in the percentage of votes won by the Liberals was won at the expense of the Labour share, and in 1960 *Must Labour Lose?* by Mark Abrams and Richard Rose appeared. Labour had lost much of the middle-class support it had received in the late 1940s, while the Conservatives had proved successful in winning back an important degree of working-class support. Sympathy for the trade unions was weakened by the 1955 rail strike and the 1958 bus strike. The Conservatives also made use of new techniques of media electioneering, including hiring a public relations firm.

Once re-elected, the Conservatives, however, proved unable to maintain their record for effective economic management. Macmillan increasingly looked weak, not least as a result of his failure to enter the EEC. However, he fell in October 1963 for a more mundane reason: a prostate illness. He was replaced by

the 14th Earl of Home, the Foreign Secretary, who relin-
quished his peerage to re-enter the Commons as Prime
Minister, becoming Sir Alec Douglas-Home (1903–95). Both
the method of selection, a closed process dominated by party
grandees, especially Macmillan, and the choice of the aristocratic Home, rather than more accessible politicians, were
bitterly criticized as out of date, and by some Conservatives as
well as Labour.

This political situation was exploited by Labour under
Harold Wilson. He was to be revealed in office as a fixer,
largely concerned to keep his Cabinet together, but, in 1963–4,
he was able to portray himself as the leader able to take Britain
forward, in particular by linking science and socialism so as to
provide effective planning and solutions. Condemning in 1964
what he termed 'thirteen wasted years' of Conservative
government, Wilson sought the mantle of John Kennedy, the
recent Democratic President of the US. He looked very
modern and democratic in contrast to the aristocratic Douglas-
Home.

Politics, 1964–79

The general election of 15 October 1964 led to a narrow
victory for Labour: by 44.1 per cent and 317 seats to 43.4 per
cent and 304 for the Conservatives. In large part, this victory
was due to a strong increase in the Liberal vote at the expense
of the Conservatives, albeit yielding the Liberals only nine
seats. The Conservatives seemed dated. The impact of repeated
attacks by satirists, in the age of *That Was The Week That Was*
and *Private Eye*, is difficult to assess, but cannot have been
helpful. The electorate had become wealthier in the 1950s, but
the percentage willing to vote Labour in 1964 was only slightly
below that of 1951. The Conservatives were again to discover
in 1997 that rising real wealth under their government did not
prevent a Labour victory. Yet, whatever the inability of the
Conservatives to respond effectively to socio-cultural shifts,
their vote remained over 40 per cent.

Labour came to power with high hopes, including schemes to use planning to improve economic performance, harness new technology, and end the 'Stop-Go' cycle. In 1965, the government produced the National Plan, an optimistic blueprint for growth, but Labour policies lacked a sound economic basis, not least because Wilson refused to tackle acute balance of payments problems by devaluing the currency. Instead, he sought to follow a balancing act across the policy front: in defending sterling, keeping a British military presence east of Suez, and also supporting American policy in Vietnam but without sending British troops there.

On 31 March 1966, Wilson won re-election over the lacklustre Conservatives, now led by Edward Heath, by 48 per cent and 364 seats to 41.9 per cent and 253; but the problems of the economy rapidly reasserted themselves, and in November 1967 the pound was devalued by 14.3 per cent after strenuous attempts to prevent the inevitable that called Wilson's judgement into question. Britain's lessened international status was further shown by the rejection of a second application to join the EEC, Wilson's failure to mediate in the Vietnam War, and the drawing up of plans for Britain's withdrawal from east of Suez. The failure of his attempt to improve industrial relations and reform the trade unions in 1969, by giving government powers to demand strike ballots or impose cooling-off periods, encouraged a sense of broken hopes.

Yet, the Wilson years were also seen as a time of social advance in which the government fostered a mood for progressive change. Liberalization of the laws concerning abortion, homosexuality, capital punishment, censorship and divorce, and the passage of the Race Relations Act in 1965, were all intended to transform Britain into a more tolerant and civilized society. This, when taken together with important reforms in the education system, including the changeover to comprehensive education (however questionable in hindsight), and the establishment of the Open University, as well as the deep-seated concern for such disadvantaged groups as the elderly and handicapped, reveal a government guided by a genuine humanitarian imperative. Increased pensions and reform of the Rent Act made a major difference to much of the population.

Defying the opinion polls, the general election of 18 June 1970 was won by the Conservatives under Heath, who, like Wilson, pushed through changes in what he saw, often misguidedly, as an attempt to modernize Britain. The decimalization of the currency in 1971 so that the pound was composed of 100 new pence in place of twenty shillings, each divided into twelve pence, discarded centuries of usage and contributed to inflation. The Local Government Act of 1972 drastically altered the historic territorial boundaries of local government. This Act constituted an important symbolic breach with the past, which formed a major contrast with the US, where the role of the individual states offered, and still offers, a continuance of older English roots that, ironically, have become attenuated in Britain. Joining the European Economic Community, to which Britain acceded in 1973, was central to Heath's consensualist plan to modernize Britain and to make it more effective internationally and domestically.

At the same time, Heath's government made the first concerted effort to reduce the scope of government action in post-war Britain, a policy that reflected a reaction against the failure of the planning experiments of both Conservative and, especially, Labour governments in the 1960s to revitalize Britain's flagging economic fortunes. When he came to office, Heath outlined an economic policy different from that of Wilson, one that was more prudent and far less ready to intervene in the economy, not least in a refusal to subsidize inefficient industries. Income tax and public spending were to be cut alongside a move away from corporatism and towards, instead, encouraging individual effort. This was the policy described as that of 'Selsdon Man', named after Conservative planning sessions at Selsdon Park, Surrey, in January and February 1970. However surprisingly, this stance paralleled aspects of 1960s social liberalism. The critical Wilson referred to Conservative ideas as 'Stone Age economics'.

The Conservatives regarded their policies as essential in order to help Britain compete effectively within the EEC. John Davies (1916–79), the outgoing Director-General of the Confederation of British Industry (CBI), was appointed head of a large Department of Trade and Industry, and Davies announced that taxes were not well spent propping up 'lame ducks': failing industries. Industrial corporatism was reversed, and the legislative and administrative structures dismantled. Seven of the regional development agencies were abolished.

As, however, with Northern Ireland (see p. 238–9), events blew policy not only off course but also back the way it had come. In February 1971, the government intervened to nationalize Rolls-Royce, Britain's leading manufacturer of aero-engines, when it was threatened with bankruptcy. Later in the year, Upper Clyde Shipbuilders was rescued under pressure from a union work-in and following an initial government refusal to provide support. These U-turns contributed to a sense of a weak government responding to pressure (ensuring that Thatcher in the 1980s was to be determined to stand firm), while the Industry Act of 1972 was designed to provide for manufacturing companies that were in difficulty. Unemployment rose to over a million, a shock after three decades when it had been generally low.

Under Heath, the immediate problems of economic management hit hard, putting great pressure on the balance of payments. Government expenditure and inflation surged ahead. The money supply (provision of money and credit) was greatly expanded, rising 20 per cent between 1971 and 1973. Public spending also shot up, by nearly 50 per cent in real terms, during the government's period of office, in large part in an attempt to reflate the economy, an attempt that was launched in the summer of 1971 and that persisted until 1973.

Efforts to create a more regulated context for industrial relations by means of the Industrial Relations Act of 1971 and a de facto incomes policy were blown apart by the National Union of Mineworkers (NUM), setting the scene for a decade of crisis in governability as successive governments found themselves forced into a corner by the excesses of trade union power. In 1972, the NUM staged the first national coal strike since 1926 in pursuit of a large pay claim. Mass picketing closed access to coal stocks, and the government declared a state of emergency, only to give in. The attitude of the NUM was particularly serious because oil and gas supplies from the North Sea were not yet available.

In February 1974, faced by a new NUM wage claim, Heath called a general election to bolster his position and try to overawe the miners, but, on 28 February, although he had a bigger percentage of the popular vote, Labour won more seats (301 to 297), and Wilson regained power once the Liberals had rejected a coalition with the Conservatives. In the general election held on 10 October 1974, Wilson won a larger parliamentary majority, but it was still modest. Moreover, due to extra-parliamentary problems he was unable to govern effectively, and in 1974–6 Wilson completed the process of dissolution begun by Heath: an economy, state and society that had been muddling through for decades, operating far below the level of effectiveness of other countries, but, nevertheless, at least avoiding crisis and breakdown, slid into chaos. With wages rising rapidly, but controls on prices and dividends, there was a massive fall on the stock market, and there was no incentive to invest. As a result of this economic illiteracy, 1974–6 was the closest that Britain has yet come to the fall of capitalism, which, indeed, was sought by some of the NUM leadership. The issue was not only 'Who governs Britain?', the question asked by Heath in 1974 when he sought to defeat the miners, but 'Could Britain be governed?'.

Wilson resigned unexpectedly in March 1976, to be succeeded by James Callaghan, the Foreign Secretary, who, unlike the 'hard left', did not believe that it would be possible to resist economic pressures by a policy of state socialism:

nationalizations, high taxation and tariffs. Instead, he advocated pragmatism and was willing to rethink the Keynesian prescriptions of the previous thirty-five years. When the IMF, to which Britain had to go for a loan in 1976, demanded cuts in government spending, and, in the face of pressure from the 'hard left' for a siege economy, they were imposed by Callaghan. As a result, confidence was restored and the pound rallied.

Yet, a crisis in industrial relations culminated in the 'Winter of Discontent' of 1978–9. Widespread strikes against the norm of an increase that year of 5 per cent in pay created a sense of crisis. Hospitals were picketed, the dead unburied in Liverpool, and troops called in to shoot rats swarming round accumulated rubbish. The large number of simultaneous strikes, the practice of secondary picketing, the violence and mean-mindedness of the picketing (which included the turning away of ambulances), and the lack of interest by the strikers in the public, discredited the rhetoric and practice of trade unionism. In one quarter alone, 16.5 million working days were lost to labour disputes.

The government also lost control of the parliamentary arithmetic of support when it failed to push through devolution in Scotland and Wales. A Scotland and Wales Bill introduced in 1976 proposed assemblies with control over health, social services, primary and secondary education, development and local government, but with no taxation power and with the Westminster Parliament retaining the veto. The Bill met opposition from Scottish and Welsh nationalists, who felt it did not go far enough, but, more substantially, from Conservatives, who saw it as a threat to Britain, and some Labour MPs. In order to secure the passage of the Bill, the government had to concede referenda, but, held on 1 March 1979, they found the overwhelming majority of the Welsh who voted doing so against devolution, while, in Scotland, although the majority of the votes cast was for devolution, it was not the necessary 40 per cent of those on the electoral register.

Labour failure and opposition to trade union disruption led to a surge in support for the Conservatives under the largely unknown Margaret Thatcher, who had become Party leader in 1975 in a determined rejection of Heath and his policies. In the general election of 3 May 1979, Thatcher won power with a majority of forty-three seats, helped by a vigorous campaigning style in which she used photo opportunities and advertising agencies. The country had voted for change, although it was not clear what that change would be.

The Thatcher Years

Margaret Thatcher, Prime Minister from 1979 to 1990, remains a figure of great controversy. She held continuous office for longer than any other Prime Minister in the age of mass democracy, indeed than any since the 2nd Earl of Liverpool in 1812–27. She was more hated on the left than any other Conservative Prime Minister, and 'Thatcherite' became a term of abuse to a degree that 'Heathite' could never match. Furthermore, she aroused strong negative passions within her own party: Heath hated her, and the 'One Nation' paternalists who had dominated the party since Churchill replaced Chamberlain in 1940, were appalled at what they saw as her divisive language and politics. Thatcher, in her turn, had clear contempt for those Conservatives she called the 'wets', and a dislike of a tradition, ethos and practice of compromise and consensus, that, she felt, had led to Britain's decline. Indeed, she attacked what she termed 'the progressive consensus'.

In practice, as with all politicians, there was much compromise: Thatcher was not the most Thatcherite. Indeed, there was to be criticism that her rhetoric of 'rolling back the state' was misleading, and that government expenditure did not fall as anticipated. Nevertheless, there was a stated determination to persist that was different in degree and style from that of her predecessors.

Economic problems interacted with fiscal policies, notably major cuts in public expenditure in the budgets of June 1979,

March 1980 and March 1982. Indeed, recession and deflation at the start of the 1980s hit hard and helped make much of the economy uncompetitive. Unemployment rose greatly as manufacturing contracted. In terms of public perception, these were 'real' jobs. They were predominantly male and in traditional industrial tasks such as metal-bashing.

Thatcher's response defined her government: 'The lady's not for turning' she told the 1980 party conference, and the delegates loudly applauded. She remained adamant in 1981 despite urban rioting from April, especially in Brixton and Liverpool, but was saved politically by the division in the opposition, as the Social Democratic Party was formed in March 1981, breaking away from a leftward-moving Labour, and, the following year, by the successful handling of the Falklands War. The latter increased Thatcher's already strong sense of purpose and self-confidence, her disinclination to adapt to the views of others. The war also cemented her already strong relations with party activists, relations that were improved by Thatcher's care of her image. Indeed, Thatcher began the late-twentieth-century 'image' revolution for politicians, notably with hiring consultants and with changes to her voice and hair.

Her strong support in the Conservative Party outside Parliament enabled Thatcher to push through an agenda that had not hitherto enjoyed widespread support within the Conservative Party, especially privatizations of nationalized industries. Success opened the way for new goals. Thatcher became less cautious, but, aside from her specific policies, she was always keen on the very process of striving, indeed believed it to be ennobling as well as necessary.

Having won a much larger parliamentary majority, of 144 seats, in the general election of 9 June 1983, when the Social Democratic–Liberal Alliance won nearly as many votes as Labour (although far fewer seats), Thatcher faced opposition from the NUM. Under the leadership of Arthur Scargill (1938–), the union mounted in 1984–5 what was really a political strike designed to defeat the government and forward revolutionary socialism. This was a key moment in the political history of Britain. The miners, however, split over the strike, in part due to Scargill's divisive and authoritarian policies and the intimidation and violent picketing by the strikers of those who continued to work, notably of Nottinghamshire miners by their Yorkshire counterparts; brought home by television reporting, this also helped to alienate much of the public.

Meanwhile, Thatcher focused the government's resources, especially the police, on defeating the strike, which collapsed as poverty and helplessness sapped support. The ability to draw on French electricity generating capacity through a new cable under the English Channel was also significant.

Due to the defeat of the strike, which was called off in March 1985, Thatcher's recasting of labour away from heavy industry and mining, and the traditional heroisms of trade union history, and towards new industries in which the workforce had different social and political values, had been taken a long way forward. Whereas there had been twenty-eight coal mines in South Wales in 1984, there were only seventeen in the whole of Wales in 1987, and fewer than 1,000 miners in mid-Glamorgan by 1992.

Instead of trade unions, nationalized industries and council houses, Thatcher wanted a property-owning democracy in which corporatism was weak and capital supreme. Institutions and opinions that resisted were marginalized, and one centre of opposition, the Labour-controlled Greater London Council under Ken Livingstone (1945–), was abolished in 1986. This was part of a wider process of governmental centralization that, however, was accompanied by the sale of most of the nationalized industries and much of the council housing. Widespread share and home ownership became the coping stones of the new property-owning democracy, helping Thatcher win re-election on 11 June 1987, albeit less comfortably than in 1983. She still had an overall majority of 101 and there was no comparison with 1951 and 1970 when, in each case, Labour governments had lost the third election in a row.

Thatcher's success owed much to the weakness and divisions of the opposition. The Labour Party had drifted to the left in the 1970s and was affected by 'entryism' by far-left groups, so that there was little to choose in the 1980s between the views of some Labour MPs and those of Western European Communists. This situation, however, helped to lead to four successive Labour failures in the general elections of 1979, 1983, 1987 and 1992. The attempt to create a collectivist society by means of state action, a new-model society planned in accordance with socialist principles, was rejected by the electorate. Ironically, in law and order, social welfare and education, the Conservatives pursued a more interventionist and regulatory approach.

Labour's was the most unimpressive record of any political party since the decline of the Liberals after the First World War, and one achieved despite serious economic difficulties for the Conservative governments in the early 1980s and the early 1990s. In each case, unemployment rose greatly. These recessions, however, did not lead to a revival of left-wing radicalism, and the circulation of the Communist daily newspaper, the *Morning Star*, fell below 10,000. Moreover, throughout the 1990s and 2000s well under 1 million working days per quarter were lost to labour disputes, a figure well below that in the 1980s. Yet, successive public opinion polls in the 1980s and early 1990s also revealed clear support for the welfare state, notably the NHS, which showed that the impact of Thatcher's ideas on the wider public was limited. Only so much recasting was possible.

If the emphasis is on aggregate national trends, it is too easy to forget the local pattern of economic and social fortunes. In particular, the crisis in mining led to peaks in unemployment. Moreover, it was not simply that unemployment was highest in these areas, as well as in those that focused on heavy industry such as steel or shipbuilding, for example Consett, Corby and Sunderland. An additional problem was that these areas had the greatest percentage of households with a low weekly income, which ensured that per capita expenditure on income support was highest there. Alongside the decline of heavy industry, more recent spheres of growth, such as the chemical and car industries, also decayed. Indeed, British Leyland, which controlled much of the car industry, proved far from robust. Plagued by bad labour relations and poor management, the decline of British Leyland was symptomatic of the failure of corporatist solutions and the decline of much British industry.

The resulting regional contrasts were clear. Average annual household income in Wales in 1991–2 was £22,015, lower than in the north of England or Scotland. Whereas in 1994 the average weekly earnings of a working man were £419.40 in south-east England, they were £327.80 in northern England. The south east also paid a disproportionately high percentage of taxation, and thus benefited from Thatcher's major cuts in income tax. The standard rate of income tax fell from 33 per cent in 1979 to 25 per cent in 1988. Cuts in other forms of taxation also benefited the south east disproportionately, as did the benefit from the privatization share issues.

Transfer payments to regions with a weaker economy became a key element in public finances, and an important aspect of the dependence of these regions on government. Scotland was a particular beneficiary of transfer payments, thanks to the Barnett formula for such transfers devised for the Callaghan government in 1978. Like Wales, it was also over-represented in Parliament, in both cases to the marked advantage of Labour. The north east of England also became a dependency region, with a particularly high percentage of state employees.

Manufacturing decline was matched by shifts in economic activity and a rise in the service sector, and this process led to a major change in the experience of work, a change linked to cultural and political developments. Management, research and development jobs were increasingly separate from production tasks: the former concentrated not in traditional manufacturing regions, but in south-east England, in areas such as the M4 corridor west of London, near Cambridge, and, to a lesser extent, in New Towns in southern England, such as Harlow, Milton Keynes and Stevenage.

The Establishment in general became more focused on London and the south east, with the world of money and services becoming more important than traditional industrial interests. Despite the attempt at the regional relocation of part of Whitehall, notably with Health and Social Security jobs going to Newcastle and both the Royal Mint and the Driver and Vehicle Licensing Agency moving to south Wales, no other part of the country saw office development to compare with that of London's Docklands in the 1980s. Its development, notably that of Canary Wharf, became a key image of Thatcherism, so that the IRA attack in 1996 was a symbolic strike at the legacy of Thatcherism. With the creation of the London Docklands Development Corporation in 1981 (abolished in 1998), Docklands' regeneration was put under the control of central government, rather than the left-wing local government. Governmental support played a role, notably in the development of the transport infrastructure, but the goal was business activity, which contrasted with the Millennium Dome built downstream at Greenwich in the late 1990s.

Yet, as a reminder of the variety concealed within aggregate regional indices – a variety that was central to the very diverse experience of change – there was, and is, also much poverty in the south east, not only in many parts of London, for example Tower Hamlets, but also along the Thames estuary, in the Medway towns, and in some places on the south coast. There were also important and persistent local and regional contrasts elsewhere in England as well as in Wales, Scotland and Northern Ireland.

Thatcher believed strongly in the need to cut (and indeed in the value of cutting) personal taxation, seeing this as a way to return money to those who had earned it and thus to provide economic incentives and to help strengthen personal freedoms.

Corporation tax was also cut. A combination of rising real earnings, lower inflation and taxation, and easier and cheaper credit encouraged spending. Spending became a major expression of identity and a significant leisure activity. The move to twenty-four-hour shopping and the abolition of many restrictions on Sunday trading were symptomatic of this shift: the attempts in the 1930s to rally local ratepayers across Britain to oppose the Sunday opening of cinemas seemed long distant. Shopping patterns in the 1980s also reflected social and cultural trends in other respects, contributing to the sense of flux under Thatcher, despite her attempts to strike resonate notes of continuity.

Lax credit controls and low taxes led, however, in the late 1980s, to a consumer boom that resulted in inflation and imports. Simultaneously, the political position of the government came under acute pressure as a result of the Community Charge (commonly known as the Poll Tax), the proposed introduction of a flat-rate local tax, which caused a furore and also reflected the long-standing difficulty in creating a tax system to support local government, a difficulty that still continues. To Thatcher, the Community Charge represented a way to reduce the radicalism of Labour councils by making them responsible to electorates, all of whom would be affected by the financial consequences of their radicalism. The Community Charge also represented a means to reward her supporters, 'our people', who paid a disproportionate share of the existing taxation as they tended to own their own homes and to live in more expensive accommodation.

However, public agitation, which included a riot in London's Trafalgar Square in March 1990, sapped confidence in Thatcher's ability to guide and respond to the public mood and led Conservative MPs to fear their chance of re-election. Mounting opposition within the Conservative Party took fire over European integration, with Thatcher facing criticism from Cabinet colleagues, notably Geoffrey Howe. She fell as Prime Minister and leader of the Conservative Party in

November 1990, to be replaced by John Major after an election conducted among Conservative MPs.

Politics, 1990–2010

Winning a narrow, and partly unexpected, success in the general election of 9 April 1992, a majority of twenty-one on 42 per cent of the vote (compared to 34 per cent for Labour and 18 for the Liberal Democrats), Major remained Prime Minister until defeated by Labour under Tony Blair in 1997. In office, Major suffered greatly from a disunited ministry that lost public confidence, and from a sense that he could not control developments, which contributed to a lack of personal authority. The savage recession of the early 1990s, which rapidly sent unemployment up, was followed by serious Conservative divisions over Europe, the humiliating failure in September 1992 to defend sterling's place in the Exchange Rate Mechanism and, finally, an atmosphere of sleaze arising from MPs receiving money from interested parties in order to raise questions in Parliament. The Major government also ran out of steam. It had no flagship proposals that grabbed public attention and, instead, campaigns, such as 'Back to Basics' in late 1993, lacked support. The Community Charge was brought to an end in 1993, although privatization continued, notably with the mishandled splitting up of the rail system between the network and the train companies. However, these and other policies were overshadowed by a sense of failure. Yet, the Conservatives did not replace Major, notably in July 1995 when he was re-elected leader.

In the general election held on 1 May 1997, Labour won a big majority, the Conservatives losing all their seats in Scotland and Wales. Labour won 418 seats on 43.4 per cent of the votes. The geography of the results was particularly striking as Labour made major gains in southern England. Tactical voting for Labour reflected a willingness of voters to trust Tony Blair and his presentation of a reformed Labour. However, although Labour's share of the vote had risen by 10.8 per cent, and was particularly apparent in the middle class, this rise was among a smaller turn-out. Indeed the Conservatives won more support in 1992 than Labour did in 1997: what was notable in 1997 was the readiness of Conservative supporters not to vote and of a middle- and working-class coalition of support for Labour that had a resonance of its triumph in 1945.

Party leader from July 1994, Blair won on the platform of 'New Labour', moving away from collectivist solutions based on interventionism and state planning, and prepared to embrace aspects of Thatcherism, not least the marketplace and modest rates of taxation. In 1995, Clause IV of the Labour party's 1918 constitution – its commitment to public ownership of the means of production, distribution and exchange – was abandoned at Blair's instigation after a ballot of party members, and, once in power, the industries privatized under Thatcher and Major were not renationalized, although a measure of public control was reintroduced in the rail industry.

The new government moved rapidly to introduce constitutional change. Referenda in Scotland and Wales in 1979 had not led to devolution, but in 1997 referenda resulted in the establishment of an Assembly in Cardiff and a Parliament in Edinburgh, with the latter wielding powers of taxation. In the 1997 general election 22 per cent of the Scottish votes cast had been for the Scottish National Party (SNP). In 2007, an SNP government gained power in Edinburgh. By then, constitutional judgments and documents such as the report produced by the Calman Commission on the future of Scotland were beginning to talk about shared sovereignty as a constitutional government. Moreover, polls in the late 2000s indicated that about 84 per cent of Scots identified themselves as Scottish not British, if asked to choose.

Devolved government was also reintroduced in Northern Ireland, as part of a settlement that involved the decommissioning of arms by the IRA and the Protestant paramilitaries. In December 1993, talks between the UK and Irish governments had led to the Downing Street Declaration: the two

Prime Ministers, John Major and Albert Reynolds (1932–), agreed to a shared sovereignty that would guarantee the rights of Nationalists, while Unionists were assured that they would not be forced into a united Ireland. A paramilitary ceasefire, declared in 1994, breached in 1996 and resumed in 1997, provided a basis for negotiations, and in 1998 the Good Friday Agreement laid the basis for the resumption of provincial self-government. After the Agreement was endorsed by a refer-endum, an Assembly and a Northern Ireland Executive were both created. Power-sharing between the loyalist Democratic Unionist Party and the republican Sinn Fein worked at the governmental level, while significant transfers of money from Whitehall propped up a very large public sector. However, splinter paramilitary groups continued, with the 'Real IRA' killing twenty-nine in the Omagh bombing in 1998, and violent vandalism remaining a problem in many areas. Those who are unemployed in Northern Ireland are far more likely to resort to violence than their British counterparts.

In the event, the 'New Labour' project proved superficial and redundant, unable to effect significant improvement in the economy, and contributing, instead, to a serious crisis in public indebtedness, as government borrowing rose to sustain far higher expenditure on the welfare state. Moreover, under Blair, Labour abandoned its caution about economic individualism and personal affluence and its focus instead on state management and public investment. Indeed, under Blair, personal borrowing and indebtedness both rose to unprece-dented heights. It was symptomatic of this trend that the Blair government actively supported plans for a change in the gambling regulations and for the construction of a super-casino, a major departure from the Nonconformist roots of the Labour movement.

Blair had sought to temper traditional Labour policies in pursuit of a middle or 'third' way that rejected socialism and trade union dominance in reconciling social democracy with the need to work with market economics. In practice, however, the interventionist role of government remained pronounced. Blair's options were limited by the nature of his parliamentary party, part of which was unconvinced by his policies, and by his focus on foreign policy, especially after the terrorist attacks on the US on 11 September 2001.

However, there was also a serious clash between his talk of self-reliance and the reality of a politics that remained keen to see legislation and government as the solution to problems. Both this and the widespread failure to solve these problems, for example in health and education provision and standards, contributed to a sense of malaise. A combination of self-righteousness and sleaze (if not widespread corruption) on the part of the Blair government did not help, and the sense of mismatch between claims and achievement became increasingly stark. Delivery frequently fell short of New Labour rhetoric, as with the attempt to deal with feral youth through ASBOs (Anti-Social Behaviour Orders) and other law-enforcing mechanisms.

Blair was re-elected on 7 June 2001 and 5 May 2005, in large part thanks to Conservative unpopularity, which reflected the failure to produce an attractive political formula for their own supporters, let alone other voters. Indeed the Conservatives were still greatly affected by the extent to which their supporters did not vote. Their successive leaders, William Hague (1961–), Iain Duncan Smith (1954–) and Michael Howard (1941–), all proved to have politically vulnerable images. Hague proved a brighter leader and better House of Commons performer than Blair, but suffered from an uncertainty over whether to advocate policies that appealed to core supporters or to back a 'modernization' approach aimed at winning over uncommitted voters. The Conservatives found it difficult to gain a favourable public image. Their divisions helped Labour to paint them as far more extreme than was in fact the case. Hague's election call in 2001 to 'save the pound' did not excite the country, although it captured the extent to which Blair's willingness to enter the Eurozone threatened national sovereignty.

The 2001 election left Labour with a commanding majority of 167, even though there had been a 1.8 per cent swing against it in votes as the Conservative share rose. Labour success owed much to support from the Liberal Democrats in marginal seats. Despite the increase in their number of seats in 1997 and 2001, the Liberal Democrats were unable to gain a benefit from Conservative weakness that in any way approached that seized by Labour.

The fall in turn-out in the 2001 election to 59 per cent, the lowest since 1918 (and less than 40 per cent for those aged between eighteen and twenty-four) was a reflection of a sense that there was little difference between Labour and the Conservatives, limited support for change in favour of the latter, and widespread dissatisfaction with politicians; it was not a testimony to confidence in the government. The sense of alienation felt by 'Old' Labour supporters was important, as was dissatisfaction with the Conservatives. Nevertheless, victory meant that Labour did not need to attract Liberal Democratic support by holding out the prospect of proportional representation. This issue became of greater importance with the rise of political extremism in the shape of the British National Party, which had three members elected to Burnley Council in 2002 and two Members to the European Parliament in 2009.

The 2005 election was a reprise of that of 2001. The Conservatives did better, but again failed to achieve a breakthrough. Moreover, the Liberal Democrats won 63 seats, a major limit to an attempt to analyse politics in terms only of Labour and Conservative, and also a challenge to any Conservative attempt to overturn Labour.

However, confidence in Labour's intentions, integrity and competence was badly hit by its years in office. War in the Middle East, notably the decision to attack Iraq in 2003, further compromised Blair's popularity, and Blair's refusal to condemn Israel's tactics during its attack on Lebanon in 2006 helped to lead to his promise to leave office, and then to his resignation in June 2007.

Blair's lacklustre Labour replacement, Gordon Brown, managed to take public confidence in the office of Prime Minister and the political system to renewed depths. Keen to take the credit for being Chancellor of the Exchequer when the economy grew in the late 1990s and early 2000s, he proved less willing to acknowledge the role of British governmental policies in contributing to the harsher impact of the 2008–9 recession in Britain than in many other states. The figures for July 2009 were an unemployment rate of 7.9 per cent, a fall of industrial production by 9.3 per cent, compared to a year earlier, and an atrocious trade balance. By September 2009, the national debt stood at £804.4 billion, equivalent to over £25,000 for every family in Britain. In response, David Cameron, Michael Howard's replacement as Conservative leader, moved to emphasize austerity, reversing an earlier pledge to match Labour's spending plans.

Brown was also criticized for problems that he did not cause but that he mishandled, notably the provision of adequate equipment for troops in Afghanistan and real and alleged corruption by parliamentarians. Both issues came to great prominence in 2009 as Brown lost control of the political agenda.

The political atmosphere is extremely uneasy. There are major concerns about the sustainability of current assumptions, whether in the shape of pension provisions (under mounting pressure from greater longevity), an NHS able to meet public requirements (and not see hospital patients killed by bugs), schools able to provide safe environments and to teach literacy and numeracy, the ability to maintain Scotland's place in the United Kingdom, or expectations of the international influence that Britain can, or should, have.

The last point has been accentuated by the clear inability of the European Union to meet British expectations concerning the direction of European policy, by Britain's growing marginality within the larger and more federal EU, and by particular concerns about domestic terrorism, related in large part to international tensions over Islamist fundamentalism. These concerns were strengthened by the suicide bombings in London in 2005, by later anxieties over terrorism and by pressure from some Muslims for changes to British foreign policy, pressure seen in by-elections in Brent and Leicester in 2003, and in Tower Hamlets in the general election in 2005.

None of these issues can be readily accommodated to a comfortable or conventional account of national history. Terrorism helped ensure that the Home Office mission, outlined in the Public Service Agreements issued in 2000, was greatly challenged. This objective was 'to build a safe, just and tolerant society, in which the rights and responsibilities of individuals, families and communities are properly balanced, and the protection and security are maintained'. In 2010, the precariousness of this 'protection and security' remained readily apparent.

Writing about the recent past, indeed the present, let alone the future, is always a precarious activity. There is the danger that predictions will be proved misplaced, but also the risk that what appeared significant no longer seems so, while the prioritization of issues in the recent past can be contested. This ability to contest views will be addressed at greater length in the next chapter. It is, indeed, one of the defining features of modern British society and history, although scarcely a distinctive feature.

9
CONTESTING THE PAST

Using History

History is both what happened and how we see it. The second is usually implicit in popular works, unstated and revealed only by the way in which the author has handled the subject. This is mistaken, for how we see history is important not only to the impact made by the past but also to the very way in which the latter is organized, understood and thus, in a way, created and composed in action. To give a personal example, *Scotland for Ever!* Lady Butler's epic painting of the heroic British cavalry charge of the Scots Greys at the Battle of Waterloo in 1815, formed the endpapers of *The Living World of History* (1963), a popular children's history that certainly did not suggest that Britain's future lay with European unity, indeed made no mention of the European Economic Community; and, instead, presented the Victorian period as the great age of British achievement. That was a book I was given and read as a child, and British history then seemed so clear and comforting; as indeed it appeared to Hugh Gaitskell, the leader of the Labour opposition, when, in 1962, he contrasted 'a thousand years of history' with membership of the EEC, which he opposed.

Subsequently, whether with Thatcher's 'Victorian values' or Blair's 'A Young Country' and 'Cool Britannia', the teaching and contents of British history became more vexed a subject than it had been for much of the period covered by this book, and contrasting understandings of the past were actively pressed as part of political debate. Moreover, the situation has varied considerably over the last three decades. Under the Conservative governments of Margaret Thatcher and, later, John Major from 1979 to 1997, there were efforts to argue a continuation with the past, not least in terms of a robust patriotism that was particularly asserted by Thatcher.

This assertion was linked to her wish to revive appreciation of pre-1945 values and achievements, particularly those of the Victorians, whom she saw as responsible for Britain's economic transformation and for Britain's past strengths and glory. Her appeal to what was the less recent past also owed much to her active rejection in policy terms of conspicuous continuity with the more recent past of social welfarism, state control of the economy and national decline. To Thatcher, these were all linked, and the post-war Labour governments, those of 1945–51, 1964–70 and 1974–9, were particularly at fault. Instead, Thatcher offered an earlier Britain as a basis for identity and continuity and did so in order to argue that her political opponents represented a recent past that had been a deviation from both national interests and true Conservatism.

The Thatcher government was also committed to the role of British history in education. In 1988, history was included in the national curriculum, the state prospectus for education, in large part due to the strong advocacy of Kenneth Baker, the Education Secretary, and later an active writer of effective popular histories of Britain. This inclusion was linked to a commitment to emphasize British political history, and the working group established to advise the minister on the curriculum was instructed accordingly. The group, however, was unhappy with this, and, instead, recommended multicul-turalism in the treatment of British history; but a dissatisfied Thatcher required that the report go out to further consul-tation, which led to a stronger focus on British history.

In academic circles, the Thatcherite account of national interests and of the past was also related to a positive re-evaluation of the Conservative leaders who preceded Churchill and of the strand of Conservatism that was displaced by him, with more favourable treatments of Neville Chamberlain, Lord Halifax and their allies. This re-evaluation, nevertheless, was certainly not linked to Thatcherism in foreign policy as her effort to increase ideological commitments, notably against communism, and to push the bounds of possibility, clashed with the pre-1940 policies of appeasement and the emphasis on prudence. Moreover, Thatcher very much identified with Churchill as the true patriot and national prophet.

In domestic policy, however, there was a clearer parallel of Conservative academics and Thatcher's politics in terms of a self-conscious rejection of elements of the 'big government' of 1945–79. Thus, Correlli Barnett's study *The Audit of War: The Illusion and Reality of Britain as a Great Nation* (1986) argued that Labour's expenditure on welfarism, particularly the policies of the Attlee governments of 1945–51, compromised the economic and military future of the country by lessening investment in both industry and the armed services. This sense of betrayal drew on another historical work, Martin Wiener's *English Culture and the Decline of the Industrial Spirit* (1981), which appealed to Thatcherite critics of the Conservative 'wets' who favoured paternalism, social welfare and Keynesian (stimulus) economics, with its argument that the economic past (and therefore future) had been betrayed by elitist liberal opposition to entrepreneurialism, including a cultural 'perversion' of entrepreneurialism.

Under Labour in power from 1997, there was, in turn, a fresh transformation in historical consciousness. The espousal of new policies under the self-conscious 'New Labour' platform was also linked to a process of asserting a new identity, for Labour and Britain, that included a different historical consciousness to that which had hitherto prevailed for the Labour Party. Class-based analyses and trade union sentiment were pushed aside as Blair, party leader from 1994 to 2007, made an explicit pitch for the middle ground and for an inclusive account of Britain, one in which 'Old' Labour and the Conservatives alike were to be marginalized as extremist. Blair deliberately broke with the past and embraced the idea of the new, as in 'New Britain'. Indeed, in 1997, Peter Mandelson, Blair's Svengali, declared 'We are defining ourselves by the future.' A decade later, in marking the re-establishment of devolved government in Northern Ireland, Blair referred to the need 'to escape the heavy chains of history. To make history anew.' Similar remarks were made by him on other occasions, as when he apologized for the slave trade. An unwillingness to acknowledge history while trading on it was at the root of the unsellability of the 'Britishness' propounded by 'New Labour'.

These attitudes reflected a rejection of national exceptionalism and, less explicitly, of the powerful social and cultural impact of custom, tradition and heritage. Empire and war were downplayed as themes in British culture and history by 'New Labour', while history itself became less important as a subject at school. The Parekh Report of the Commission on the Future of Multi-Ethnic Britain of 2000, a report from a commission whose chairman was to become a Labour peer, pressed for a sense of heritage adapted to the views of recent immigrants. In November 2003, Jack Straw, the Foreign Secretary, blamed British colonialism for many of the world's international disputes, a view that minimized not only the good it had brought, but also the extent to which British imperialism was usually one in a sequence of imperial conquests, notably in India.

More generally, there is, in political discussion, education and the media an overly critical and somewhat ahistorical account of the British empire, one that reflects the extent to which the overthrowing of British rule is important to the foundation accounts of so many states, for example India. In particular, there is a failure to understand the extent to which Britain was not the conqueror of native peoples ruling themselves in a democratic fashion. There is also a misleading tendency to blame British imperial rule for many of today's pressures and problems which, in reality, stem from modernization and globalization. Moreover, as an empire, Britain engaged with rival empires that are correctly seen as tyrannies, a description that does not fit the varied contours and purposes of British imperial rule. This is particularly the case with Britain's leading role in opposition to the genocidal tyranny of Nazi Germany.

There was also, across the political spectrum, the political tendency to read the past to satisfy the present, as seen by politicians' use of arguments about appeasement at Munich (1938) and failed intervention at Suez (1956) to justify or condemn foreign policy episodes, notably the invasion of Iraq in 2003: supporters of action against Saddam Hussein presented any failure to act as another case of Munich, while critics referred to Suez and Vietnam.

The frequent use of Churchill as a rhetorical ploy indicated the lack of knowledge of the complexity of the past: the Churchill that was seen as a point of reference was that of 1940 (ennobling defiance of Hitler) and not 1915 (failure at Gallipoli) nor 1919 (failed intervention in the Russian Civil War). Thus, the complexity of his record was collapsed into a sound bite. Thatcher frequently referred to 'Winston' without mentioning that he was not only a Conservative leader but also a reforming Liberal Home Secretary. Interviewed by *BBC History* in March 2007, John Reid, the (Labour) Home Secretary, chose Churchill as his hero, without noting his Liberal and Conservative roles. Instead, Reid sought to annex Churchill as 'a bit of a rebel' who became a reforming Home Secretary.

The pillaging of the past continued and also served to create an account of history. Thus, in 2008–9, the 'lessons of the 1930s' were much deployed in discussion of the serious recession of these years. With the Labour government resorting to deficit financing, and borrowing and spending vast sums on supporting the economy through stimulating demand by 'quantitative easing', there was a return of interest in the ideas of John Maynard Keynes (1883–1946), who, in the early 1930s, had turned away from the idea that markets are automatically self-correcting and, instead, urged such remedies. Both ideas and example were debated in public, for example on the radio and in the press. Moreover, the use of Keynes served critics of Conservatism who argued that Britain had taken a wrong turning under Thatcher and that this was demonstrated by their reading of the 1930s and the 2000s, a reading that, however, failed to appreciate the dangerous consequences of large-scale deficit financing for the currency, fiscal system and economy.

Patriotic Myth

That the past was both used and controversial is scarcely a surprise, but it directs renewed attention to the question of how best to write about it, and, indeed, what to cover. Past treatments also invite attention to the issue of whether there should be a major theme at the close of this book. Comforting public myths do not capture the indeterminate nature of change, nor the controversies of the past, but a powerful public myth was for long part of British culture. In particular, a progressive move towards liberty was discerned in Britain past and present. Evolutionary change was held to be the hallmark of the British political system.

> Rule, Britannia, rule the waves;
> Britons never will be slaves.

James Thomson's (1700–48) lines for the masque *Alfred* (1740), lines that became the anthem of British maritime greatness, remained resonant while Britain was the world's leading naval power, which it was until replaced by the US during the Second World War. These lines looked towards 1902, when Arthur Benson's (1862–1925) words for 'Land of Hope and Glory', the first of Edward Elgar's *Pomp and Circumstance* marches, were first heard as part of the Coronation Ode for Edward VII. Three years later, the successful poet Henry Newbolt (1862–1938) produced a history, *The Year of Trafalgar*, capturing the mood of national celebration and exceptionalism.

As with Thomson's lines, produced at a time of war with Spain, much of the expression of national identity was for long focused on antipathy to what was constructed as a different world, that of Continental autocracy and Catholicism, a world that by its difference defined the nature of Britishness. National identity indeed was moulded during war with France and Spain. There was declared war with the former in 1702–13, 1744–8, 1756–63, 1778–83, 1793–1802, 1803–14 and 1815, undeclared war in 1743–4 and 1754–6, and hostile relations at other times. The role of conflict with France in defining British identity helps explain the importance of conflict with Germany for the sustaining of this identity in the twentieth century and, in turn, raises the question of the consequences today of the lack of a clear national enemy in opposition to which unity and identity can be asserted.

War with France was the context in which British identity was created and the empire expanded. Just as English identity had owed a lot to the medieval Hundred Years War with France, the sense of war with Catholicism stemming from the Reformation, and to war with Spain from 1585 to 1604 and again in the 1620s and 1650s, so the Britain created with the parliamentary union of Scotland with England and Wales in 1707 was baptized in talk of national values that were at war with those of France. The experience of the Napoleonic Wars in particular underscored a patriotic discourse on British distinctiveness while simultaneously creating a new iconography of national military heroes focused on Nelson and Wellington. By the 1800s, 'God Save the King', originally a Jacobite song, had come to be called the national anthem.

The resonance of these wars was long-standing and particularly important throughout the nineteenth century, with London, both national and imperial capital, the setting for a memorialization of identity through victory. Nelson's Column, Waterloo Station, the tombs of national heroes in St Paul's Cathedral, Wellington's funeral: sites and occasions contributed directly to a sense of national exceptionalism that was still potent at the time of the world wars but that had its last nostalgic hurrah for Churchill's funeral in 1965 and had largely been forgotten by 2010.

At the same time, the nineteenth century also saw a fleshing out of an understanding of national greatness that did not focus so closely on triumph in war. Victorian Britain displayed a clear perception of national uniqueness, nationalistic self-confidence, and a xenophobic contempt for foreigners, especially Catholics, although the Catholic hierarchy was restored in England in 1850 and in Scotland in 1878. This xenophobia was not a matter of hostility towards foreignness itself, but rather to what was seen as backward and illiberal. The latter were defined in accordance with British criteria (a process that is more generally true), but these criteria were also seen as of wider applicability for the rest of the world. Religious toleration, freedom of speech, parliamentary government, and a free press were all regarded as important to British liberty, and as ways in which Britain set a progressive example.

For England, these values were portrayed as a seamless web that stretched back to the supposedly free and democratic village communities of Angles and Saxons, applauded by John Richard Green (1837–83) in his *Short History of the English People* (1874), and this tradition and belief system was still apparent in the highly popular history books of Arthur Bryant (1899–1985) in the mid-twentieth century, and in the equivalents for children by R.J. Unstead (1915–88), both of which, again, I read. Indeed, Unstead's books were given as school prizes and Bryant was a speaker at Prize Day.

There was a related Scottish narrative, not least with an emphasis on William Wallace, Robert the Bruce, and the 'war of independence' from England from the 1290s. This was not in the Victorian period and early twentieth century a form of victim history in which all ills were blamed on England, but rather an account of why Scotland was a fit partner in Union, and not a colony.

An idealization of democracy as inherently British, or English and Scottish, was in line with the politics of the spreading franchise: the extensions of the right to vote were seen as arising naturally from the country's development. To offer another historical strand, empire was given an historical component by being presented as both apogee and conclusion of an exemplary historical process begun with ancient Rome.

This sense of superiority and the positioning of Britain in an exemplary fashion as the end-product of historical progress were also reaffirmed through a combination of the notion of Britain as the leader of civilization with the precepts of Social Darwinism: the idea of an inherent competitiveness leading to the survival of the fittest, which was seen as a way to affirm Britain's success. Thus, an emphasis on meritocracy in British society was linked to a confidence in Britain's global merit. Heroic nationalism was a theme across social classes and for all generations, and the emphasis was on the obligations of the patriot (generally male, but with exemplary female equivalents, notably Britannia, Elizabeth I, Queen Victoria, Elizabeth Fry, Grace Darling, Florence Nightingale and Emmeline Pankhurst), not the rights of the citizen: in short, on fulfilling individual potential through service to a greater good.

The literary world testified powerfully to this theme. Charles Kingsley (1819–75), a clergyman who was Regius Professor of Modern History at Cambridge from 1860 to 1869, wrote a number of historical novels glorifying heroes from the English past. These included *Westward Ho!* (1855), an account of the Elizabethan struggle with Philip II of Spain, in which the Inquisition and the Jesuits appear as a cruel inspiration of Spanish action, and *Hereward the Wake* (1866), about valiant resistance to the Norman Conquest. The latter is largely forgotten while the former has recently been revived by film, notably in *Elizabeth: The Golden Age* (2007).

The British Dimension

Parliamentary government was regarded as a key characteristic of Britishness, one that Britain exported to its Dominions overseas. This characterization was appropriate because Britain, established in 1707, was created by Act of Parliament, and thus by the politics that led to that Act. Britain was a parliamentary creation, unlike the very different entities of England, Scotland or Wales, the last of which had been incorporated into the English realm as a result of an Act of Parliament in 1536. Northern Ireland, linked to Britain in the United Kingdom, is a relict of the Act of Union with Ireland which came into force in 1801. Britain, the united expression of what would otherwise have been a federal state, therefore lacks a deep history comparable to England, Scotland and Wales, and much of its history is covered in this book. Indeed, much that we associate with one of the constituent parts of Britain is of no relevance for another. Magna Carta (1215), a key event in English history, means nothing in Scotland, which was then an independent kingdom, while, conversely, the Declaration of Arbroath (1320) was a key event in Scottish, but not English history.

That is not the sole misunderstanding. There is also a tendency, both abroad and in England, to see British and English history as interchangeable, indeed of Britain as a greater or another England, both of which are far from the case. This misunderstanding is shared by many of the English. There is, of course, no perfect balance in the history of Britain. For example, the currently fashionable 'four nations' approach to the history of the British Isles (English, Scots, Welsh, Irish) devotes insufficient attention to England, which is by far the preponderant nation in terms of population, and increasingly so; and there is also a more general failure to devote sufficient space to the history of the localities and regions of England. The West Country, London or the West Midlands, and the outer South East, have more people than Wales, Scotland and Northern Ireland respectively, but they receive less attention in coverage of national history.

Moreover, processes common to at least two of the parts of the British Isles, such as Roman attack, the 'Barbarian' invasions, feudalism, the Protestant Reformation and the civil wars of the 1640s, played out very differently in the distinct states of the British Isles, as they also did across Western Europe. Indeed, the relevant units for the Reformation are as much France and Scotland, or England and Sweden, as Britain. Thus, despite retrospective attempts to create a common memory for Britain prior to the union of the crowns in 1603 and, even more, parliamentary union in 1707, there was none.

This is a key point in the modern struggle over national identity, as many Scots and Welsh correctly see their identity as more historically grounded than that of Britain, and indeed deploy the past accordingly. The recovery of their views is therefore important to the history of modern Britain. As a result, to begin British history prior to 1707 is a political legacy of dubious historical value, and one moreover that will look increasingly invalid as separatism increases. A focus on 1707 underlines the problematic nature of the relationship between British and Scottish history as the end then of Scottish independence and the Scottish Parliament can create among Scots a sense of loss and powerful dispossession.

Starting British history at 1707, roughly twice the period covered in this book, puts the focus on a world that is not as remote as if searching for political or cultural origins in Anglo-Saxon (and Scottish and Welsh) forests, which was where seventeenth-century English commentators searched for the origins of English liberty. Indeed, there was much already in existence in the 1700s and, newly confirmed by the Act of Union and the politics of the surrounding decades, that was important throughout the period of this book and that seems somehow familiar now. The ideas of limited government, representative politics, accountable monarchy, the rule of law, and an absence of religious persecution (Catholics would not all have agreed), were all affirmed from 1689. Indeed, the 1701 Act of Succession that excludes Catholics from the throne remains in force. Partly as a result, these ideas have all been part of Britain's deep history. Indeed, their roots were longer-lasting in at least part of Britain.

Thus, the Common Law, with its stress on trial by jury and on equality under the law, both still important today, was an important aspect of English distinctiveness, and, from the twelfth century, this was true of both the content of the law and the way it was administered. English Common Law was particularly suited to the protection of rights and liberties, and it encouraged a respect for the character and continuity of English political society. At the same time, the legal tradition was very different in Scotland where there was a basis, instead, in Roman law.

A Democratic Public History

Looked at more positively – and the interplay of positive and critical themes and approaches is a key element in this chapter, and one that repays reiteration – legal, governmental and political practices were, and are, not simply of constitutional and political force, but also reflected and sustained assumptions that constitute essential aspects of a history and identity that was handed on to immigrants and to new generations, notably a belief in fairness and in accountability. These assumptions provide an historical basis for a democratic culture in British history and in Britain today. This culture therefore is not simply grounded in constitutional provisions such as the restrictions on royal (and thus governmental) authority that followed the expulsion of James II (of England) and VII (of Scotland) in

1688–9, the so-called Glorious Revolution. This proved the key background to the parliamentary Acts of Union and also of the political world that prevailed until mass politics and the change in the role of government brought a slower-moving governmental and political transformation from the 1900s on. Partly as a result of the handing on of a set of historically grounded values, we see a situation in which, although modern British democratic culture is not particularly acute in its knowledge of historical facts, it reflects, nevertheless, a pervasive historicism of continuing values that are grounded in past events and practices.

The quest for freedom, the defence of liberty, and the respect for both law and individual rights, do not provide both narrative and analysis for the entire thrust of British history, but they do manage this for important episodes of which the British are proud. These episodes are then joined to present an account of a benign progress towards liberty in what is referred to as the Whig interpretation of British history, a view that is the basis for the way in which the British have tended to present their history.

Moreover, this quest, this defence and this respect do offer a noteworthy example both to the present and, more generally, across the world. It is the peculiar greatness of British history that those who fought gloriously for national independence, most especially in 1805 against Napoleon and, even more, in 1940 against Hitler, were also asserting values that were more noble and uplifting than those of the nation's enemies, while also helping to forge a sense of national unity. That Napoleon and Hitler were subsequently defeated in large part by the efforts of Britain's allies, notably Russia, Prussia and, despite being reluctant, Austria in 1812–14, and principally by the Soviet Union and the US in 1944–5, did not lessen the key role of Britain in maintaining both struggles when others did not, keeping opposition alive and also in still playing a major role at the close.

The situation is very different now. While there was particular concern over whether the Blair and Brown governments knew how best to define and sustain a viable interpretation of the national interest and national interests, more generally the very sense of national identity is being challenged strongly. This situation has led to tension over how best to present national history. Here we are talking not only of specifics, such as the treatment of the slave trade or of imperialism, for both of which there are misguided and ahistorical apologies, but also of the general interpretation and presentation of national history, as well as of the extent to which any single nation or country could, or should, be marked out alongside the state in British history.

In particular, the arguments for Irish, Scottish and Welsh nationalism rest partly on the notion that Britishness is an extension of Englishness – or, at least, is employed by the English to that end – and therefore that it is of limited value. This, however, is a thesis that makes little sense of the processes by which Britishness has been defined and redefined, and has included, comprehended and drawn on, more than just Englishness, which was certainly the case in the nineteenth century, but far less now. In practice, multiple identities exist; and individual identities do not necessarily exclude all others, a key conclusion for any history of modern Britain and a parallel to the situation in the US. Although many Scots claim that it is increasingly difficult because Britishness is not defined as multinational, or at least in their eyes, it is possible to be British and either English or Scottish or a Londoner or of Pakistani origins, or Catholic; and so on. Appreciating this for the present means that the past should also be seen in this light.

Moreover, an engagement with complexity is appropriate when looking to the past. For instance, differing themes are provided by the presentation of Britain's leading role in the Atlantic slave trade in the eighteenth century, as it is one of the ironies of British history that the country also played the leading role in ending that trade the following century, both legislating against first the slave trade and then slavery, and then using the Royal Navy and diplomatic pressure to stamp out both across the world.

This double role indicates the extent to which the national past can resonate with very different themes. Unfortunately, in offering an overall account, both the government and much public history, notably that served up on television, consistently manifest a maladroit and misleading reluctance to accept the variety of possible interpretations. As always, what is stressed tends to reflect current interests and needs, rather than the multiplicity of differing accounts. Thus, the recent governmental emphasis in the 2000s on Britishness represents a deliberate attempt to strengthen and sustain a sense of national identity in the face of what were seen as challenging tendencies, notably the rise of radical Islam.

Yet, at the same time, as a reminder of the range of explanations possible for many historical episodes, the policy can be discussed in terms of the determination of the Labour government of the 2000s, heavily dependent on Scottish support, to resist the separation of England and Scotland advanced by the Scottish Nationalists, as well as to oppose calls for greater commitment to English interests. As a consequence, the language of Britishness became an assertion of long-term values very much in relation to the needs of the present day, a familiar process.

The Decline of Britishness

With the creation in 1997 of a Scottish Parliament and Executive, however, the drift became very much away from a British identity, not least as separatism became an incremental process. Just as this identity was created by Act of Parliament so it may well be dissolved by another, with, yet again, Parliaments in Edinburgh and London playing the key role. On 24 September 2009, indeed, BBC Radio 4's flagship *Today* programme referred to 'our devolved nations'. Two years earlier, Radio 4 had dropped the UK-themed music until then played at the 6.30 a.m. start of broadcasts.

In recent decades, the long tradition of British history that prevailed for a quarter-millennium from the Act of Union with

Scotland has largely collapsed. Empire disappeared, particularly from the granting of independence to India in 1947, as, soon after, did Britain's leading maritime role. Indeed, it became apparent that British history in many respects had meant British empire history, and much of it passed with the loss of empire. Until 1947, Britishness was quintessentially imperial, and 'Empire' meant an international Britishness, not an island one.

Conversely, the late 1940s saw the beginning of a new, provincialized state which, as 'Great Britain', came into being to run a global colonial and trading system that has since disintegrated. As a result, the 'Little Britishness' characteristic of the post-war period, and associated in particular with Thatcher, is of very recent origin and not as deeply rooted as is generally implied. Looked at differently, there is still a great deal of point in England, but it is unclear how far there still is in Britain. From the Scottish perspective, Scotland has been regionalized from the 1940s as Great Britain is no longer seen as a multinational polity. There is certainly less English interest now in Scottish culture than was the case in the Victorian period. In the nineteenth century, and even the 1930s, Sir Walter Scott (1771–1832) and Robert Burns (1759–96) were very significant writers for English school curricula, but by the 1960s both had been discarded

Moreover, as discussed in the last chapter, cultural and religious continuity was greatly compromised in the 1960s, notably with the decline in the position, popularity and relevance of the Established Churches. In addition, Americanism and globalization compromised native styles, whether in food or in diction, with all that they meant for national distinctiveness and continuity.

Furthermore, all too much of the quest for freedom, defence of liberty, and respect for both law and individual rights has been neglected or distorted in recent decades by governmental and institutional priorities and interests. In particular, a combination of the communitarian solutions pushed by the left, the major inroads of European federalism and a lack of trust in the individual has transformed the political and legal culture of the country. For example, parliamentary government has been greatly eroded by the rise of European institutions, notably the European Parliament and courts, and by the incorporation of European law.

Indeed, in 1993, a leading English historian, W.A. Speck (1938–), published a *Concise History of Britain, 1707–1975* in which he claimed that his chronology 'spans the whole history of Britain in the precise sense', as membership of what became the European Union was, he argued, a partial surrender of British sovereignty. This sense of discontinuity carried forward the 1962 remark by Hugh Gaitskell, the leader of the Labour Party, then in opposition, that such membership would mean 'the end of Britain as an independent nation'. Thus, the recent past has very much seen a recasting of the legacy of the distant past, a recasting that has attracted limited attention, and mainly only from those critical of the process. Nevertheless, whereas some changes, notably the end of empire, have not led to much of a sense of dislocation for many Britons, particularly for the growing numbers who did not experience imperial greatness, this is not the case as far as European integration is concerned.

A widespread failure to appreciate the extent and consequences of the recasting represents a key misunderstanding of Britain's past. Alongside many Britons, foreigners in particular, sold by the 'heritage industry' an impression of ancient ceremonial, historic cities and long continuity, have often failed to appreciate that most British people neither have tea with the queen nor commit murders in picturesque villages. *Midsomer Murders* (1997–), for example, is highly popular in many foreign markets, including Germany and Scandinavia, as is *Morse*. That poverty or poor housing scarcely feature makes these series similar to more historic series, such as *Poirot* and *Miss Marple*, both based on the bestselling novels of Agatha Christie; but also reflects a different brand of escapism because

Midsomer Murders is very much one located in the present. Moreover, Britons, and, even more, foreigners, frequently do not understand the extent to which there have been sweeping changes in recent decades, notably in culture, society and living arrangements.

A widespread lack of appreciation of the extent of change is linked to a major source of criticism of Britain, namely its supposed association with outdated social and political practices, notably social division, class control and the role of the monarchy. The balanced constitution on which eighteenth- and nineteenth-century British commentators prided themselves, a constitution praised by many contemporary foreigners, is now rejected as an undesirable legacy for a democratic age. This approach has been taken further in the world of Hollywood, in which the British, those of the present and, even more, their forebears, repeatedly appear as the villainous opponents of democratic tendencies, as well as being personally, psychologically and sexually repressed and repressive.

Again, this account is misleading, notably because it simplifies the past, giving it a misleading aggregate description, while also inscribing on the British characteristics that might be more generally true of the entire age, for example the role of inherited privilege in the eighteenth century. Yet, the strength of visual impressions in films such as *The Patriot* (2000), with its very hostile, and highly misleading, account of British conduct during the War of American Independence, works more powerfully on modern audiences than the balancing arguments of scholars.

So also, more insidiously, as another form of simplification of the past, does the impression, created by television, film and historical novels, that people in the past were like us, an approach particularly seen with the rendition of classic novels, such as those of Jane Austen, Charles Dickens and Anthony Trollope, as well as with reconstruction dramas based on what did occur or implying that they are thus based. This approach removes the distance of the past and encourages the view that people would have behaved like us. Thus, when they did not, they can be criticized or made to appear quaint or ridiculous, which, indeed, is how Dickens treated historical episodes.

Britain, of course, is not alone in receiving this treatment, but it is particularly pronounced in the treatment of British history because of the strength and accessibility of its literary tradition and the extent to which this tradition has become common property. It was always thus. Dickens was very popular with American readers, so modern Anglo-American co-productions of television series based on Austen novels are in a long tradition. As a result, the past appears clear.

Like the frequent denunciations of British imperialism, this last feature, however, leads to a lack of engagement with the past for its own sake, and this absence of specificity captures a key problem with British history. Where it most attracts attention, it is frequently misconstructed, in a new version of the Whiggishness often decried by scholarly commentators. The highly misleading perception of the First World War in terms of the war poets of the period, such as Wilfred Owen and Siegfried Sassoon, is a notable instance, and one that tells us more about anti-war values from the 1960s on, than about the character of the war and the impression it made on all contemporaries.

Indeed, the grasping of the past in the image of the present represents an unwillingness to think historically that is an important indication of a desire for simplicity that says much about current popular culture. In particular, there is a desire to emote about the past, which is an obvious result of being asked to empathize with figures from history. This process of empathy is carried further forward by the current vogue for genealogy, which indeed accounts not only for a television genre, but also for the largest category of visits to archives and of hits on online archival sources. Thus, the past is seen in a dialogue with the present, with the emotional as much as intellectual drives of the latter inscribed in history.

The misleading character of much of this process is neglected, not least the extent to which important elements of the recent past no longer command such sympathetic attention, notably the role of religion. The space devoted to the latter in this book reflects the importance to the last 160 years of shifts in religious commitment and in the religious paradigm for social values. This is particularly true of Victorian values and of the major changes seen in the 1960s. These points scarcely exhaust the subject. For example, the marked rise in the number of Catholics in Britain (due to Irish immigration) and the restoration of the Catholic hierarchy represented a key, and highly controversial, feature of the 1850s for many contemporaries, and one that linked both circumstances in the localities to wider cultural, political and ideological issues.

A very useful exercise for readers is to consider how far they would offer a different prioritization for the issues tackled in this book, and, more significantly, why; specifically whether the decision reflects an engagement with the period or, rather, factors more pertinent to an understanding of the present world. Having considered this for the issues tackled, the same approach can be adopted to their organization and my coverage.

In practice, once great, Britain had a more noble and more distinctive history than is often allowed for, but it is also a history that has been superseded by, and in, a very different age. The greatness of the past is sadly missing in the present. If there is cause for optimism, then it lies in the freedoms and tolerance that still thrive, the ability, independence and resilience of individuals, the varied and rich achievements of the culture, and the beauty, charm and comfort of so much of the landscape that yet survives the advance of concrete. It is also possible to write a history of modern Britain without being worried about criticizing the present government or particular governments of the past. Whether this freedom of expression will continue in the decades ahead is less clear. The presentist pressures of conformity with norms judged politically appropriate leave only limited room for hope on this head.

SELECTED FURTHER READING

The emphasis on books cited is on recent works, and earlier works can be followed up through their footnotes and bibliographies, but it is more useful to encourage readers to turn to sources from the period. Newspapers offer much, and many libraries will hold newspapers, either in hard copy or on microfilm. It is very instructive to read national newspapers, such as *The Times* and the *Observer*, which survive in widely held microfilm editions, while local newspapers show how national developments, such as the spread of the railway, affected communities and were perceived. For example, Manchester Central Library holds microfilm of eighty-eight newspapers from this period.

It is also useful to turn to visual images, such as caricatures, for example those in *Punch* and *Private Eye*.

Maps are important, as changing editions of the Ordnance Survey show some aspects of how areas have altered. Historical atlases can hold much of value, for example Simon Foxell's *Mapping London: Making Sense of the City* (London,

2007). Specialized works include Robert Woods' and Nicola Shelton's *An Atlas of Victorian Morality* (Liverpool, 1997). Historical geography, a key element, is best approached through the articles in the *Journal of Historical Geography*. The local and regional perspective often receives insufficient weight, but the Longman series 'A Regional History of England' includes valuable works, as do local history publications such as the transactions of the Birmingham and Warwickshire Archaeological Society, the Cumberland and Westmorland Antiquarian and Archaeological Society and the Historic Society of Lancashire and Cheshire. Literary sources provide many insights and readers should turn to Collins, Orwell and other writers. Simon Dentith, *Society and Cultural Forms in Nineteenth-century England* (Basingstoke, 1999) and David Daiches (ed.), *The New Companion to Scottish Culture* (Edinburgh, 1993) contain valuable introductions.

General

Black, J., *Britain Since the Seventies* (London, 2004)

Childs, D., *Britain Since 1939* (London, 2002)

Harkness, D., *Ireland in the Twentieth Century: Divided Island* (London, 1995)

Mohan, J., *A United Kingdom?Economic, Social and Political Geographies* (London, 1999)

Pittock M., *The Road to Independence? Scotland Since the Sixties* (London, 2008)

Smout, T.C., *A Century of the Scottish People, 1830–1950* (London, 1986)

Prologue

Davis, J., *The Great Exhibition* (Stroud, 1999)

Chapter 1

Daunton, M.J. (ed.), *The Cambridge Urban History of Britain, Vol. 3, 1840–1950* (Cambridge, 2000)

Englander, D., *Landlord and Tenant in Urban Britain, 1838–1918* (Oxford, 1983)

Freeman, M.J. and Aldcroft, D.H. (eds), *Transport in Victorian Britain* (Manchester, 1988)

Halliday, S., *The Great Stink of London: Sir Joseph Bazalgette and the Cleansing of the Victorian Metropolis* (Stroud, 1999)

Pollard, S., *Britain's Prime and Britain's Decline: The British Economy, 1870–1914* (Cambridge, 1988)

Priestley, J.B., *English Journey* (London, 1933)

Rubinstein, W.D., *Capitalism, Culture and Decline in Britain, 1750–1990* (London, 1990)

Chapter 2

Barker, R., *Politics, People and British Political Thought Since the Nineteenth Century* (London, 1994)

Belchem, J., *Popular Radicalism in Nineteenth-century Britain* (London, 1995)

Biagini, E., *Gladstone* (London, 1999)

Fraser, W.H., *A History of British Trade Unionism 1700–1998* (London, 1999)

Hawkins, A., *British Party Politics 1852–1886* (London, 1978)

Jenkins, T., *Disraeli and Victorian Conservatism* (London, 1996)

Jenkins, T., *The Liberal Ascendency 1830–1886* (London, 1994)

Machin, I., *The Rise of Democracy in Britain, 1830–1918* (London, 2001)

McWilliam, Robin, *Popular Politics in Nineteenth-century England* (London, 1998)

Packer, I., *Lloyd George* (London, 1998)

Powell, D., *The Edwardian Crisis: Britain, 1901–1914* (London, 1996)

Chapter 3

Boyce, D.G., *The Irish Question and British Politics* (London, 1996)

Hirst, D., *Welfare and Society 1832–1991* (London, 1991)

Kidd, A., *Society and the Poor in Nineteenth-century England* (London, 1999)

McIvor, A., *A History of Work in Britain 1880–1950* (London, 2001)

McLeod, H., *Religion and Society in England 1850–1914* (London, 1996)

Mingay, G.E., *Land and Society in England 1750–1980* (London, 1994)

Taylor, D., *Crime, Policing and Punishment in England 1750–1914* (London, 1998)

Tosh, J., *A Man's Place: Masculinity and the Middle-class Home in Victorian England* (New Haven, Connecticut, 1999)

Chapter 4

Beckett, I., *The Great War, 1914–18* (Harlow, 2001)

Liddle, P.H., *The British Soldier on the Somme 1916* (Camberley, 1996)

Porter, A., *The Oxford History of the British Empire, Vol. III: The Nineteenth Century* (Oxford, 1999)

Chapter 5

Booth, A., *British Economic Development Since 1945* (Manchester, 1996)

Martin, J., *The Development of Modern Agriculture: British Farming Since 1931* (London, 1999)

Saint, A. (ed.), *London Suburbs* (London, 1999)

Simmons, I.G., *An Environmental History of Twentieth-century Britain* (London, 2002)

Chapter 6

Dorling, D., *A New Social Atlas of Britain* (London, 1995)

Gladstone, D., *The Twentieth-century Welfare State* (London, 1999)

Goulbourne, H., *Race Relations in Britain Since 1945* (London, 1998)

Holt, R., *Sport and the British: A Modern History* (Oxford, 1989)

Lowe, R., *The Welfare State in Britain Since 1945* (London, 1998)

Tranter, N.L., *British Population in the Twentieth Century* (London, 1995)

Chapter 7

Bartlett, C.J., *British Foreign Policy in the Twentieth Century* (London, 1989)

Greenwood, S., *Britain and the Cold War* (London, 1995)

Loughlin, J., *The Ulster Question Since 1945* (London, 1998)

McIntyre, W.D., *British Decolonisation 1946–1997* (London, 1998)

Ovendale, R., *Anglo-American Relations in the Twentieth Century* (London, 1998)

Young, J., *Britain and European Unity 1945–1999* (London, 2000)

Chapter 8

Brown, C., *Religion and Society in Twentieth-century Britain* (Harlow, 2006)

Campbell, J., *Edward Heath* (London, 1993)

Hall, L., *Sex, Gender and Social Change in Britain Since 1880* (London, 2000)

Hewison, R., *Culture and Consensus: England, Art and Politics Since 1940* (London 1995)

McAleer, J., *Popular Reading and Publishing in Britain, 1914–1950* (Oxford, 1992)

Pimlott, B., *Harold Wilson* (London, 1992)

Smart, N., *The National Government, 1931–40* (London, 1999)

Thorpe, A., *A History of the British Labour Party* (London, 1997)

Wood, I., *Churchill* (London, 1999)

INDEX

Note: Where more than one page number is listed against a heading, page numbers in bold indicate significant treatment of a subject

Abortion Act (1967) 272
Adams, Richard 158
Addison, Christopher 24
Afghanistan 241, 248, 305
Africa 128–9, 130, **131–3**, 134, 183, 217–18, 220, 241
agriculture 4–5, 24–6, 66, 142, 150, 159, 171, 235
Albert, Prince xi, xii, 86
Alma-Tadema, Sir Lawrence 43
Anglo-Irish Treaty 72, 73
'Angry Young Men' 269
architecture 17–19, 31, 43, 266, 267–8
armed forces 127, 132, 141, 211–12, 234-5
Armstrong, William 26–7
art and culture 17, 18–19, 35, 36, 38–9, 41–3, 266, 279
Artisans' Dwellings Act (1875) 52
ASBOs (anti-social behaviour orders) 205, 303

Asquith, Herbert 67–8, 142
Atlantic (Anglo-American) Alliance 284
Attlee, Clement 156, 228, 229, 250, 281, 309
Austen, Jane 324, 325

Baden-Powell, Robert 119
Baldwin, Stanley, 1st Earl Baldwin of Bewdley 22, 76–7, 209
Balfour, Arthur 53, 62, 63
Balfour Declaration (1917) 143
Barlow, W.H. 14
Barnado, Thomas 96
Barnett, Correlli 309
Barry, Sir Charles 18
Barry, Sir J.W. 19
Bazalgette, Joseph 88
The Beatles 155, 255, 270, 271, 275
beer-brewing industries 12–13
Belgium 9

Betjeman, John 21
Bevan, Aneurin 151, 190
Beveridge, Sir William 187–8
Blair, Tony 177, 192, 204, 237, 245, 246, 259, 281, 305, 308, **300–4, 309–10**
Blitz 211, 216–17, 223
Boer War 60–1, 63, 119, 131–3, 135
Booth, William and Catherine 96
Boy Scout movement 114, 119
bricks and brickmaking industries 23
British Broadcasting Corporation (BBC) 79, 261, 282, 321
British Empire xii–xiii, xv, xvi, **118–46, 207–10** 218, 248, 277, 310, 322, 323
  decolonization 225, 226–8, 228–35, 240–1 251
  see also the Commonwealth; foreign policy
British Empire Exhibition (1924) xvii
British National Party (BNP) 257, 304
British Nationality Act (1948) 183
British Overseas Airways Corporation 282
'Britishness' 7, 310, 313, 314–15, 316–18, 321–6
  see also 'Englishness'; nationalism
Britten, Benjamin 267
Brown, Ford Madox 38–9, 43
Brown, Gordon 177, 192, 237, 246, 259, 305–6
Browning, Robert 40
Bryant, Arthur 314, 315
Burne-Jones, Edward 43
Butler, R.A. 284
Butterfield, William 18

Callaghan, James 240, 291–3
Cameron, David 158, 305
Campaign for Nuclear Disarmament (CND) 232, 242, 247
capital punishment 264, 272, 288
Cardwell, Edward 129
Carlile, Wilson 96
Carr, Jonathan Dodgson 13
Catholic Church 56, 72, **108**, 109, **111**, 242, 268, **274**, 314, 326
  in Northern Ireland 237, 238, 239
Cecil, Robert, 3rd Marquess of Salisbury 17, 53, 60
censorship 142, 224, 263, 288
Chamberlain, Austen 74, 75
Chamberlain, Joseph 31, 61
Chamberlain, Neville 80, 212, 214, 309
chemical industries 9
childbearing and childbirth 102, 175–6, 178, 179, 185, 263, 272, 288
Childers, Erskine 137
Christie, Agatha 266, 269
Church Army 96
Churchill, Winston 36, 37, 119, 145, 154, 229, 284, 285, 309, 311, 314
  Second World War and 212, 213, 215, 219, 220, 224
cinemas 20, 23, 38, 106, 153, **164–5, 249–50,** 299
Citizens' Charter (1991) 280
class structure
  consumerism and 153
  economy and 194–5, 199–200, 271–2
  imperialism and 120
  'New Elite' 26–7
  politics and 63–4, 65, 67, 75–6, 283, 286

social segregation ('underclass')
    167–8, 199–200
social tensions and 95, 112–14
upper classes 199
see also middle-classes;
    working-classes
Clean Air Acts (1956, 1968) xviii,
    156–7
climate change 169–70
coal mining industries 6–7, 8–9,
    91–2, 137, 142, 152, 282, 296
labour relations 79–80, 223,
    225, 291, 294–5
coalition governments 50, 67–70,
    75, 81–3, 142, 187
Cold War 225–6, 228–9
Collins, Wilkie 39, 44, 103
Colonial Laws Validity Act (1865)
    135
commerce 8, 10–11, 46, 299
Common Market *see* European
    Economic
    Community/European
    Union (EEC/EU)
Commonwealth 182–3, 218, 231,
    240, 241, 284
see also British Empire; foreign
    policy
Commonwealth Immigrants Act
    (1968) 183
communism 209, 250, 285
Community Charge ('Poll Tax')
    299–300
Como, Perry 251
Compton-Burnett, Ivy 266
conscription 68, 121, 143, 213,
    224, 264, 277
Conservative Party
    agriculture and 150
    'Blair Years' and 303, 304, 305
    Boer War and 60–1, 63
    environmental issues and 158
    First World War 70

housing and 154–6
leadership:
    Anthony Eden 229, 285, 286
    David Cameron 305
    Edward Heath 235, 236,
        289–91
    Harold Macmillan 151, 154,
        231, 284, 285, 286
    John Major 244–5, 259, 280,
        285, 302, 308
    Margaret Thatcher 162, 177,
        180, 189, 200, 203, 241,
        243, 253, 254, 258, 280,
        282, 283, 285, **293–300**,
        308
Stanley Baldwin 77–9
    nationalism and 59, 66, 73
    Second World War and
        aftermath 285–7
    social welfare and 30, 51–3
    taxation and 59
    voting (political franchise) and
        47–8, 49–50
    in Wales 57
consumerism 7, 33, **36–9**, 46, 150,
    153, **168–9**, 198, , 261, 272,
    274, 280–1, 299
    television and 46, 161, 251–2,
        255, 263, 295
Contagious Diseases Acts (1864,
    1866, 1869) 101–2
Cookson, Catherine 265
Costain, Richard 23
Cottrell, Stephen 274
Countryside Commission 157
Countryside and Rights of Way
    Act (2000) 171
County and Borough Police Act
    (1856) 93
Coward, Noël 269
Cresy, Edward 86
Crimea War (1853–4) 122–4
Crofters' Holding Act (1886) 59

Crosland, Anthony 203
Czechoslovakia 212

Darwin, Charles 44, 108–9
Davies, John 290
de-industrialization 10, 158–9, 195–7
Dean, James 255
Defence of the Realm Act (1914) 142
Defence White Paper (2003) 247
Definition of Time Act (1880) 52
Democratic Unionist Party 302
democratization 167, 252, 261, 280, 281
Derby, Edward, 14th Earl xiii
Dickens, Charles 3, 11, 32, 39, 95, 121, 265, 324, 325
disease 51, 85–91, 98–9, 101–2, 186, 193–4
Disraeli, Benjamin 36, 48, 49–50, 51–2, 133–4
Divorce Reform Act (1969) 177–8, 272
Dominions 117, 135, 141, 230
Douglas-Home, Sir Alec 285, 287
Douglas-Home, William 269
Downing Street Declaration (1993) 301–2
Du Maurier, Daphne 267

Eastlake, Sir Charles 42
economy
    change to service economy 197, 198–9, 297–8
    class structure and 194–5, 199–200, 271–2
    Crisis (1929–31) 33, 81–3
    free trade 31, 208, 224, 228, 243, 250
    international status 32–3, 248–9
    National Debt 60
    recession (2008–9) 305
    sterling 233, 248, 284, 288, 289, 292, 300
    transfer payments 297
    see also taxation
Eden, Anthony 229, 285, 286
education xii, 50, 95, 97, 98, 104, 200–4, 264, 271, 277, 288, 308–9
    Education Acts (1870, 1918, 1944, 1988, 1992) 50–1, 200–1, 201–3, 204,
Edward VII, King 60, 86
Edward VIII, King 177
EEC/EU see European Economic Community/Union)
egalitarianism 282–3
electricity 15, 27, 30–1, 89, 162, 251, 282, 295
Elgar, Edward 22, 110, 265, 313
Eliot, George 39, 103
Elizabeth II, Queen 268, 279
Elswick Ordnance Company 26–7
Emergency Powers (Defence) Act (1940) 224
energy resources 8–9, 20, 152–3, 160, 161–2
'Englishness' xvii–xviii, 265–6
    see also 'Britishness'; nationalism
Environment, Department of 157
environmental issues 29, 91, 156–62, 165–6, 168–70
Equal Citizenship, National Union of Societies for 106–7
Equal Pay Act (1970) 272–3
European influence on Britain 252–6
European Economic Community/Union (EEC/EU) 180, 227, 228, 232, 233, 235–7, 243, 244–6, 254, 289, 305, 307, 322–3

European Free Trade Association (EFTA) 228

factories 20–1, 101, 158–9
  Factory Acts (1860, 1874) 93
Falklands War (1982) 231, 241–2, 258, 294
fascism 209, 285
Fawcett, Millicent 105
Festival of Britain (1951) 267–8
fiction 20, **39–40**, 210, 264–5, 266–7, 315–16, 324–5
First World War, (1914–18) 32, **67–70**, 118, **138–43**, 247, 325
  see also Second World War
Fleming, Alexander 185–6
food and drink 13, 24, 25, 98, 121–2, 152, 217, 224
Foot, Michael 242
Football Association 37
foreign policy 45, 240–8, 284, 303, 311
  see also British Empire; Commonwealth
Foster, Myles 17
France 7, 9, 127, 130, **136**, 214, 222, 233, 242, **258**, **313–14**
free trade 31, 208, 224, 228, 243, 250
Friends of the Earth 158

Gaitskell, Hugh 233, 284, 307, 323
Gaskell, Elizabeth 39
Geddes, Sir Eric 74, 201
gender issues 276–7
General Strike (1926) 80
George VI, King 279
Germany xvi, 9, 31, 136–7, **138–42**, 143
  Second World War and 210–18, 219, 220–3, 311, 319
Gilbert and Sullivan 40, 134

Gissing, George 39
Gladstone, William 36, 46–7, 48, 49–50, 62, 134
Glasgow 6
Good Friday Agreement (1998) 239, 302
Government of India Acts (1919, 1935) 145, 208–9
Graham, Billy 268, 275
Grainger, Percy 265
Great Exhibition (1851) xi–xii
Greater London Council (GLC) 295
Green Belt (London and Home Counties) Act (1938) 153
Green, John Richard 314
Green Party 157
Greenpeace 158
Greenwood, Walter 267
'Greenwood' Housing Act (1930) 152
Gulf Wars (1991, 2003) 230, 246

Hague, William 303
Hardy, Thomas 25, 39, 103
Harris, Augustus 40
Havelock, Henry 126
Hawtrey, Charles 40
health and medicine
  advances in 87, 98–100, 185–6
  comparison with United States 193
  life expectancy 178–9, 193
  mental health xiv, 186
  National Health Service (NHS) 188, 190–4, 282–3
  social welfare and 189–90, 192, 193
    see also public health
Heath, Edward 150, 235, 236, 239, 288, 293
Henderson, Arthur 69, 114
Henty, G.A. 119

'heritage industry' 323–4
Hindus 184
Holidays with Pay Act (1938)
    252–3
Holtby, Winifred 265
Home Government Association
    54
Home Rule Bill (1914) 66
Home Rule League 54
Hore-Belisha, Leslie 164
housing
    pre-1930s 15–17, 20–4, 52, 66
    the thirties onwards 150–1, 152,
        153–6, 168–9, 171, 180, 188,
        189, 249
Housing Act (1980) 189
Housing and Town Planning Act
    (1919) 24
Human Rights Act (1998) 280
Hunt, William Holman 42
Hunting Act (2004) 171
Huntley and Palmer 13
Huxley, Aldous 173

immigration 95, 108, 115, 174,
    181–5, 205, 257, 275, 310
Imperial Trade Preference (1932)
    208
imperialism xv, xvi, 55, 59,
    118–22, 311
India
    immigration from 183
    independence 225, 227, 230,
        240
    India Act (1858) 125–6
    Indian Mutiny (1857–9) 119,
        124–7, 127–8
    influences 121–2
    as part of British Empire 131,
        135, 145, 207–8
Industrial Relations Act (1971)
    290–1
industrialization 7–11

Industry Act (1972) 290
Infant Life Preservation Act
    (1929) 263
International Monetary Fund
    (IMF) 240, 292
Iraq 242, 246, 247, 304, 311
Ireland
    Irish Local Government Act
        (1898)
    migration to England and Wales
        6, 9, 108, 181–2
    nationalism (Home Rule) 53,
        54–5, 56, 66, 70–3, 135, 144
    urbanization 6
    see also Northern Ireland
Irish Republican Army (IRA) 71,
    72–3, 237, 238–40, 301, 302
ITV (independent television
    channel) 269

Jagger, Mick 271
James, P.D. 165–6
Japan xvi, 118, 127, 136, 196, 203,
    208, 219–20, 222, 225, 232
Jarrow March (1936) 151
Jenkins, David (bp. of Durham)
    274
Jenkins, Roy 236
Jews 27, 51–2, 108
Johns, Captain W.E. 119
Kelvin, William, 1st Baron of
    Largs 15
Kennington, Thomas 42
Keynes, John Maynard 312
Kingsley, Charles 315–16
Kipling, Rudyard 60, 120
Kyoto Protocol (1997) 169

labour conditions 8, 91–2
Labour Party
    class structure and 75–6, 283,
        286
    communism and 285

European integration and 233, 235, 236
Falklands War and 242
First World War 69
formation 63
immigration and 183–4
leaderships:
  Gordon Brown 177, 192, 237, 246, 259, 305–6
  Harold Wilson 156, 203, 233, 235, 287, 288, 289, 291
  James Callaghan 240, 291–3
  Ramsay MacDonald 77, 80–1, 82
  Tony Blair 177, 192, 204, 237, 245, 246, 259, 281, 305, 308, **300–4, 309–10**
Liberalism and 48–9, 62–3, 66–7
Second World War and aftermath 210, 214, 262, 281–2
social welfare and 30, 228–9
'Thatcher Years' and 295–6
in Wales 57, 64
Labour relations 113, 243, 284, 286, 288, 292, 296–7
  coal mining industries and 79–80, 223, 225, 291, 294–5
Laing, John 23
'Land of Hope and Glory' (Benson) 313
Land League 58
landscape 4–5, 156, 157–60, 166
Landseer, Edwin 41–2
Lansbury, George 114
Lavers, G.R. 273
Law, Andrew Bonar 75, 76
Lawrence, D.H. 263, 271
leisure pursuits
  cinemas 20, 23, 38, 106, 153, **164–5, 249–50**, 299
  consumerism and 36–9
  dance halls 106

holidays 28, 180, 253
middle-classes 27, 37, 165, 253
music halls and theatre xiv, 38, 40–1, 119, 268–9
regulation of 37, 263–4
science 44
sports and outdoor pursuits 27–8, 29–30, 36–8, 253–4
Lewis, C.S. 268
Liberal Democrats 304
Liberalism
  1924 Election 77–8
  class structure and 67, 65, 76
  First World War 68–70
  Labour Party and 48–9, 62–3, 66–7
  Lloyd George leadership 24, 36, 64–6, **68–9, 73–5, 80**, 112, 113, 142, **144**, 214
  religion and 50, 54–5, 61
  Second World War and aftermath 285
  social welfare and 30, 64–7, 70
  voting reform and 46–7, 49–50
  in Wales 57, 64
libraries and reading rooms 38, 57, 268
Licensing Act (1872) 93
Lipton, Thomas 8
Lisbon Treaty (2007) 237
Liverpool 6
Livingstone, Ken 295
Lloyd George, David 24, 36, 64–6, **68–9, 73–5, 80**, 112, 113, 142, **144**, 214
Lloyd, Marie 38
Local Government Acts (1888, 1972) 289
London 19, 27, 40, 217, 223, 257, 306
  political and economic role 249, 295, 298
  population 6

public health and 86, 87–8, 157, 158–9
London Docklands Development Corporation 298
London Green Belt Act (1959) 154
London Passenger Transport Board 282
Lubetkin, Berthold 266
Lytton, Edward Bulwer xv

Maastricht Agreement (1991) 245
MacDonald, Ramsay 77, 80, 81–2
Mackintosh, Charles Rennie 19
Maclise, Daniel 42
Macmillan, Harold 151, 154, 231, 284, 285, 286
Major, John 244–5, 259, 280, 285, 302, 308
Manchester 6, 18, 90
Mandelson, Peter 310
Manson, James Bolivar 266
Marks and Spencer 8
marriage and divorce 103–4, 106, 177–8, 181, 263, 272, 277, 288
Marx, Karl 112
Mason, Sir Josiah 97
mass-production 10–11, 22, 119
Maternity and Child Welfare Act (1918) 98
Maxwell, James Clerk 15
merchant shipping 196–7
Metaliferous Mines Acts (1872, 1875) 93
Metropolitan Water Act (1852) 88
Middle East 144–5, 207, 218, 226, 242, 246, 247, 304, 311
middle-classes 56–7, 153, 179, 194, 195, 270–1
  cultural expression 38, 44
  leisure pursuits 27, 37, 165, 253
  politics and 44, 47, 61, 78, 283, 286
  public health and 86, 93, 97

rise of suburbia and 21–2
  see also class structure; working-classes
Midwives Act (1902) 98, 102
migration 6–7, 9, 13, 25, 26, **33–4**, 45, 108, 151, 152, **179–80**, 181–2
Military Service Act (1916) 68
Millais, John Everett 43
Milner, Alfred 131
Mines Regulation Act (1908) 93
Modernism 264–5, 266, 267–8, 279
'modernization' 3–4, 235, 246, 289, 303, 311
monarchy xi, xiii, 20, 60, 86, 122, 133–4, 177, 178, 279
Moore, Henry 217
Morris, William 18–19, 43
Morton, Charles xiv
Mosley, Sir Oswald 209, 210, 285
Mother's Union 104
motor cars 15, 20, 21, 31, 33–4, **162–8**, 251, 297
multiculturalism 184–5, 256–7, 258–9, 310
Munich Agreement (1938) 210–11, 212, 311
museums xii, 57, 151
music xii, 36, 38, 267
  the Church and 110
  music halls xiv, 38, 119
  patriotism and 312–13, 314
  popular 106, 119, 251, 255, 269–71
  traditional 22, 265–6
Muslims 175, 184–5, 242, 257, 306

National Children's Home 96
National Electricity Scheme 31
National Health Service (NHS) 188, 190–4, 282–3

National Insurance Acts (1911, 1946) 65, 73, 188, 190–1 283
National Parks Commission 156
National Plan (1965) 288
National Trust 27, 29–30
National Union of Mineworkers (NUM) 291, 294–5
nationalism
    Conservative Party and 59, 66, 73
    declining distinctiveness and 258–9
    devolution and 292, 301–2, 310
    identity through victory 314
    Ireland 53, 54–5, 56, 66, 70–3, 135, 144
    regionalism ('sense of place') and 265, 267
    rural leisure pursuits and 28, 29–30
    Scotland xiv, 55, 58–9, 135, 174, 286
    Wales 55, 56–8, 174, 286
    see also 'Britishness';
        'Englishness'
Naval Defence Act (1889) 131
'New Elite' 26–7
New Towns Act (1946) 154
New Zealand 128
Newbolt, Henry 313
newspapers and the press 7, 11, 13, 44–6, 119
NHS (Family Planning) Act (1967) 176
Nonconformity 57, 108, 109, 111, 262, 268, 273
North Atlantic Treaty Organization (NATO) 227, 232, 234, 250, 284
Northern Ireland 6, 237–40, 242, 301–2, 310, 316
    see also Ireland; Scotland; Wales
Norwood Report (1943) 202

Offences Against the Person Act (1861) 263
O'Neill, Captain Terence 237
Orwell, George xvii, 250, 267
Osborne, John 198–9
Owen, Wilfred 140, 325

Palmerston, Henry, 3rd Viscount 44–5, 50
Pankhurst, Emmeline and Christabel 105
Parliament Act (1911) 65
Parnell, Charles 54
Parry, Sir Hubert 110
patriotism 253–4, 258, 312–16
Paxton, Joseph xi–xii
Pinero, Arthur Wing 40, 103
Plimsoll, Samuel 52
poetry 39–40, 313
Poland 181, 212, 213
police force 56, 93, 107, 276
Political and Economic Planning (pressure group) 281
politics
    the twenties 75–81
    National Government (1931) 164, 209, 262
    National Government (1940) 212, 213, 214, 215, 219, 220, 224
    the forties to sixties 281–7
    the sixties to seventies 240, 287–93
    'Thatcher Years' 241–4, 249, 253, 254, 258, 280, **293–300**, 308–9
    modern Britain 300–6
    accountability and rights 280–1
    class structure and 44, 47, 48–9, 61, 63–4, 65–6, 75–6 78, 113, 283, 286
    coalition governments 50, 67–70, 75, 81–3, 142, 187

culture and society and 261–306
extremism 257, 304
growth of press and 44–5
morality and 263–4, 272–3
privatization and nationalization 283
radicalism 74, 209, 250, 285
voting (political franchise) 36, 44–5, 46, 49–54, 100, 104–6
see also Conservative Party; Labour Party; Liberalism
pollution 157, 160, 161, 165–6
population
birth rates 185
growth 5–7, 85, 115, 137, 149, **173–6**, **178–80**, 257
mortality rates 88–9, 90–1, 98, 187, 188–9
rural areas 5, 25, 26, 180
postal service 19
poverty 17, 42, 99, 187, 298
the Church and 108, 111–12
the Poor Laws and 91–4
social welfare and 187, 188–9
see also working-classes
Powell, Enoch 278
Presley, Elvis 251, 255
Priestley, J.B. 22, 121, 265, 269
Primrose League 53
Prison Act (1877) 52
Proclamation to the People of India (1858) 122
Provisional IRA 238–40
public health 16, 51, 52, **85–91**, 92, 93, 97, 98, 151, 157, 158–9, 167, **185–94**
Public Health Acts (1848, 1871) 51, 86
public houses 93–4
Public Service Agreements 306
Pugin, Augustus 18

Race Relations Act (1965, 1968, 1976) 278, 288
radio 31, 79, 153
railways xii, 3–4, 9, **11–15**, 19, 21, 27, 112, 131, 142, 163, 282
Rathbone, Eleanor 106–7
Rattigan, Terence 269
Reform Acts (1832, 1867,1884) 46, 48
religion and the Church (Anglican)
architecture and art 18, 43
disestablishment of 54–5, 66, 107
education and social welfare 50–1, 95, 96, 97, 109, 177
middle-classes and 112
in modern Britain 176–7, 184–5, 274, 275, 322
politics and 50, 54–5, 61
poverty and 108, 111–12
pre-sixties 107–12, 262, 268
Religious Census (1851) xv, 109
the sixties and 273–6
Victorian era xv, 4
in Wales 57
Rent Act (1968) 289
Restriction of Ribbon Development Act (1935) 153
Reynolds, Albert 302
Ridley, Nicholas 244
Robertson, Thomas 40
Robinson, John 273
Rolls-Royce 290
Romanes, George 100
Rossetti, Dante Gabriel 43
Rowntree, (Benjamin) Seebohm 273
rural areas
environmental issues 29
indentity 29–30, 170–1
Labour Party and 76
leisure pursuits and 27–8

population 5, 25, 26, 180
preservation and 29–30
public health and 91
social tensions and 28–9
transformation of 24–6
urban life impacts on 170–1
Victorian era 4–5
Rushdie, Salman 184–5
Ruskin, John 18
Russell, Bertrand 232
Russell, John, 1st Earl Russell 50
Russia 9, **122–4**, 127, 130, 138,
141, 144, 145, 212, 220, 222,
225–6

Sainsbury, John 8
Salvation Army 96
Sassoon, Siegfried 140, 325
Sayers, Dorothy L. 250, 266
Scargill, Arthur 294–5
Scotland
devolution and 292, 301, 321,
322
engineering and shipbuilding 6
history of Britain and 316–18
housing 169
nationalism and xiv, 55, 58–9,
135, 174, 286
rural areas 26, 58–9
townscapes in 22
see also Wales; Northern Ireland
Scott, Sir George Gilbert 14, 18
Scott, William Bell 35
Scottish Conservative
Associations, National Union
of 52
Scottish Home Rule Association
(SHRA) 58
Scottish Patriotic Association 58
Second World War xvi, 181,
194–5, 210, 213–25, 262,
267–8, 281–2
see also First World War

service economy 197, 198–9,
297–8
Sex Discrimination Act (1976)
276
sex and sexuality 101–2, 103, 106,
176, 181, 194, 263, 266, 271–3
homosexuality and lesbianism
256, 263, 272, 273, 274, 276,
277, 288
Sexual Offences Act (1967) 272
Shaw, George Bernard 17, 41
Shaw, Norman 18
shipbuilding 6, 9–10, 137, 196,
234, 290, 296
Shore, Peter 236
Sikhs 184
Single European Act (1986) 244,
246
Sinn Fein 71, 72, 302
slate industries 13
Smith, Iain Duncan 303
Snow, Dr John 87
social criticism 94–5
Social Democratic Party 294
*Social Insurance and Allied
Services* report (1942) 187–8
social welfare
the Church and 51, 96, 109, 177
health and medicine and
189–90, 192, 193
institutionalization of 52, 61,
98, 161, 188, 228, 256, 296,
309
politics and 30, 51–3, 64–7, 70,
228–9
poverty and 187, 188–9
social segretation ('underclass')
167–8, 199–200
women and 101
socialism 63–4, 74, 114
Special Areas Act (1934) 151
Speck, W.A. 323

sport and outdoor pursuits 27–8, 36–8, 253–4
Stanford, Sir Charles Villiers 110
Statute of Westminster (1931) 145
steel industries 9, 91, 137, 195
Stephenson, Robert xiii, xiv, 35
Stephenson, Rev. Thomas 96
Stopes, Marie 106
Straw, Jack 310
Street, G.E. 18
Suez Crisis (1956) 196, 229, 311
Sullivan, Sir Arthur 40, 110
Sumner, John Andrew Hamilton, Viscount 145–6
Sunningdale Agreement (1973) 239
suburbia, rise of 4, 20–4, 33, 149, 173, 251
sixties
  cultural changes 261, 262, 278–81
  gender roles 276–8
  music 269–71
  religion 273–6
  sexuality and hedonism 271–3
  society and culture before 262–9

taxation
  advertising 44
  building materials 16–17
  food imports and 61–2
  health and medicine and 192, 283
  newspapers 44, 45
  north-south contrast 297
  'People's Budget' (1909) 64–5
  as a political issue 59, 73, 280
  'Thatcherism' and 298–9
  to fund wars 60, 133, 225
  see also economy
telegraph xiv, 19, 31
television 168, 171, 178
  British history and 25, 67, 140, 321, 324, 325
  'Britishness' and 265, 269
  cinema and 165
  consumerism and 46, 161, 251–2, 255, 263, 295
  gender issues and 277
  Television Act (1954) 46
temperance movement (teetotalism) 28, 96
Temple, William (Archbp.) 111
Tennyson, Alfred 39–40
terrorism 73, 237, 238, 239–40, 246, 257, 298, 302, 305
Terry, Ellen 40
textile industries 10, 101, 107
Thatcher, Margaret 162, 177, 180, 189, 200, 203, 241, 243, 253, 254, 258, 280, 282, 283, 285, 293–300, 308
theatre and plays 40–1, 268–9
the thirties 33, 81–3, 150–3, 187–8, 192, 267, 282
time, standardization of 8, 14, 52
Tippett, Michael 267
Tory Party see Conservative Party
tourism and travel 252–3
Town and Country Planning Acts (1932, 1944, 1947, 1969) 153, 154
Town Planning Act (1909) 65
townscapes 8, 13, 16, 17–19, 65, 155–6, 166
Trade Disputes Act (1906) 65
trade (foreign) 8, 24–5, 31, 32, 61–2, 76–7, 120, 150, 217
trade unions 63–4, 65, 69, 75–6, 79–80, 101, 113, 114, 286, 288, 291
transportation 4, 19, 28, 30, 162–8, 282
  see also motor cars; railways
Treaty of Accession (1972) 235
Treaty of Paris (1856) 124
Treaty of Rome (1957) 228

Treaty of Versailles (1919) 143
Trollope, Anthony 102–3, 121, 324
Trunk Roads Programme (1929)
    163–4
Tudor Walters Report (1918) 24
Tyneside 89

unemployment 106, 284, 290, 294,
    296, 300, 305
    Crisis (1929–31) 81
    government provision for 65,
        73–4, 176, 187–8, 190, 198
    late 2000s 205
    'Thatcher Years' 294
    the thirties 151, 187–8, 192,
        267, 282
    Unemployment Act (1934) 190
United States
    foreign investment and 248
    health and medicine 193
    influence on Britain 146,
        249–52, 255–6, 268, 269, 322
    manufacturing output 31
    relationship with 121, 145, 212,
        218–21, 227, 230, 231,
        233–5, 241, 243, 285
    terrorism and 246, 247, 303
Unseaworthy Ships Act (1876) 52
Unstead, R.J. 314–15
urbanization 4, 5, 6, **20–4**
    commuting and 19
    housing 15–17, 20–4
    leisure pursuits and 37–8
    migration and 45, 90
    rise of suburbia 20–4, 33
    rural areas and 170–1
    social welfare and 30
    townscapes 8, 13, 17–19, 31,
        155–6, 166
    wildlife and 159

Vaughan Williams, Ralph 22, 265,
    266

Victoria, Queen xi, xiii, 20, 122,
    133–4
'Victorian values' xiv–xv, 4, 308,
    326
Vindication of Scottish Rights,
    National Association of xiv,
    58
voting (political franchise) 36,
    44–5, 46, 47–8, 49–54, 100,
    104–6

Wales 15, 101, 154, 165
    coal mining industries 6–7, 9,
        91–2, 152, 295
    de-industrialization 195
    devolution and 292, 301
    disestablishment of the Church
        in 55, 66, 111
    history of Britain and 316, 317
    migration from Ireland and
        England 6–7
    nationalism 55, 56–8, 174, 286
    Nonconformity 108, 111
    politics and 57–8, 64
    slate industries 13, 90
    use of English language 56–7,
        174
    see also Northern Ireland;
        Scotland
Walton, Sir William 265
water supplies 87–90, 160, 168, 185
Waterhouse, Alfred 18
Waterhouse, J.W. 43
welfare state 52, 187, **189–90**, 191,
    192, 195, 250, 283, 284, 285,
    296, 302
Wells, H.G. 20, 65, 98
Wentworth, Patricia 156–7, 272
West Indies 275
Wiener, Martin 309
Wilde, Oscar 29, 40, 41
Wilkinson, Ellen ('Red Ellen')
    151, 202

Wilson, Harold 156, 203, 233, 235, 287, 288, 289, 291
Wine and Beerhouse Act (1869) 93
Wodehouse, P.G. 269
Wolfenden Commission (1957) 263
women 100–7, 223, 274, 276–7, 315
working-classes 95, 153, 175, 267
  the Church and 111, 112
  health and medicine 179, 187, 188–9
  leisure pursuits 36–7, 38–9, 93–4, 253
  'middle-class lifestyles' 197
  politics and 47, 48–9, 64, 65–6, 75–6 78, 113, 283
  see also class structure; middle-classes; poverty
Workmen's Compensation Act (1897) 52

youth culture 255, 269–71